Microsoft® ACCESS 97

Step by Step

Other titles in the *Step by Step* series:

*Microsoft Excel 97 Step by Step
*Microsoft Excel 97 Step by Step, Advanced Topics
*Microsoft FrontPage 97 Step by Step
 Microsoft Internet Explorer 3.0 Step by Step
 Microsoft Office 97 Integration Step by Step
*Microsoft Outlook 97 Step by Step
*Microsoft PowerPoint 97 Step by Step
 Microsoft Team Manager 97 Step by Step
 Microsoft Windows 95 Step by Step
 Microsoft Windows NT Workstation version 4.0 Step by Step
*Microsoft Word 97 Step by Step
*Microsoft Word 97 Step by Step, Advanced Topics

Step by Step books are also available for the Microsoft
Office 95 programs.

* These books are approved courseware for Certified Microsoft
  Office User (CMOU) exams. For more details about the CMOU
  program, see page xvii.

Microsoft®

ACCESS 97

Step by Step

Catapult

Microsoft Press

PUBLISHED BY
Microsoft Press
A Division of Microsoft Corporation
One Microsoft Way
Redmond, Washington 98052-6399

Library of Congress Cataloging-in-Publication Data
Microsoft Access 97 step by step / Catapult, Inc.
     p.   cm.
   Includes index.
   ISBN 1-57231-316-1
   1. Microsoft Access.   2. Database management.   I. Catapult, Inc.
QA76.9.D3M5566 1997
005.75'65--dc20   96-38986
                                                 CIP

Printed and bound in the United States of America.

6 7 8 9 WCWC 2 1 0 9 8

Distributed to the book trade in Canada by Macmillan of Canada, a division of Canada Publishing Corporation.

A CIP catalogue record for this book is available from the British Library.

Microsoft Press books are available through booksellers and distributors worldwide. For further information about international editions, contact your local Microsoft Corporation office. Or contact Microsoft Press International directly at fax (206) 936-7329.

FoxPro, Microsoft, Microsoft Press, and Visual Basic are registered trademarks and FrontPage and Outlook are trademarks of Microsoft Corporation.

Other product and company names mentioned herein may be the trademarks of their respective owners.

Companies, names, and/or data used in screens and sample output are fictitious unless otherwise noted.

For Catapult, Inc.
Managing Editor: Diana Stiles
Writer: Charles Freeman
Project Editor: Annette Hall
Technical Editors: John Cronan;
  Cynthia Slotvig
Production/Layout: Jeanne Hunt, Editor;
  Anne Kim
Indexer: Jan Wright

For Microsoft Press
Acquisitions Editor: Casey D. Doyle
Project Editors: Laura Sackerman;
  Maureen Williams Zimmerman

Catapult, Inc. & Microsoft Press

Microsoft Access 97 Step by Step has been created by the professional trainers and writers at Catapult, Inc., to the exacting standards you've come to expect from Microsoft Press. Together, we are pleased to present this self-paced training guide, which you can use individually or as part of a class.

Catapult, Inc., is a software training company with years of experience in PC and Macintosh instruction. Catapult's exclusive Performance-Based Training system is available in Catapult training centers across North America and at customer sites. Based on the principles of adult learning, Performance-Based Training ensures that students leave the classroom with confidence and the ability to apply skills to real-world scenarios. *Microsoft Access 97 Step by Step* incorporates Catapult's training expertise to ensure that you'll receive the maximum return on your training time. You'll focus on the skills that can increase your productivity the most while working at your own pace and convenience.

Microsoft Press is the book publishing division of Microsoft Corporation. The leading publisher of information about Microsoft products and services, Microsoft Press is dedicated to providing the highest quality computer books and multimedia training and reference tools that make using Microsoft software easier, more enjoyable, and more productive.

Table of Contents

Table of Contents

Table of Contents

Opening a table, see Lesson 1, page 13

Viewing and creating relationships, see Lesson 4, page 77

Linking to external databases, see Lesson 6, page 111

Basing a form on a table, see Lesson 9, page 164

Creating a new table, see Lesson 4, page 65

Relating tables, see Lesson 4, page 78

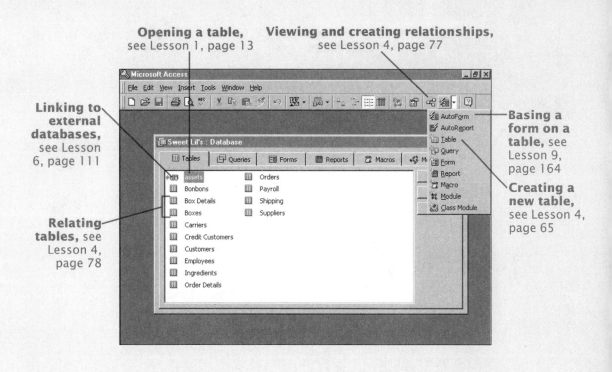

Sorting in Datasheet view, see Lesson 3, page 43

Filtering by selection, see Lesson 3, page 44

Setting and changing field properties, see Lesson 4, page 74

Creating a new table by adding data to a blank datasheet, see Lesson 4, page 69

Moving to different records, see Lesson 1, page 11

Adding new records, see Lesson 4, page 67

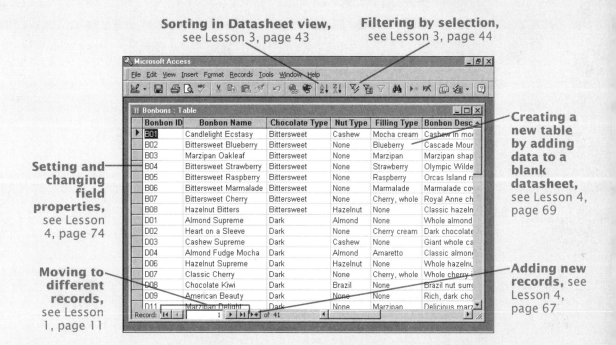

Sorting a query in Datasheet view, see Lesson 7, page 135

Finding specific records, see Lesson 2, page 36

Switching views with the View button, see Lesson 7, page 134

Changing field names in a query, see Lesson 8, page 150

Basing a report on a parameter query, see Lesson 3, page 46

Creating parameter queries for criteria, see Lesson 8, page 158

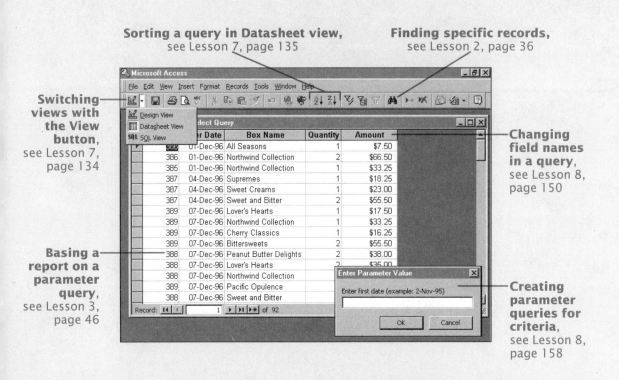

Using junction tables to join two tables, see Lesson 5, page 106

Joining tables in a query, see Lesson 7, page 140

Calculating totals in a query, see Lesson 8, page 146

Setting query criteria, see Lesson 7, page 134

Creating calculated fields, see Lesson 8, page 152

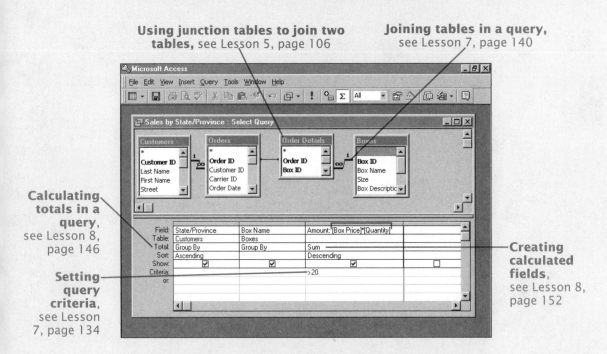

Creating a Command Button to open a related form, see Lesson 9, page 167

Entering and editing records in subforms, see Lesson 2, page 30

Using a subform, see Lesson 2, page 30

Setting validation properties that will check a date, see Lesson 5, page 88

Creating a Combo Box control, see Lesson 5, page 91

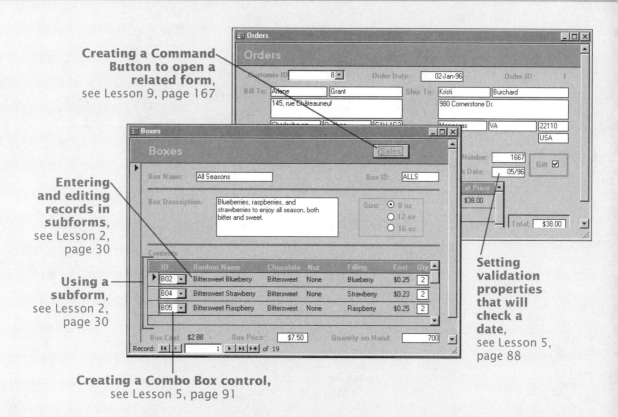

Copying the format with the Format Painter, see Lesson 10, page 193

Adding an unbound picture to a form, see Lesson 10, page 187

Formatting controls, see Lesson 10, page 187

Aligning controls, see Lesson 10, page 194

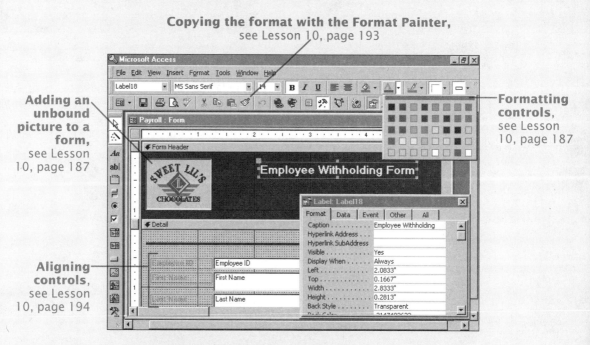

Using the new Report Wizard to create a report and add an automatic print date, see Lesson 11, page 205

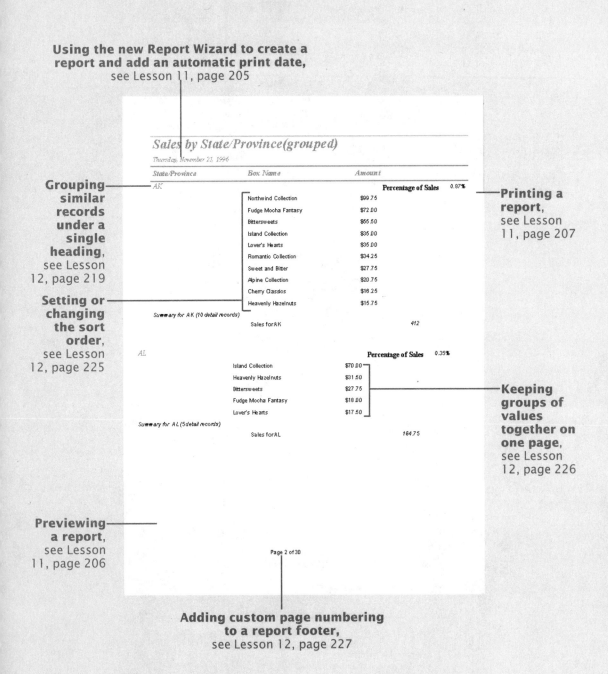

Grouping similar records under a single heading, see Lesson 12, page 219

Setting or changing the sort order, see Lesson 12, page 225

Printing a report, see Lesson 11, page 207

Keeping groups of values together on one page, see Lesson 12, page 226

Previewing a report, see Lesson 11, page 206

Adding custom page numbering to a report footer, see Lesson 12, page 227

Finding Your Best Starting Point

Microsoft Access is a powerful database management program than you can use to efficiently create and manipulate database systems. With Microsoft Access Step by Step, you'll quickly and easily learn how to use Microsoft Access to get your work done.

 IMPORTANT This book is designed for use with Microsoft Access 97 for the Windows 95 and Windows NT version 4.0 operating systems. To find out what software you're running, you can check the product package or you can start the software, click the Help menu at the top of the screen, and click About Microsoft Access. If your software is not compatible with this book, a Step by Step book for your software is probably available. Many of the Step by Step titles are listed on the second page of this book. If the book you want isn't listed, please visit our World Wide Web site at http://www.microsoft.com/mspress/ or call 1-800-MSPRESS for more information.

Finding Your Best Starting Point in This Book

This book is designed for readers learning Microsoft Access for the first time and for more experienced readers who want to learn and use the new features in Microsoft Access 97. Use the following table to find your best starting point in this book.

If you are	Follow these steps
New... to computers to graphical (as opposed to text-only) computer programs to Windows 95 or Windows NT	**1** Install the practice files as described in "Installing and Using the Practice Files." **2** Become acquainted with the Windows 95 or Windows NT operating system and how to use the online Help system by working through Appendix A, "If You Are New to Windows 95, Windows NT, or Microsoft Access." **3** Because additions and deletions of data have a cumulative effect on your database, the most effective approach is to work through the lessons sequentially, from Lesson 1 through Lesson 12.
Switching... from Paradox from dBASE V for Windows from Lotus Approach	**1** Install the practice files as described in "Installing and Using the Practice Files." **2** Because additions and deletions of data have a cumulative effect on your database, the most effective approach is to work through the lessons sequentially, from Lesson 1 through Lesson 12.
Upgrading... from Microsoft Access for Windows 95	**1** Learn about the new features in this version of the program that are covered in this book by reading through the following section, "New Features in Microsoft Access." **2** Install the practice files as described in "Installing and Using the Practice Files." **3** You can use the table of contents and the *Quick*Look Guide to locate information about general topics. You can use the index to find information about a specific topic or a feature from Access for Windows 95.
Referencing... this book after working through the lessons	**1** Use the index to locate information about specific topics, and use the table of contents and the *Quick*Look Guide to locate information about general topics. **2** Read the Lesson Summary at the end of each lesson for a brief review of the major tasks. Lesson Summary topics are listed in the same order as they are presented in the lesson.

Certified Microsoft Office User Program

The Certified Microsoft Office User (CMOU) program is designed for business professionals and students who use Microsoft Office 97 products in their daily work. The program enables participants to showcase their skill level to potential employers. It benefits accountants, administrators, executive assistants, program managers, sales representatives, students, and many others. To receive certified user credentials for a software program, candidates must pass a hands-on exam in which they use the program to complete real-world tasks.

The CMOU program offers two levels of certification: Proficient and Expert. The following table indicates the levels available for each Microsoft Office 97 program.

Software	Proficient level	Expert level
Microsoft Word 97	✔	✔
Microsoft Excel 97	✔	✔
Microsoft Access 97		✔
Microsoft PowerPoint 97		✔
Microsoft Outlook 97		✔
Microsoft FrontPage 97		✔

Microsoft Press offers the following books in the *Step by Step* series as approved courseware for the CMOU exams:

Proficient level:
Microsoft Word 97 Step by Step, by Catapult, Inc. ISBN: 1-57231-313-7
Microsoft Excel 97 Step by Step, by Catapult, Inc. ISBN: 1-57231-314-5

Expert level:
Microsoft Word 97 Step by Step, Advanced Topics by Catapult, Inc.
   ISBN: 1-57231-563-6
Microsoft Excel 97 Step by Step, Advanced Topics by Catapult, Inc.
   ISBN: 1-57231-564-4
Microsoft Access 97 Step by Step, by Catapult, Inc. ISBN: 1-57231-316-1
Microsoft PowerPoint 97 Step by Step, by Perspection, Inc. ISBN: 1-57231-315-3
Microsoft Outlook 97 Step by Step, by Catapult, Inc. ISBN: 1-57231-382-X
Microsoft FrontPage 97 Step by Step, by Catapult, Inc. ISBN: 1-57231-336-6

Candidates may take exams at any participating Sylvan Test Center, participating corporations, or participating employment agencies. Exams have a suggested retail price of $50 each.

To become a candidate for certification, or for more information about the certification process, please call 1-800-933-4493 in the United States or visit the CMOU program World Wide Web site at http://www.microsoft.com/office/train_cert/

New Features in Microsoft Access 97

The following table lists the major new features in Microsoft Access that are covered in this book. The table shows the lesson in which you can learn how to use each feature. You can also use the index to find specific information about a feature or a task you want to do.

To learn how to	See
Work with Office Assistant	Lesson 1
Switch between views of an object with the View button	Lesson 3
Create a hyperlink to jump to another part of the database	Lesson 6
Add a Tab control to a form	Lesson 10
Work with the Publish To The Web Wizard	Lesson 12
Export objects in HTML format	Lesson 12

Corrections, Comments, and Help

Every effort has been made to ensure the accuracy of this book and the contents of the practice files disk. Microsoft Press provides corrections and additional content for its books through the World Wide Web at

    http://www.microsoft.com/mspress/support/

If you have comments, questions, or ideas regarding this book or the practice files disk, please send them to us.

Send e-mail to

    mspinput@microsoft.com

Or send postal mail to

    Microsoft Press

    Attn: Step by Step Series Editor

    One Microsoft Way

    Redmond, WA 98052-6399

Please note that support for the Microsoft Access software product itself is not offered through the above addresses. For help using Access, you can call Microsoft Access AnswerPoint at (425) 635-7050 on weekdays between 6 a.m. and 6 p.m. Pacific time.

Visit Our World Wide Web Site

We invite you to visit the Microsoft Press World Wide Web site. You can visit us at the following location:

http://www.microsoft.com/mspress/

You'll find descriptions for all of our books, information about ordering titles, notice of special features and events, additional content for Microsoft Press books, and much more.

You can also find out the latest in software developments and news from Microsoft Corporation by visiting the following World Wide Web site:

http://www.microsoft.com/

We look forward to your visit on the Web!

Installing and Using the Practice Files

The disk inside the back cover of this book contains practice files that you'll use as you perform the exercises in the book. For example, when you're learning how to import a Microsoft Excel spreadsheet, you'll open one of the practice files—an Excel spreadsheet file—and then convert the spreadsheet to a Microsoft Access table. By using the practice files, you won't waste time creating the samples used in the lessons—instead, you can concentrate on learning how to use Word. With the files and the step-by-step instructions in the lessons, you'll also learn by doing, which is an easy and effective way to acquire and remember new skills.

 IMPORTANT Before you break the seal on the practice disk package, be sure that this book matches your version of the software. This book is designed for use with Microsoft Access 97 for the Windows 95 and Windows NT version 4.0 operating systems. To find out what software you're running, you can check the product package or you can start the software, and then on the Help menu at the top of the screen, click About Microsoft Access. (If you need some help starting the software and so on, see Appendix A, "If you Are New to Windows 95, Windows NT, or Microsoft Access.") If your program is not compatible with this book, a Step by Step book matching your software is probably available. Many of the Step by Step titles are listed on the second page of this book. If the book you want isn't listed, please visit our World Wide Web site at http://www.microsoft.com/mspress/ or call 1-800-MSPRESS for more information.

Install the practice files on your computer

Follow these steps to install the practice files on your computer's hard disk so that you can use them with the exercises in this book.

 NOTE If you are new to Windows 95 or Windows NT, you might want to work through Appendix A, "If You Are New to Windows 95, Windows NT, or Microsoft Access," before installing the practice files.

In Windows 95, you will also be prompted for a username and password when starting Windows 95 if your computer is configured for user profiles.

1 If your computer isn't on, turn it on now.

2 If you're using Windows NT, press CTRL+ALT+DEL to display a dialog box asking for your username and password. If you are using Windows 95, you will see this dialog box if your computer is connected to a network. If you don't know your username or password, contact your system administrator for assistance.

3 Type your username and password in the appropriate boxes, and then click OK. If you see the Welcome dialog box, click the Close button.

Close

4 Remove the disk from the package inside the back cover of this book.

5 Insert the disk in drive A or drive B of your computer.

6 On the taskbar at the bottom of your screen, click the Start button.

The Start menu opens.

...and then click Run.

Click Start...

7 On the Start menu, click Run.

The Run dialog box appears.

8 In the Open box, type **a:setup** (or **b:setup** if the disk is in drive B). Don't add spaces as you type.

9 Click OK, and then follow the directions on the screen.

The Setup program window opens with recommended options preselected for you. For best results in using the practice files with this book, accept these preselected settings.

10 When the files have been installed, remove the disk from your drive and replace in the package inside the back cover of the book.

A folder called Access SBS Practice has been created on your hard disk, and the practice files have been put in that folder.

Microsoft
Press
Welcome

Camcorder
Files On The
Internet

NOTE In addition to installing the practice files, the Setup program has created two shortcuts on your Desktop. If your computer is set up to connect to the Internet, you can double-click the Microsoft Press Welcome shortcut to visit the Microsoft Press Web site. You can also connect to this Web site directly at http://www.microsoft.com/mspress/

You can double-click the Camcorder Files On The Internet shortcut to connect to the *Microsoft Access 97 Step by Step* Camcorder files Web page. This page contains audiovisual demonstrations of how to do a number of tasks in Access, which you can copy to your computer for viewing. You can connect to this Web site directly at http://www.microsoft.com/mspress/products/337/

Using the Practice Files

Each lesson in this book explains when and how to use any practice files for that lesson. When it's time to use a practice file, the book will list instructions for how to open the file. The lessons are built around scenarios that simulate a real work environment, so you can easily apply the skills you learn to your own work. For the scenarios in this book, imagine that you have been asked to serve as the Microsoft Access specialist for a small candy manufacuring and marketing company, Sweet Lil's. Sweet Lil's has been using computers for some time, but most of their systems have been built in a haphazard way without a consistent application of standards. They have recently decided to convert all of their existing systems over to a central database using Microsoft Access as the standard development tool. Your job in the company is to master Microsoft Access and apply it efficiently to a wide variety of situations.

For those of you who like to know all the details, here's a list of the files included on the practice disk:

Filename	Description
Lessons 1 through 12	
Sweet Lil's.mdb	This is the main database file which contains all of the tables, queries, reports and macros used in this book.

Filename	Description
Lesson 9	
Assets.dbf	A dBASE IV file used to demonstrate retrieving and working with external data.
Payroll.xls	A Microsoft Excel spreadsheet used to demonstrate importing a table.
Lesson 10	
Sweet Lil's logo.bmp	A Microsoft Paint file used to demonstrate inserting and editing images.

Uninstalling the Practice Files

Use the following steps to delete the practice files added to your hard drive by the Step by Step program.

1 Click Start, point to Settings, and then click Control Panel.

2 Double-click the Add/Remove Programs icon.

3 Select Microsoft Access Step by Step from the list, and then click Add/Remove.

   A confirmation message appears.

4 Click Yes.

   The practice files are uninstalled.

5 Click OK to close the Add/Remove Programs Properties dialog box.

6 Close the Control Panel window.

Need Help with the Practice Files?

Every effort has been made to ensure the accuracy of this book and the contents of the practice files disk. If you do run into a problem, Microsoft Press provides corrections for its books through the World Wide Web at

http://www.microsoft.com/mspress/support/

We also invite you to visit our main Web page at

http://www.microsoft.com/mspress/

You'll find descriptions for all of our books, information about ordering titles, notices of special features and events, additional content for Microsoft Press books, and much more.

Conventions and Features in This Book

You can save time when you use this book by understanding, before you start the lessons, how instructions, keys to press, and so on are shown in the book. Please take a moment to read the following list, which also points out helpful features of the book that you might want to use.

 NOTE If you are unfamiliar with Windows, Windows NT, or mouse terminology, see Appendix A, "If You Are New to Windows 95, Windows NT, or Microsoft Access."

Conventions

- Hands-on exercises for you to follow are given in numbered lists of steps (1, 2, and so on). An arrowhead bullet (▶) indicates an exercise that has only one step.
- Text that you are to type appears in **bold**
- A plus sign (+) between two key names means that you must press those keys at the same time. For example, "Press ALT+TAB" means that you hold down the ALT key while you press TAB.

The icons on the next page identify the different types of supplementary material.

Notes labeled	Alert you to
Note	Additional information for a step.
Tip	Suggested additional methods for a step or helpful hints.
Important	Essential information that you should check before continuing with the lesson.
Troubleshooting	Possible error messages or computer difficulties and their solutions.
Demonstration	Skills that are demonstrated in audiovisual files available on the World Wide Web.

Other Features of This Book

- You can learn how to use other Microsoft products, such as FrontPage, with Access by reading the shaded boxes throughout the lessons.

- You can learn about techniques that build on what you learned in a lesson by trying the optional One Step Further exercise at the end of the lesson.

- You can get a quick reminder of how to perform the tasks you learned by reading the Lesson Summary at the end of a lesson.

- You can quickly determine what online Help topics are available for additional information by referring to the Help topics listed at the end of each lesson. The Help system provides a complete online reference to Microsoft Access. To learn more about online Help, see Appendix A, "If You Are New to Windows 95, Windows NT, or Microsoft Access."

- You can practice the major skills presented in the lessons by working through the Review & Practice sections at the end of each part.

- If you have Web browser software and access to the World Wide Web, you can view audiovisual demonstrations of how to perform some of the more complicated tasks in Word by downloading supplementary files from the Web. Double-click the Camcorder Files On The Internet shortcut that was created on your Desktop when you installed the practice files for this book, or connect directly to http://mspress.microsoft.com/mspress/products/337/. The Web page that opens contains full instructions for copying and viewing the demonstration files.

Part
1

Entering and Viewing Data in Microsoft Access

Viewing, Entering, and Customizing Data

In this lesson you will learn how to:

**Estimated time
45 min.**

- Open a database.
- Enter and modify data using a form.
- Select an option or a check box.
- Navigate between records.
- Switch between Form and Database views.
- Use editing tools.
- Select values from a list.

When you run a business, manage an office, or even just keep track of day-to-day tasks, there are hundreds of pieces of information that you use. The most convenient place to keep that information is right at your desk. For a while you might stack paper forms in a file folder next to the phone, as long as the stack doesn't get too big. But you'll have a problem if you try to keep all the information you need at your desk—pretty soon you won't be able to find the desk!

You can use Microsoft Access to organize and store all kinds and all quantities of information and have the data you need available with only a few clicks of your mouse. In this lesson, you'll find out how to open a Microsoft Access database, use a form to add new data, and move from record to record.

Data and Databases

Data is anything you want to store and refer to again. In Microsoft Access, data can be text, numbers, dates, pictures, files, and many other types of material. For example, if you sell boxes of bonbons, you can store the names, pictures, and recipes of your bonbons, the prices and quantities of boxes, and the dates of sales, to name just a few.

A *database* is an integrated collection of data that shares some common characteristic. For example, many businesses view all the data that relates to running that business as a corporate database. Databases also assist consumer groups, educational facilities, and government organizations in managing information. Even individuals or families have uses for databases. Databases are really just a way of organizing data so that it is more useful.

In most cases, the easiest way to enter data is by using a *form*. Forms used to enter data in Microsoft Access resemble the paper forms we see in offices. You type the data in the form, and then Microsoft Access stores it in a table.

A database *table* is a collection of data about the same subject or topic stored in records (rows) and fields (columns). A *record* is a set of information that belongs together, such as all the information about a magazine subscription card or a listing in a phone book. Records are made up of individual *fields*. Each field contains a discrete piece of data. For example, a magazine subscription table would contain one field for the subscriber name, another for the address, and as many other fields as the database designer believes are necessary to completely describe a subscriber.

Setting the Scene

To attract new customers, Sweet Lil's Chocolates, Inc., a fast-growing gourmet chocolate company, started a monthly newsletter called *The Chocolate Gourmet*. The newsletter has generated so many sales that Sweet Lil's decided to switch to Microsoft Access to store data about its product lines and sales. After seeing how much time using the database has saved other departments and how many errors have been prevented, the Marketing Department wants to keep subscription information in the database as well.

You have been recruited to enter data using a new form called "Subscriptions." The Sweet Lil's database contains the form you need. You'll open the database, open the Subscription form, and enter subscription data. The records you enter will be stored in the Customers table.

Opening a Database

If you quit Microsoft Access at the end of "Installing and Using the Practice Files," or if you are just starting to use Microsoft Access 97 with this lesson, perform these steps for starting Microsoft Access and opening a database.

TIP After you have opened a database, the next time you start Microsoft Access you'll see the database name listed in the Microsoft Access dialog box. When the database name appears in the Microsoft Access dialog box, you can double-click the name to open the database.

Start Microsoft Access from Microsoft Windows 95 or Windows NT

1 On the taskbar, click the Start button.

2 Point to Programs, and then click Microsoft Access.

The Microsoft Access dialog box appears as shown in the following illustration. From here, you can create a new database, open an existing database, or start the Database Wizard, which will help you create a new database.

An Introduction to the Office Assistant

While you are working with Microsoft Office 97, an animated character called the *Office Assistant* pops up on your screen to help you work productively. The Office Assistant offers help messages as you work. You can ask the Office Assistant questions by typing your question, and then clicking Search. The Office Assistant then shows you the answer to your question.

You can close any Office Assistant tip or message by pressing ESC.

You will sometimes see a light bulb graphic next to the Office Assistant—clicking the light bulb displays a tip about the action you are currently performing. You can view more tips by clicking Tips in the Office Assistant balloon when the Office Assistant appears. These tips are tailored to how you work—when you master a particular skill, the Office Assistant stops offering help.

Clippit, an Office
Assistant, in action

The Office Assistant appears in the following situations:

- When you click the Office Assistant button on the Standard toolbar.
- When you choose Microsoft Access Help on the Help menu, or when you press F1.
- Whenever you click certain commands or try new tasks, for example, when you use Open for the first time.

Office Assistant

You can customize the Office Assistant. Use the right mouse button to click the Office Assistant, and then click Options to open the Office Assistant dialog box. You can then define when you want the Office Assistant to appear, and what kind of help you want it to offer. You can even change your Office Assistant character by clicking the Gallery tab. The Office Assistant is a shared application—any settings that you change in Microsoft Access will affect the Office Assistant in other Office 97 programs.

IMPORTANT   If the Office Assistant appears, click the Start Using Microsoft Access option. If the User Name dialog box appears, fill in your name and initials, and then click OK. On the Office Assistant, click the Close button.

For the purposes of this book, the Office Assistant will not appear in the illustrations. If you want to match the illustrations, any time the Office Assistant appears, use the right mouse button to click the Office Assistant, and then click Hide Assistant. If you want to leave Office Assistant on top to help guide you, but it is in your way, simply drag it to another area on the screen.

Open a database

In this exercise, you open the Sweet Lil's database.

1   In the Microsoft Access dialog box, be sure that the Open An Existing Database option is selected, and then click OK.

The Open dialog box appears.

Look in Favorites

2   In the Open dialog box, click the Look In Favorites button.

The names of all folders and files in the Favorites folder are displayed in the file list. Your dialog box should look similar to the following illustration.

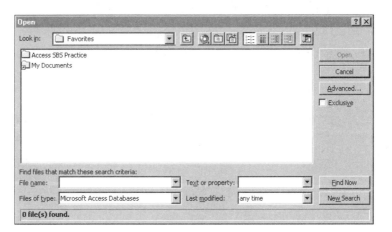

3   Double-click the Access SBS Practice folder.

4 Double-click the Sweet Lil's filename.

The Database window for the Sweet Lil's database opens. The Database window has tabs—the Tables tab lists the tables that store data about Sweet Lil's business; the Forms tab lists the forms that were created for the Sweet Lil's database; and so forth. From the Database window, you can open and work with any object in the database. The Sweet Lil's Database window looks like the following illustration.

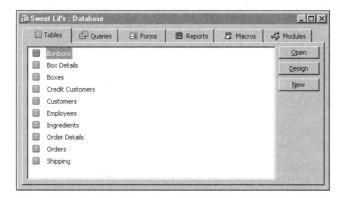

Entering and Viewing Data by Using Forms

Now that you're in the Sweet Lil's database, you can open the Subscription form to enter the subscription information for a new customer. The Subscription form contains blank boxes—*fields*—where you type the information from the paper form. A field is an area on a form where you enter data, such as a last name or an address.

The *insertion point*, the blinking vertical bar on your screen, indicates where the information appears when you type. You can move the insertion point by clicking a different field or by pressing the TAB key. In general, forms are set up so that when you press TAB, the insertion point moves through the fields from left to right or from top to bottom.

Microsoft Access fills in the current date in the Date Received field automatically so that you don't have to type the date.

Open a form

In this exercise, you open a form.

1 In the Sweet Lil's Database window, click the Forms tab.

A list of the forms in the Sweet Lil's database is displayed.

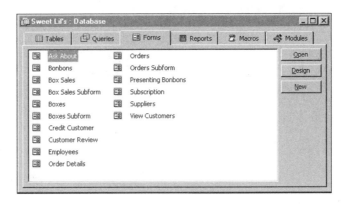

2 Double-click the Subscription form.

The Subscription form appears.

Fields —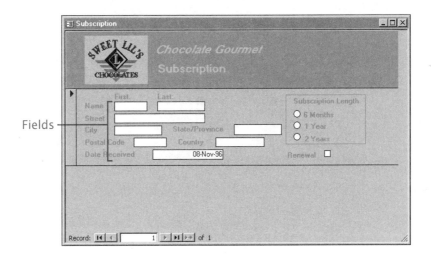

Updating the Database by Using a Form

You'll use the blank Subscription form on your screen to enter the subscription for a fan of *The Chocolate Gourmet* from Ohio. Here's what his paper subscription form looks like.

Add a name

If you make a mistake, just press the BACK-SPACE key and then retype.

You can also click anywhere in the Last Name field.

1 Type **Earl** in the First Name field.

As soon as you start typing, a new blank form appears below the one you're working in.

2 Press TAB to move the insertion point to the Last Name field.

When your hands are already on the keyboard, you press TAB to move to the next field and press SHIFT+TAB to move to the previous field.

3 Type **Lee** in the Last Name field.

Add an address

➤ Type the following address information, pressing TAB to move from field to field.

Street:	**28 Dorothy**
City:	**Fairborn**
State/Province:	**OH**
Postal Code:	**45324**
Country:	**USA**

Selecting an Option or a Check Box

When you press TAB after typing "USA" in the Country field, Microsoft Access draws a dotted line around "6 Months" in the Subscription Length field instead of displaying the insertion point.

Subscription Length is an *option group*. Because an option group presents a set of options to select from, you don't have to type the data yourself—you just select an option. In this case, Earl Lee wants a 2-year subscription.

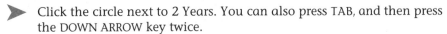

Option group

Check box

Select an option

If you press TAB in this step, be sure the insertion point is in the Country field.

 Click the circle next to 2 Years. You can also press TAB, and then press the DOWN ARROW key twice.

A dot appears in the button next to 2 Years, indicating that the option is selected. Next, you'll fill out the Renewal field.

Select a check box

The subscription for Earl Lee is a renewal. The Renewal field contains a check box. When this kind of field is selected, you see a check mark in the box.

Click the Renewal check box.

A check mark appears in the box.

TIP To clear a selected check box, click it again. If you prefer to use the keyboard, you can press the SPACEBAR to select or clear a check box.

Navigating Between Records

All the information in Earl Lee's subscription makes up one complete record. Now that you've entered Earl Lee's subscription, you're ready to move to the next record.

TIP You can move to a field by pressing TAB. If you do, Microsoft Access selects the entire value in the field. To cancel the selection and place the insertion point at the end of the field, press F2.

To move to the next record, you can also press TAB in the Renewal field of the current record.

You might be able to see more than one record at a time while you are entering data. If you can see the next record, you can move to that record by clicking in it. Whether you can see the next record or not, you can move to the next record by pressing TAB when your insertion point is in the last field in the current record (the record you're in now).

Save the record and move to the next record

➤ Click in the First Name field of the next record.

The subscription information for Earl Lee is saved automatically when you go to a new record.

Return to the previous record

You can also use the PAGE UP key to go to the first field in the first record. Then, press TAB to move to the Street field.

Looking over your first entry, you notice that you didn't type "St." in Earl Lee's street address. You'll return to the previous record to make the change.

1 In the Street field of Earl Lee's record, click after the "y" in "Dorothy" to return to the record.

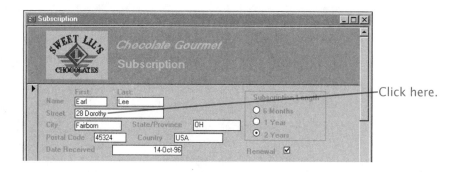
—Click here.

2 Press the SPACEBAR to insert a space after "Dorothy," and then type **St.**

You can also click Save on the File menu to save changes to the current record.

3 Click in the First Name field of the next record.

The change is saved.

While you were editing Earl Lee's record, a pencil symbol appeared in the area on the left side of the form. The pencil symbol indicates that you've changed data in the current record but that your changes aren't saved yet. If you haven't changed data in the current record, a triangle appears instead of a pencil. You can see how this works while you add the next record.

Add the second record

1 Type **Becky** in the First Name field.

2 Type the following data, pressing TAB to move from field to field.

Last name: **Sawyer**
Street Address: **260 Kent Street Station 1551**
City: **Ottawa**
State/Province: **Ontario**
Postal Code: **K1A 0E6**

Country: **Canada**
Subscription Length: **6 Months**
Renewal: **No**

Proofread your entries. When you're finished, you will close the Subscription form.

Close the form

*You can also
click Close on
the File menu.*

➤ On the Subscription window, click the Close button.

Be sure that you click the Close button on the form, not the Close button on the Microsoft Access window. When you close the form, your new entry is saved.

Click here

Opening a Table to View the Data

Just as a record is used to group similar pieces of information together, a table is used to group records together. A table organizes data into rows and columns. Each column describes some characteristic of the data (a field), and each row contains an item of the data (a record). For example, a field might contain the subscriber's last name, while a record would completely describe one person's subscription.

The records you just added using the Subscription form were saved in the Customers table in the Sweet Lil's database. In the next exercise, you look at the new records in the Customers table.

Open the Customers table

1   In the Database window, click the Tables tab.

The list of tables in the Sweet Lil's database is displayed.

13

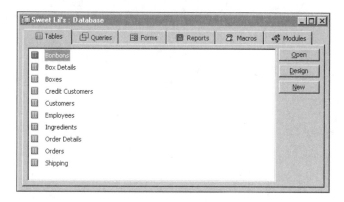

2   Double-click the Customers table.

The Customers table opens, and its records are displayed.

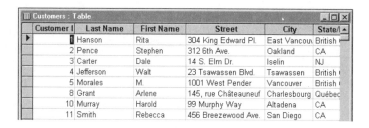

The two records you added are at the end of the list of customers. You can use the navigation buttons at the bottom of the Customers Table window to move directly to the first, previous, next, or last record.

Move to the last record

1   In the lower-left corner of the window, click the navigation button for the last record.

The last few records in the table appear. The last two records are the ones you just added for Earl Lee and Becky Sawyer. This table was set up to automatically assign customer ID numbers to all new records. Lesson 4, "Controlling Database Growth," discusses how to set up a table that assigns ID numbers.

2   To return to the Database window, click the Close button.

TIP You can use the keyboard or the vertical scroll bar to move between records, but the fastest way to move around in a large database is by using the navigation buttons and the mouse.

Understanding Views

A paper form shows one arrangement of your data. To see another arrangement, you have to look at a different paper form. A Microsoft Access form, however, provides the flexibility of two *views*, or arrangements, of your data: Form view and Datasheet view. In Form view, the fields are arranged to show each individual record to its best advantage. Datasheet view shows the same data arranged in rows and columns, like a spreadsheet, so that you can see multiple records at the same time.

Switching Between Views of a Form

You've just been put in charge of Sweet Lil's new Fudge Mocha line. You'll use the Bonbons form to update existing records for Fudge Mocha bonbons and to add records for several new bonbons.

Open a form

1 In the Database window, click the Forms tab.

   A list of the forms in the Sweet Lil's database is displayed.

2 Double-click the Bonbons form.

   The Bonbons form appears, and the record for Candlelight Ecstasy is displayed.

In Form view, the fields on the Bonbons form are arranged so that you can see all the information about an individual bonbon at a glance. For your current task, a row-and-column format would make it easier to compare fields from different Fudge Mochas.

Switch to Datasheet view

View

➤ On the toolbar, click the View down arrow, and then click Datasheet View.

   The records in the Bonbons form appear in a table layout (that is, a layout that has rows and columns). The triangle next to the Candlelight Ecstasy record indicates that Candlelight Ecstasy is the current record.

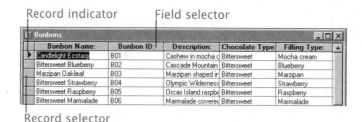

Record indicator   Field selector

Record selector

You can see that two of the bonbons in the new Fudge Mocha line—Walnut Fudge Mocha and Pistachio Fudge Mocha—are already in the database (Bonbon IDs F01 and F02). These are the records you want.

Move to a different record

▶ Click anywhere in the row for Walnut Fudge Mocha.

Now the record for Walnut Fudge Mocha is the current record. The triangle at the left edge of the datasheet is now pointing to the Walnut Fudge Mocha record. If you switch back to Form view, Walnut Fudge Mocha is the record you'll see on the form.

Switch views

The graphic on the View button changes depending on the current selection.

1   On the toolbar, click the View down arrow, and then click Form View.

The record for Walnut Fudge Mocha is displayed in Form view.

2   Click the View down arrow, and then click Datasheet View.

The form appears in Datasheet view. Walnut Fudge Mocha is still the current record.

Changing the Appearance of a Datasheet

The Bonbon Description field describes each bonbon in a sentence or two. You are going to include these descriptions in Sweet Lil's catalog, so you want to make sure that the text is just right. With the datasheet laid out as it is now, you can see only part of each bonbon's description. To read an entire description, you'd have to use the arrow keys and the HOME and END keys to scroll through the text.

Rather than doing a lot of scrolling, you decide to change the datasheet layout so that you can read the entire description at once. To change the height of a row in a datasheet, you use the *record selector* on the left side of the record. You use the *field selector* at the top of a column to change the column width.

You'll start by maximizing the Form window and then changing the row height so that you can see the entire description of a bonbon.

Change the row height

You can also double-click the Form window title bar to maximize the window.

1 Maximize the Form window.

It is easier to work in a maximized window.

2 Position the mouse pointer on the lower border of any record selector.

Bonbon Name:	Bonbon ID:	Description:	Chocolate Type:	Filling Type:	Nut Type:
Candlelight Ecstasy	B01	Cashew in mocha c	Bittersweet	Mocha cream	Cashew
Bittersweet Blueberry	B02	Cascade Mountain	Bittersweet	Blueberry	None
Marzipan Oakleaf	B03	Marzipan shaped ir	Bittersweet	Marzipan	None
Bittersweet Strawberry	B04	Olympic Wilderness	Bittersweet	Strawberry	None
Bittersweet Raspberry	B05	Orcas Island raspbe	Bittersweet	Raspberry	None

To resize a record, position the mouse pointer here.

3 Drag the border down to make the row higher.

Microsoft Access resizes all the rows. (One row cannot be sized differently from the other rows in the table.)

4 Adjust the height of the rows until you can read the complete description for Bittersweet Blueberry (Bonbon ID B02).

Change the column width

Now that you've resized the rows, you'll adjust the width of some of the columns. The Bonbon ID field and the Cost field are wider than necessary. If you make these columns narrower, you'll be able to see more of the other fields in the datasheet.

1 Position the mouse pointer on the right border of the field selector for the Bonbon ID field.

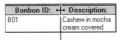

Bonbon ID:	Description:
B01	Cashew in mocha cream covered

Position the mouse pointer here.

2 Double-click the right edge of the field selector.

The column is sized to fit the widest entry in the field, including the complete field name at the top of the column.

3 At the bottom of the Datasheet window, click in the scroll bar to scroll to the right to see the rest of the fields.

Click here to scroll in large increments.

Record: |◄ ◄ 18 ► ►| ►* of 41

Click here to scroll in small increments.

17

4 Make the column for the Cost field narrower by double-clicking the right border of the field selector.

TIP You can click the arrows at either end of the scroll bar to scroll one field (one column) at a time.

Save the datasheet layout

Records are automatically saved as you move from record to record, but changes to the layout of a form or table must be saved by using the Save command.

You can save this convenient layout so that your datasheet appears this way every time you use it.

➤ On the File menu, click Save.

Scroll through the records

You're ready to work with the records in the Fudge Mocha line. But now that you've increased the height of your datasheet rows, the records you want aren't visible. You can use either the vertical scroll bar or the PAGE DOWN key to scroll through the records.

1 In the vertical scroll bar, click below the scroll box. Or, press PAGE DOWN.

Microsoft Access scrolls down one page (window).

2 Continue to click below the scroll box until you see Walnut Fudge Mocha in the list.

Each time you click below the scroll box, the box moves down the scroll bar to show your relative position in the records.

To scroll up or down one record at a time, click the arrows at the top or bottom of the scroll bar.

TIP If you hold down the left mouse button while moving the scroll box, a ScrollTip (a small box that displays information) indicates the record number that will be at the top of your display when you release the mouse and the total number of records (for example, record 187 of 322). If you know the relative position of the records you're looking for, you can move to them very quickly by dragging the scroll box. For example, if you're looking for a record in the middle of the list, drag the scroll box to the middle of the vertical scroll bar. You can see the records change as you drag the scroll box.

Speeding Up Data Entry by Using Editing Tools

You keep a database current and accurate by updating data in fields. Microsoft Access has convenient editing features that help you edit, move, copy, and delete data in fields. You'll find most of the editing features on the Edit menu and on the toolbar.

When you edit in Microsoft Access, keep in mind a principle called *select, then do*. If you want to copy, delete, or change something, you first *select* it, and *then* you *do* it by clicking the command you want on a menu or by clicking the appropriate button on the toolbar. Many menu commands show a toolbar button image to the left of the command to indicate which button corresponds to that command. Using the toolbar buttons is usually faster than clicking menu commands. Convenient keyboard shortcuts are also listed to the right of many menu commands. If you do a lot of typing, you might want to memorize the keyboard shortcuts for the commands you use frequently. Find the command method that works best for you—for example, if you want to delete text, first you drag to select the text, and then you can click Cut on the Edit menu, press the shortcut keys CTRL+X, or click the Cut button on the toolbar.

When you cut or copy text or an object, the object is placed in the Windows storage area called the *Clipboard*. When you paste, Microsoft Access pastes whatever is on the Clipboard to the current location of the insertion point. You can copy text from one field and then paste it into another field or into as many other fields as you need. That's because Windows keeps the Clipboard contents until you copy or cut something else or until you exit Windows.

Add text to a field

Market research indicates that chocolate fudge is a key ingredient for the success of your new line. You'll add the phrase "smothered in fudge" to the end of each bonbon description.

1 In the Description field for the Walnut Fudge Mocha bonbon, click between the t in "walnut" and the period.

The insertion point appears where you click.

2 Press the SPACEBAR to insert a space, and then type **smothered in fudge**

Copy text from one field to another

Rather than type the phrase again, you can copy it to the Description field for the Pistachio Fudge Mocha bonbon.

1 Select the phrase "smothered in fudge," including the space in front of "smothered" but not the period at the end.

Hint: Click in the space after the t in "walnut." Drag to select the text you want.

2 On the toolbar, click the Copy button.

Microsoft Access places a copy of the selected text on the Clipboard.

Copy

You can also click Copy on the Edit menu.

Paste

You can also
click Paste on
the Edit menu.

Cut

3 In the Description field for the Pistachio Fudge Mocha bonbon, position the insertion point between the o in "pistachio" and the period.

4 On the toolbar, click the Paste button.

The text is pasted from the Clipboard.

 NOTE You use the same steps to move text, except you click Cut instead of Copy on the Edit menu (or click the Cut button, which is to the left of the Copy button on the toolbar). The highlighted copy is removed from the text and placed on the Clipboard. Then, you can paste the text where you want it.

Add new records

Next, you'll enter records for Sweet Lil's three new Fudge Mochas—Pecan, Cashew, and Almond. You can add new records in either Datasheet view or Form view, but it's easier in Form view because you can see all the fields in a record at once.

1 On the toolbar, click the View down arrow, and then click Form View.

The Bonbons form appears in Form view.

2 Click the New Record navigation button.

New Record
navigation button

The new record is displayed following the last record in the set.

3 Type this data in the first two fields:

Bonbon Name: **Pecan Fudge Mocha**

Bonbon ID: **F03**

4 In the Description field, type **Creamy sweet mocha and nutty pecan,** and then press the SPACEBAR.

The next part of the description, "smothered in fudge," is still on the Clipboard. Instead of typing the description, you can paste it again.

You can also
click the right
mouse button,
and select Paste.

5 On the toolbar, click the Paste button.

6 Type a period at the end of the description.

Edit text

"Nutty" is redundant as an adjective for "pecan," so you'll delete it. To match the other Fudge Mocha descriptions, you want this description to start with

"Sweet creamy" rather than "Creamy sweet." You can replace the old text at the same time that you type the new text; you don't have to delete the old text first.

1   Select the word "nutty" and the space after it, and then press DELETE.

2   In the Description field, select "Creamy sweet."

3   Type **Sweet creamy**

The text you type replaces the selected text. Now your description is correct.

Selecting Data Entry Values from a List

A *value* is an individual piece of data, such as a last name, an address, or an ID number. Sometimes a database designer will add a list of correct values to some fields. If the person entering the data doesn't know or can't remember what to enter, he or she can select the appropriate value from the list. Selecting a value from a list is often quicker than typing the value yourself. But using lists has another advantage besides speed—your data is more accurate. When you select a value from a list, you know that it's spelled consistently and that it's a valid entry.

The Chocolate Type field on the Bonbons form is a special kind of field called a *list box*. List boxes display a list of values to select from. You can use either the mouse or the keyboard to select a value from the list.

The Nut Type and Filling Type fields are both *combo boxes,* which are combinations of text entry and list boxes. In a combo box, you can either type the value yourself or select it from the list.

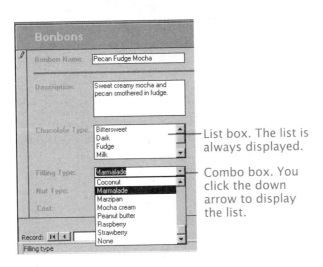

— List box. The list is always displayed.

— Combo box. You click the down arrow to display the list.

Select a value from a list

You can also press TAB to move to the Chocolate Type field.

➤ In the Chocolate Type field, click "Fudge" to select it.

Fudge is the only value in the Chocolate Type list that starts with f, so you can select Fudge by typing the first letter of the word. If the list has more than one f value, you can type f to go to the first one and then use the DOWN ARROW key to move down the list.

Select a value in a combo box

You can either type the value you want in the Filling Type combo box, or you can select a value from the list. Often, it's easier and more accurate to select a value.

You can also press TAB to move to the Filling Type field, and then press F4 to display the drop-down list.

1 Click the down arrow in the Filling Type field to display the list.

This list shows you the fillings that Sweet Lil's uses.

2 Select Mocha Cream from the list.

To select the value without using the mouse, type **mo**, the first two letters in Mocha. Because Mocha Cream is the only value that starts with those two letters, Microsoft Access selects it. If you wanted to select Marmalade instead of Marzipan, you'd type **marm**

3 Type **Pecan** in the Nut Type field, or select it from the list.

Enter the bonbon cost

➤ Type **.25** in the Bonbon Cost field, and then press TAB to move to the last field on the form.

When you exit the Bonbon Cost field, the value is automatically formatted as a currency value.

NOTE If you'd like to build on the skills that you learned in this lesson, you can do the One Step Further. Otherwise, skip to "Finish the lesson."

One Step Further: Manipulating Datasheet Views

Datasheets display all the fields and records of a table. If the table has a large number of fields, Datasheet view might be difficult because you can't see all the fields on a single screen. Two techniques that make large datasheets easier to work with are freezing and hiding columns.

Freeze a column

When you scroll to the fields on the far right of the Bonbon Table datasheet, you can no longer see the Bonbon Name field, so you can't tell which bonbon records you're viewing. It would be much easier to scroll through the data fields to the right while the Bonbon Name field remains anchored, or frozen, on the left. You can do that by freezing the column.

If your screen resolution is more than 640 x 480 pixels, you might not need to scroll and you will not see the scroll bars.

1 On the toolbar, click the View down arrow, and then click Datasheet.

2 Scroll back to the left side of the datasheet.

Click here to scroll to the left.

3 Click in any record in the Bonbon Name column.

4 On the Format menu, choose Freeze Columns.

Microsoft Access displays a bold line on the right border of the Bonbon Name column. Now the column is frozen.

5 Scroll horizontally to see the fields on the right side of the record, and then scroll to the left side of the form.

This column doesn't scroll. All other columns scroll.

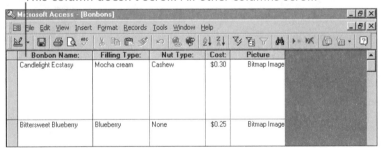

Hide a column

The Format menu also contains a Hide Columns command. When you choose the command, it hides the column that contains the insertion point.

In Datasheet view, the bonbon pictures cannot be seen. Because the pictures aren't visible anyway, you can hide the Picture column.

➤ Click the right border of the Picture column at the column heading, and drag the right border past the left border.

Microsoft Access hides the column.

Drag from here...

...to here.

23

Restore hidden columns

1   On the Format menu, click Unhide Columns.

    If the Unhide Columns dialog box indicates that the Picture column is already showing, the column might not be completely hidden. Make sure that you dragged the column's right border *all the way* to its left border.

2   Select the Picture field check box, and then click Close.

Finish the lesson

1   To continue to the next lesson, on the File menu, click Close.

2   If you are finished using Microsoft Access for now, on the File menu, click Exit.

Lesson Summary

To	Do this
Open a database	In the Microsoft Access dialog box, double-click the database you want to open. *or* In the Microsoft Access Startup window, double-click More Files. In the Open dialog box, select the folder where the database file is stored, and double-click the database filename.
Open a form	In the Database window, click the Forms tab, and then double-click the form you want to open.
Select an option in an option group	Click the option. *or* Press an arrow key until the option is selected.
Select or clear a check box	Click the check box. *or* Press TAB to move to the check box, and then press the SPACEBAR.

To	Do this	Button
Move to the next record on a form	Click the Next Record button at the bottom of the form. *or* With the insertion point in the last field, press TAB.	
Move from field to field	Click the field you want to move to. *or* Press TAB to move to the next field, and press SHIFT+TAB to move to the previous field.	
Move to the previous record in a form	Press the PAGE UP key. *or* Click the Previous Record navigation button at the bottom of the form.	
Save data	Microsoft Access automatically saves your data when you move to another record or window, close the form, or exit the program. *or* If you want to save your data at any other time, click Save on the File menu or click the Save button.	
Open a table	In the Database window, click the Tables tab, and then double-click the table you want to open.	
Switch between Form view and Datasheet view	Click the View down arrow, and then click Datasheet View or Form View.	
Change the height of rows or the width of a column in a datasheet	To resize rows, drag the lower border of any record. To resize a column, drag the right border of the column's field selector.	
Copy text from one field to another	Select the text. On the toolbar, click the Copy button. Place the insertion point where you want the text to appear. On the toolbar, click the Paste button.	

To	Do this	Button
Move text from one field to another	Select the text. On the toolbar, click the Cut button. Place the insertion point where you want the text to appear. On the toolbar, click the Paste button.	
Freeze columns	Click any record in the column you want to freeze, and then click Freeze Columns on the Format menu.	

For online information about	On the Help menu, click Contents And Index, click the Index tab, and then type
Opening databases	**opening databases**
Moving between records	**records, navigating**
Saving data	**saving records**
Opening tables	**opening tables**
Changing column widths	**resizing columns**
Hiding a column	**hiding columns**
Freezing columns	**freezing columns**
Copying text from one field to another	**copying data**
Moving text from one field to another	**moving data**

Increasing Efficiency by Using Subforms

Estimated time
40 min.

In this lesson you will learn how to:

- Use a subform.
- Use a validation message to help you enter the right data.
- Undo your edits.
- Simplify tasks by using command buttons.
- Use subforms to add and change data.
- Delete a record.

When you fill out a form, it's easy to make a small mistake that can turn into a big problem. A simple subtraction error can result in a frustrating check of the numbers; a search for a forgotten bit of information can eat up time; and there's always the possibility of writing the right information in the wrong box. What you need is a form that does calculations for you, looks up missing information, and warns you when the data you enter doesn't make sense.

Microsoft Access forms can do all this for you. In this lesson, you'll find out how to use forms that help you start and stay with the right data.

Understanding Forms That Have Subforms

In this lesson, you will use a form that has been named Boxes. The Boxes form is more complex than either the Subscription form or the Bonbons form used in Lesson 1. But when you use Microsoft Access forms, "more complex" doesn't necessarily mean "harder."

The Boxes form contains a *subform*, which is a form within a form. Because the Boxes form has a subform, you can look at all the information about the box (number of boxes in stock, total cost of the box, and so on) on the main form at the same time you look at detailed information on the subform about the candies that are in the box (what type of bonbons are in the box, how many are in the box, type of filling, individual cost of each bonbon, and so on). You can scroll through the records in the subform, adding and deleting types of bonbons, until the box contains the candies that you want.

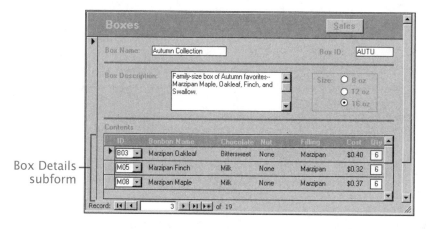

Box Details subform

The advantage of using a form that has a subform is that you can work with data from two different tables at the same time. This approach not only simplifies using Microsoft Access, it increases the reliability of the data in the tables.

When you use the Boxes form, data you enter on the main form is stored in the Boxes table. Data you enter on the subform is stored in the Box Details table. You'll learn how to create a form that has a subform in Lesson 9, "Merging Data from Two Tables onto One Form." You'll learn more about why the data is stored in separate tables in Lesson 4, "Controlling Database Growth."

Start the lesson

> If Microsoft Access isn't started yet, start it. Open the Sweet Lil's database. If the Microsoft Access window doesn't fill your screen, maximize the window.
>
> If you need help opening the database, see Lesson 1.

Focusing on Specific Data by Using a Subform

Microsoft Access forms are very versatile tools. A well-designed form can accomplish several tasks simultaneously. For example, a single form can be used to update two or more tables at once. When a form uses information from more than one table, you should create a subform. The main form is based on the data from one table, and the subform is based on the data from the second table. Using the subform structure increases the control you have over your tables and makes your database easier to maintain.

You'll use the Boxes form to add a new box of bonbons called Winter Collection to Sweet Lil's line of products. The Boxes form contains the Boxes subform. The Boxes subform can be thought of as a "window" into another set of data, which is stored in a separate table. The Boxes table stores data about all the boxes. The Boxes form draws its data from the Boxes table. The details of what makes up a particular box are stored in a table called Box Details. The Boxes subform draws its data from the Box Details table. In Microsoft Access, viewing a form and a subform together has several advantages. It is more convenient, and it makes forms easier to construct.

 NOTE   The reasons for storing the external and internal box details in separate tables are discussed in Lesson 4 "Controlling Database Growth." In general, however, this type of storage structure helps ensure the integrity of the data and simplifies database maintenance.

Open a form, and go to the new record

Restore

You can also select the Boxes form, and click the Open box in the Database window.

1   Double-click the Boxes form. Click the Restore button on the form.

The record for the All Seasons Collection—the first box in the Boxes table—appears in the main form, and the contents of the All Seasons box are displayed in the subform.

2   At the bottom of the form, click the New Record navigation button.

The new blank record appears at the end of the existing records.

Enter data in the main form

1   Type the following data in the fields on the main form:

Box Name   **Winter Collection**

Box ID   **WINT**

Box Description   **Nuts and berries coated with chocolate and fudge for those long winter evenings by the fire.**

2   In the Size option area, select 12 oz.

3 Press TAB to move to the subform.

The insertion point moves to the first field in the subform.

Locate data and enter a record in the subform

For more information about combo boxes, see Lesson 10, "Streamlining Data Entry."

The first field in the subform will contain the Bonbon ID for the first candy in the Winter Collection box. The bonbon you want is Bittersweet Blueberry, but you're not sure of its ID number. You'll use the ID combo box to find the ID you want. A *combo box* is a control area, similar to a list box or text box, in which you can either type a value or select a value from a list.

1 Click the ID down arrow to display the ID combo box list.

The list has two columns: IDs are in the first column, and the corresponding bonbon names are in the second column. When you select a row, only the ID is stored in the field. The names are there to help you make the right selection.

Box list—
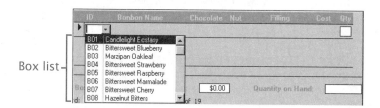

2 Select Bittersweet Blueberry.

The Bonbon ID B02 appears in the ID field; and the Bonbon Name, Chocolate, Nut, Filling, and Cost fields are filled in. The fields for which you supply information have a white background; all the other fields have a gray background.

3 Press TAB to move to the next empty field.

The insertion point skips fields that are already filled in and moves to the Qty field.

4 Type 3 in the Qty field, and then press TAB.

Microsoft Access saves the first record in the subform and moves the insertion point to the first field in the second record.

Enter more subform records

As you add the remaining bonbons to the subform in this exercise, the Box Cost field in the lower left of the main form will change for each new record because how much a box costs depends on which bonbons are in the box. When you use the Boxes form, the box cost is calculated automatically as you add bonbons to the box.

NOTE Look at the vertical scroll bar on the right side of the subform. The presence of the scroll bar means that the subform contains more records, and you can scroll through the records to view them.

1 Add the following two bonbons to the Winter Collection:

ID		Qty
B05	Bittersweet Raspberry	3
D03	Cashew Supreme	3

2 Press TAB to move to the next record in the subform.

A new, blank record appears.

3 Add the following three bonbons to the Winter Collection:

ID		Qty
D07	Classic Cherry	3
F01	Walnut Fudge Mocha	3
F02	Pistachio Fudge Mocha	3

4 Scroll through the subform to check your work. Be sure that each record is correct before continuing.

Exit the subform

Now that you've added all the bonbons to the new box, you're ready to fill in the two fields in the lower portion of the main form—Box Price and Quantity On Hand.

 Press CTRL+TAB to move to the next field on the main form.

The insertion point moves from the subform to the Box Price field on the main form. You can also move to the Box Price field by clicking that field, but when you're entering new records, it's easier to keep your hands on the keyboard than to switch between the mouse and the keyboard.

 TIP When you're using a form that has a subform, you can think of the CTRL key as the "switch form" key. Just as pressing TAB moves you to the next field in a form, pressing CTRL+TAB moves you from the subform to the next field in the main form. And just as pressing SHIFT+TAB moves you to the previous field in a subform or main form, pressing CTRL+SHIFT+TAB moves you from the subform to the previous field in the main form.

Validating Your Data

You will learn more about validation rules and how to create forms for automatic data entry in Lesson 5, "Keeping Database Information Reliable."

You've already seen a number of ways that using a Microsoft Access form can help you enter the correct data. For example, the ID combo box in the subform helps you pick the right ID by showing you bonbon names as well as IDs. After you pick a bonbon, Microsoft Access fills in fields, such as the Bonbon Name and Chocolate fields, saving you time and eliminating the possibility of data entry errors in those fields. As you're adding bonbons to the box, the cost of the box is automatically calculated and is displayed in the Box Cost field.

A form can be of even more help when you're entering data. Microsoft Access displays a message when you enter incorrect information in a form. The value you enter in a field is checked against a validation rule that was established when the table was created. If the value you attempt to enter breaks the rule, a message appears. You can't exit the field until you correct the invalid data.

Correct the data

The note you have from Sweet Lil's Marketing Department says to give the new box the special introductory price of $7.50.

1 Type **7.50** in the Box Price field, and then press TAB.

A validation message tells you the value you entered is incorrect, and gives you information about how to correct the problem.

  NOTE If the message doesn't appear, you might have incorrect data in the Box Cost field. The validation rule for the Box Price field allows those values that are at least twice as much as the value in the Box Cost field. An error message is displayed if the price is less than twice the cost. The Box Cost field is calculated automatically from the records entered in the subform.

2 Click OK.

At this point, you double-check with the Marketing Department and discover that the introductory price of the new box should be $17.50.

3 Type a **1** before the 7 in the Box Price field, and then press TAB.

Microsoft Access accepts this price, adds a dollar sign, and moves the insertion point to the Quantity On Hand field.

4 Type **0** (zero) in the Quantity On Hand field.

This is a new box type, so you don't have any in stock yet.

Undoing Your Edits

In Microsoft Access, you can use the Undo button to reverse changes you make to the current field or record. Because there are different types of actions that you might want to undo, the ToolTip for the Undo button changes to reflect the most recent reversible action. For example, if your most recent action was to enter data, the Undo button is labeled the Undo Typing button. If your most recent action was to delete a field, the available Undo action will be Undo Delete.

Undo your most recent action

1 Select "Nuts and berries" at the beginning of the Box Description field for the Winter Collection, and then type **Berries and nuts**

2 Place the insertion point in front of the word "fire," type **roaring** and then press the SPACEBAR.

3 On the toolbar, click the Undo button.

The word "roaring," your most recent change, is deleted.

Undo

You can also choose Undo on the Edit menu.

Undo all edits in the current field

After making numerous changes to the text in a field, you might decide that you prefer the original text. Rather than restore the original text one change at a time, you can undo all the changes to that field at once.

➤ On the Edit menu, click Undo Current Field/Record.

All the edits you made to the Box Description field since moving the insertion point into the field are undone. The Undo button becomes the Undo The Current Field button.

Using a Command Button

Sometimes one task turns into many related tasks. For example, you might be looking at information about the contents of a product on one form and realize that you also want to see sales information for the product. So you open a sales form and find the appropriate sales information. These related tasks can require a number of steps, and you might need to repeat these actions many times.

A *command button* (a button that initiates a series of commands) condenses related tasks into a single step. A command button can be used to perform one action or a series of actions, depending on how you define the button. Command buttons can be used to either execute macros or run programs written in Visual Basic for Applications, which is a special programming language. A *macro* is a recording of a list of tasks or a set of keystrokes. When a macro is played, Microsoft Access performs the prescribed actions very quickly, thus improving productivity. How to create a macro and assign it to a command button is covered in Lesson 10, "Streamlining Data Entry."

Use a command button to go to a specific record

The Sales command button on this form executes a macro called Show Box Sales. The Sales command button was added to the form when the form was created, and the Show Box Sales macro was assigned to the Sales command button. In this exercise, you'll use the Sales command button to check the sales of one of Sweet Lil's best sellers: the Autumn Collection. The Autumn Collection is the third record in the Boxes form.

1   To the right of the word "Record," in the lower-left corner of the window, select the current record number, and then type **3**

Record indicator

2   Press ENTER.

The record for the Autumn Collection is displayed.

3   At the top of the Boxes form, click the Sales command button.

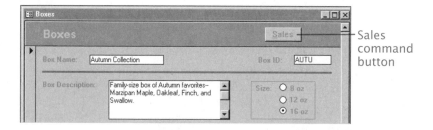

Sales command button

The Box Sales form appears. Just as the Boxes form has a subform, the Box Sales form has a subform called Daily Sales. The main form shows the name of the box at the top and the total sales for the box at the bottom of the form. The subform shows daily sales for the box.

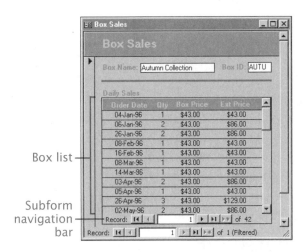

Box list

Subform navigation bar

You can also click Close on the File menu.

4 Scroll through the records in the Daily Sales subform to see all the sales.

5 To close the Box Sales form, click the Close button.

6 To close the Boxes form, click the Close button.

Maintaining Your Database by Entering Data in Forms

In most databases, the only real constant is that data is constantly changing. You add records when you have to keep track of new people or things. You change records when the data changes. And you delete records when you no longer need to track the people or things represented by the records. Most data entry should be accomplished through forms. When designing a database, it is a good idea to use forms for entering data, rather than directly changing the tables. This method allows you, as the database designer, to build in controls to increase security.

In the following exercises you find and delete records. Sweet Lil's receives this note in the morning's mail:

Dear Sweet Lil's:

My son buys your chocolates frequently and loves them. In fact, he told me that he recently gave you my name to add to your customer list. I'm trying to lose some weight, so please don't add me to your list. No need to waste the catalog.

Thank you,

Francois Marcus

Find the record you want to delete

In this exercise, you find Francois Marcus in the Customers table.

1 Open the View Customers form.

2 Click in the Last Name field

Find

3 On the toolbar, click the Find button.

The Find In Field dialog box appears. The title bar of the Find In Field dialog box shows the name of the field you're searching: Last Name.

4 In the Find What box, type **Marcus**

You have the option of searching in all the fields for Marcus. Because you know the value is in the Last Name field (the current field), you can make the search go faster by searching only in that field. The dialog box should look like the following illustration.

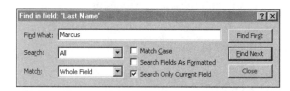

5 Click Find First.

The record for a Francois Marcus is displayed. This appears to be the record for the customer you need to call, but you must make sure there's not another customer who has the same name.

6 Click Find Next.

Microsoft Access displays a message indicating that it cannot find another Marcus.

7 Close the Find In Field dialog box.

Delete a record

Delete Record

You can also choose Delete Record on the Edit menu.

1 On the toolbar, click the Delete Record button.

2 When a message appears asking you to confirm the deletion, click Yes.
The record is deleted.

3 Close the View Customers form.

Find a record when you are missing details

As soon as you delete the record for Francois Marcus, you get a call from a clerk in Sweet Lil's Shipping Department. He's having trouble reading the address on a shipping label. All he can make out is part of the street name, which starts with "Stew." He asks whether you can use this information to find the name and address of the customer.

1   Open the Customer Review form.

2   In the Customer Review form, click in the field that contains the street address (the first line in the address).

> You don't have to go back to the first record in the table—you can use the Find button when you are in any record.

3   On the toolbar, click the Find button.

> The Find In Field dialog box appears. The Find What box still contains your last entry, Marcus.

4   In the Find What box, type **Stew**

5   Click the Match down arrow, and select Any Part Of Field.

> Because Stew is only part of the street name, you want to search for Stew no matter where it occurs in the field.

6   Click Find First.

> Microsoft Access finds an address that has "Stewart" in the street address.

You can make a search case-sensitive (find only text that has the same uppercase and lowercase letters) by selecting the Match Case check box. For example, if you want to find McDaniel and not Mcdaniel, use the Match Case check box.

7   Click Find Next.

> Microsoft Access finds a second record that has "Stew" in the address.

8   Click Find Next again.

> Microsoft Access doesn't find another "Stew," so you have two possible customers for the Shipping Department.

9   Click Close to close the Find In Field dialog box.

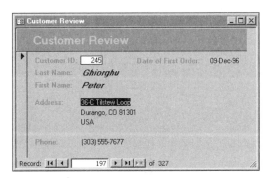

10   Close the Customer Review form.

NOTE   If you'd like to build on the skills that you learned in this lesson, you can do the One Step Further. Otherwise, skip to "Finish the lesson."

One Step Further: Replacing Data

In many instances, you will not only want to find data, you will want to replace the data with more up-to-date information. In addition to finding data, Microsoft Access can assist you with quickly replacing data that meets certain criteria. For example, if you know that a customer address has changed, you can combine the process of finding and replacing the data into one step.

Replace data meeting known criteria

Sweet Lil's has merged its Marketing and Acquisitions Departments. All employees are now members of the Marketing Department. You need to replace all Acquisitions entries in the Department Name field of the Employees table with the word "Marketing."

1 Make sure the Tables tab is selected in the Database window, and then double-click the Employees table.

2 Click anywhere in the Department Name field, and then click the Replace command on the Edit menu.

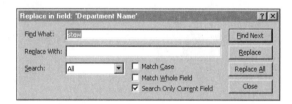

3 Type **Acquisitions** in the Find What field and **Marketing** in the Replace With field.

4 Click Replace All.

   All instances of Acquisitions in the Employees table are replaced with Marketing. A message appears, indicating that the Replace operation cannot be undone.

5 Click Yes.

6 Close the Replace In Field Department Name dialog box.

7 Close the Employees table.

Find and replace data simultaneously

You have already seen how Microsoft Access can help you to quickly locate data. In some cases, you might not know exactly which records you need to replace. For example, if some characters of the field are missing, you might need to use wildcard characters to find the data. *Wildcard characters* are special symbols that can be used to substitute for unknown characters. For example, if you are searching for a record that contains the letters "man" as the last three characters, but you are not sure whether the name is Freeman or Friedman, you can search with the * wildcard character. The * character replaces a group of characters, so searching for F*man find records that contain either spelling.

This morning, the Sweet Lil's Marketing Department received a call from a customer, V.J. Bernstein. She said she was recently married, and her last name is now Grable. The customer hung up before the clerk could find out how the customer spelled Bernstein. The Marketing Department has asked you to help find and replace the record.

1 Double click the Customers table to open it in Datasheet view.

2 Click anywhere in the Last Name field.

3 On the Edit menu, click Replace.

4 Type ***stein** in the Find What field, and then type **Grable** in the Replace field.

5 Click the Find Next button.

   The record for V.J. Bernstein is located. The customer address is the same.

6 Click the Replace button.

   The last name is changed to Grable.

7 Close the Replace in Field Last Name dialog box.

8 Close the Customers table.

Finish the lesson

1 To continue to the next lesson, on the File menu, click Close.

2 If you are finished using Microsoft Access for now, on the File menu, click Exit.

Lesson Summary

To	Do this	Button
Add a record	Click the New Record navigation button at the bottom of the form.	
Move from a main form to a field on a subform	Click the field in the subform. *or* In the last field on the main form before the subform, press TAB.	
Move from a subform to the next field on a main form	Click the field in the main form. *or* Press CTRL+TAB.	

To	Do this	Button
Move from a subform to the previous field on a main form	Press CTRL+SHIFT+TAB.	
Undo your most recent changes	On the toolbar, click the Undo button. *or* On the Edit menu, click Undo.	↺
Undo all edits in the current field	On the Edit menu, click Undo Current Field/Record.	
Go directly to a specific record	Type the record number in the Record Number box at the bottom of the form, and then press ENTER.	
Delete a record	Click in any field in the record to select it. Then click the Delete Record button.	▶✕
Find a record	On the toolbar, click the Find button, and fill in the dialog box.	🔍

For online information about	On the Help menu, click Contents And Index, click the Index tab, and then type
Adding records to a form	**new record**
Undoing changes	**undo**
Deleting records	**delete record**
Finding records	**find record**

Viewing Only the Information You Need

Estimated time
45 min.

In this lesson you will learn how to:

- Sort records.
- Specify a set of related records by using a filter.
- Report only the information you need.
- Preview and zoom in on report details.
- Print a report.
- Create mailing labels.

Databases can be very large and describe a wide variety of details. However, when you consult a database, you don't want all the available information at once. When you're interested in milk chocolate, you don't want to look at data about bittersweet chocolate. When you're interested in your Canadian customers, you don't want to see data about customers in the United States. As a user of the database, you will ask questions to narrow your search to the information you want; Microsoft Access will provide the answers.

While you're viewing data in forms, you can focus on the information you're interested in without wading through irrelevant data. In this lesson, you'll learn how to make sure that Microsoft Access displays only the data you want to see.

41

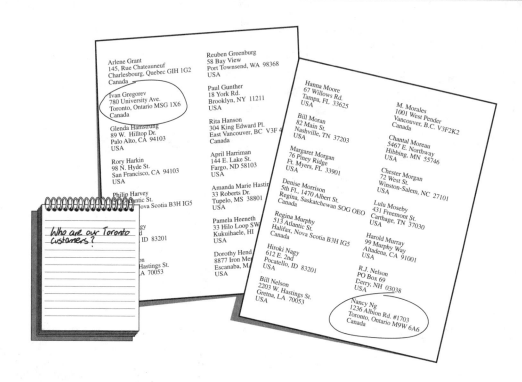

Organizing Your Data

Microsoft Access is more helpful than a filing cabinet or a pile of paper, because when you use Microsoft Access, you can find just the records you need, and you can *sort* (rearrange in a specified order) them the way you want them. Whether your database contains hundreds, thousands, or even millions of records, Microsoft Access finds exactly what you ask for and sorts the data to meet your requirements.

For quick searches, when you're looking for only one record, you use the Find button on the toolbar. When you want to see a particular group of records, such as all the employees hired after a certain date, you create a *filter* to tell Microsoft Access which records you want. When you create a filter, you give Microsoft Access a set of *criteria* or characteristics that describe the records you want to see. Microsoft Access then displays the records in a form or in a form datasheet.

You can sort records alphabetically, numerically, chronologically, or by a specified characteristic. For example, you could sort your customers alphabetically by last name.

Start the lesson

▶ If Microsoft Access isn't started yet, start it. Open the Sweet Lil's database. If the Microsoft Access window doesn't fill your screen, maximize the window.

If you need help opening the database, see Lesson 1.

Putting Records in Order by Using the Sort Button

In addition to using Microsoft Access to keep track of candy orders, Sweet Lil's maintains employee records in a table called Employees. You use the Employees table to conduct annual employee performance reviews. You'll find it easiest to keep your view of the Employees table sorted into departments so you can review the employees a department at a time.

To see the Employee table grouped by department, you sort the table by the Department field.

Sort on the Department field

1 Make sure the Tables tab is in front, and then double-click the Employees table.

2 Click in the Department Name field.

43

Sort Ascending

3 On the toolbar, click the Sort Ascending button.

The records are sorted by department, in ascending alphabetical order, from A to Z.

First Name	Last Name	Title	Extension	Department Na	Birthda
Ursula	Halliday	Buyer	677	Acquisitions	7,
Donna	Petri	Buyer	678	Acquisitions	5,
Rowen	Gilbert	VP Planning	679	Acquisitions	8/1
Mary	Culvert	VP Marketing	134	Marketing	12/1
Jerome	Woods	Marketing Agen	135	Marketing	3,
Nora	Bromsler	Marketing Agen	136	Marketing	5,
Dale	Wilson	Designer	137	Marketing	9/3
Hans	Orlon	VP Operations	787	Operations	5,
Charles	Beatty	Administrative A	788	Operations	10,
Elizabeth	Yarrow	Administrative A	777	Operations	9,
Frederick	Mallon	Shipping Coordi	546	Shipping	7,
Adrienne	Snyder	Shipping clerk	547	Shipping	12,
Henry	Czynski	Shipping clerk	548	Shipping	6/1
Robin	Saito	Shipping clerk	549	Shipping	3/1

Employees : Table

Record: 1 of 14

Narrowing Your View by Using Filters

For a demonstration of how to create and use filters, double-click The Camcorder Files On The Internet shortcut on your Desktop or connect to the Internet address listed on p. xxvi.

In Microsoft Access, you can limit the number of records you see by using a filter. A *filter* is a set of criteria you apply to records to sort them. Filters do not change your data. Instead, they adjust your view of the data, so that only the information you need is visible. Filters are not saved when the table or form is closed. If you want to save a particular view of your data, you use a query, which is like a saved filter that you can use again and again. Queries are covered in Lesson 7, "Getting Answers to Questions About Your Data."

View only employees in the Marketing Department

Mary Culvert, Sweet Lil's vice-president of Marketing, has decided to call a meeting of the Marketing Department managers. She wants you to use Microsoft Access to quickly send them all a meeting notice. In this exercise, you use a filter to identify the Marketing Department managers.

Find

1 Be sure you are in the Department Name field.

2 Click the Find button to locate a record containing Marketing in the Department Name field.

3 In the Find What box, type **Marketing**, and make sure the Search Only Current Field option is selected.

4 Click Find First, and then click Close.

*Filter By
Selection*

5 On the toolbar, click the Filter By Selection button.

Because you selected Marketing in the Department Name field, the filter locates all employees in the Marketing Department. The navigation area at the bottom of the window indicates that you are viewing filtered data.

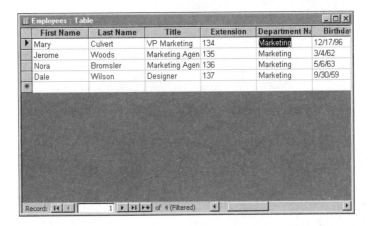

Add another criteria

The Marketing staff at Sweet Lil's are classified as either managers or sales personnel. Now that you have filtered the Employees table for the department, you also need to see whether the employee is a manager. To add another criteria to the filter, you use the Filter By Form button. The Filter By Selection button works only for simple filters. When building filters that have more than one criteria, it is necessary to use the Filter By Form feature.

Filter By Form

1 On the toolbar, click the Filter By Form button.

A blank row that has a column for each field is displayed; the word "Marketing" is highlighted in the Department Name column.

2 Scroll to view Classification data.

3 Click in the Classification column.

A down arrow appears, which indicates that the column has a drop-down list.

4 Click the Classification down arrow, and then select Manager.

5 On the toolbar, click the Apply Filter button.

Apply Filter

	Employee ID	First Name	Last Name	Title	Extension	Departmei
►	1	Mary	Culvert	VP Marketing	134	Marketing
	9	Dale	Wilson	Designer	137	Marketing
*	(AutoNumber)					

45

6 Scroll to view the Classification column.

7 On the Employees table, click the Close button, and then click No to close the table without saving your changes.

Communicating Through Reports

After you have organized your data, you might want to share the data with others or make a paper record of the results. Sharing data in this way is done through reports. Reports are similar to forms in that they draw data together from tables or queries. You can create reports yourself by using the Design window, or you can use one of the predefined report types available in the Report Wizard. Creating reports is covered in more detail in Lesson 11, "Customizing a Report."

> ## Sharing Reports Through Microsoft Outlook
>
> If you are using Outlook 97, an easy way to share reports with other users is by either importing the report to the Notes folder or saving it to a Shared folder.

View data in report

You must set a default printer before you can print or preview reports. See Access help for more information.

The Sales manager has created a report to show sales for the month of November 1996. You will now view this report.

1 In the Database window, click the Reports tab.

2 Double-click the Sales By Box report.

A message appears asking you to enter the dates for the period you want the report to cover.

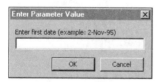

3 Type **1-Nov-96** as a starting date, and then press ENTER.

Microsoft Access recognizes a number of ways to enter dates. For example, you could have used 11/1/96, another United States format. The Canadian (English) format is 1/11/96.

To find out
which country
your computer
is set for, open
the Windows
Control Panel,
and double-click
the Regional
Settings icon.

4   In the next dialog box, type **30-Nov-96** as an ending date, and then press ENTER.

Microsoft Access collects the appropriate data and opens the report in Print Preview. Your toolbar has changed.

Look at a whole page at once

The report is magnified in Print Preview so that you can clearly read the data. In Print Preview you can switch to a detailed view by using the magnifying-glass pointer. You use the pointer to zoom out when you want to see how the data is laid out on the whole page, and to zoom in to see the magnified view.

Zoom

➤   Click the magnifying-glass pointer anywhere on the report. Or, click the Zoom button on the toolbar to display the whole page.

Zoom in on the data

You can also
switch views by
clicking the
Zoom button.

The layout looks fine. Now you'll make sure that you have the data you want.

➤   Click anywhere on the report. Or, click the Zoom button on the toolbar.

Now you're looking at the magnified view again.

Move around the page

1   Use the vertical scroll bar to move up and down the page, and use the horizontal scroll bar to move from left to right.

Two Pages

2   Click the Two Pages button to change to a two-page view of the report. You might have to maximize the window to view the pages.

TIP   If you want your report to have wider margins, click Page Setup on the File menu, and then on the Margins tab, change the margins.

Printing a Report

When you print a report, you can print the entire report, you can specify a range of pages or individual pages you want to print, and you can specify how many copies you want to print. If you print more than one copy, you can have Microsoft Access collate the copies for you.

IMPORTANT   If you have a printer connected to your computer, you can print the Sales By Box report now. If you don't have a printer connected to your computer, you can skip to step 3.

Print a report from Print Preview

If you want to use the default print settings, you can also click the Print button on the Standard toolbar.

1 On the File menu, click Print.

The Print dialog box appears. You want to print one copy of the whole report, so you don't need to change any of the settings in the Print dialog box.

2 Click OK.

3 Close the Sales By Box report.

 TIP When you double-click a report in the Database window, Microsoft Access opens it in Print Preview so that you can see how the report will look on the page before you print it. To print a report without opening it first in Print Preview, select the report in the Database window, and then click Print on the File menu or click the Print button on the toolbar.

Creating Mailing Labels

To create mailing labels, you use a Microsoft Access wizard. A *wizard* is like a database expert who asks you questions about the form or report you want and then builds it for you according to your answers. You use the Form Wizard to build forms and the Report Wizard to build reports. You can use the Label Wizard to create mailing labels.

Create mailing labels

After you examine the Sales By Box report, you decide to promote the two slowest-selling boxes by discounting them in a special mailing to all customers. You want to create mailing labels and print the labels sorted by postal codes. Because you just printed the Sales By Box report, the Database window still shows the list of reports.

1 Click New.

The New Report dialog box appears.

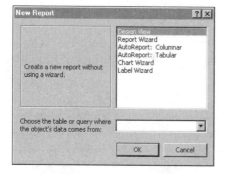

2 In the New Report dialog box, select Label Wizard.

3 Click the Choose The Table Or Query Where the Object's Data Comes From down arrow, and then select Customers.

The Customers table contains the names and addresses you want to print in the mailing labels.

4 Click OK.

The Label Wizard dialog box appears.

Select the mailing label size

You can choose from a wide range of label sizes, listed in either U.S. measurements (inches) or metric measurements. If you have label stock on hand, use the stock number to help you select the label size you want.

In the Label Type area, you can select the label paper type: sheet feed or continuous feed.

 Select Avery number 5260 (scroll down to find it), or the label stock you have available, and then click Next.

The Label Wizard displays a dialog box for formatting the text in your labels.

Choose the text font and color

You can use this dialog box to change the appearance of your mailing labels. For now, accept the default choices.

 Click Next.

Define the label text

1 In the Available Fields box, double-click the First Name field.

The field is added to the first line of your mailing label.

2 Press the SPACEBAR to add a space between first names and last names.

You'll type spaces and punctuation marks between the fields. These spaces and punctuation marks will appear on the label.

3 Double-click the Last Name field.

Microsoft Access adds the Last Name field to the first line of your mailing label, after the space you typed.

4 Press ENTER to move to the second line of the mailing label.

5 Add the following fields to the second, third, and fourth lines of the mailing label. If you make a mistake, select the line, and press the BACKSPACE key to remove the item from the mailing label.

Line	Field
Second	Street
Third	City, State/Province, and Postal Code fields in the third line. Type a comma between the City and State fields, and use a space between the State and Postal Code fields.
Fourth	Country

6 Click Next.

The Prototype Label box in the Label Wizard should look like this.

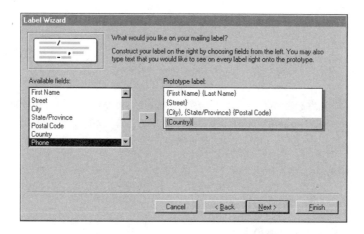

Sort the labels

You can sort the labels in the Label Wizard. When you select the field to sort in the Label Wizard, the wizard will sort the labels when they print. You want to sort the labels by postal code.

1 In the Available Fields list, select Postal Code, and click the single right-pointing arrow button between the two list boxes to have the Label Wizard sort by postal codes. Click Next.

2 The Label Wizard suggests the name of Labels Customers for the report. Accept that name by clicking Finish.

The labels appear as they will print on the page. Scroll through the labels.

TIP If the labels don't appear to be evenly lined up, the problem might be a mismatch between your printer driver and the label size or format. Try different label sizes.

Close the mailing label report

When you created the Labels Customers report, you saved the definition of the mailing labels, but not the actual names and addresses that print on the labels. The data that prints on the labels is stored in the Customers table. When Sweet Lil's adds a new customer, the customer information is added to the Customers table. The next time the Labels Customers report is printed, Microsoft Access will take the most current data from the Customers table to print the labels.

The report was automatically saved as Labels Customers when you created it, so you do not need to save it again.

 Close the Labels Customers report.

Your new report appears in the list of reports in the Database window. Now, whenever you need mailing labels for your customers, you can print this report.

 NOTE If you'd like to build on the skills that you learned in this lesson, you can do the One Step Further. Otherwise, skip to "Finish the lesson."

One Step Further: Creating More Complex Filters

It's spring 1997. In late 1996, Sweet Lil's launched a marketing promotion in Canada. Now, it's time to decide whether to expand the promotion for the United States by studying how successful the Canadian campaign is. Using filters allows you to quickly find and look at particular records. This exercise shows you more ways to specify information for your filter.

Identify new customers in Canada

Create a filter that shows Canadian customers added on or after November 15, 1996, the first day of the promotion.

1 Open the Customer Review form. Be sure that Form view is displayed.

You want to be in Form view because you use the Filter By Form button to create a complex filter.

Filter By Form

2 On the toolbar, click the Filter By Form button to begin building your filter.

The Filter By Form dialog box looks different, because you are building the filter in Form view.

3 Press TAB four times; the insertion point is between Address and Phone.

A down arrow appears to the right of the insertion point.

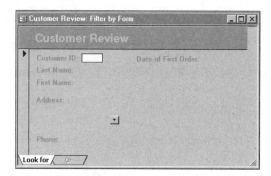

4 Click the down arrow, and select Canada.

Canada appears as a criteria in the Filter By Form dialog box. You could run a simple filter now by clicking the Apply Filter button, but for this exercise you'll add another, more complex criterion and a sort order.

Apply an Advanced Filter/Sort

1 On the Filter menu, click Advanced Filter/Sort.

The Customer ReviewFilter1 window opens, displaying the filter criteria you set in the previous steps. Next, you'll add criteria for Date Of First Order, and then sort the filtered records.

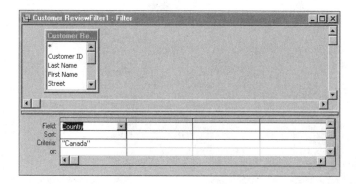

2 Press TAB to move to the next empty Field box in the criteria grid.

3 Click the down arrow for the empty Field box. In the drop-down list, scroll down, and then select Date Of First Order.

4 Click in the Sort box below Date Of First Order. Then, click the Sort down arrow and select Descending.

The records are sorted so that you see the newest customers (those that have the most recent date of first order) first. You want to see only those records for on or after November 15, 1996.

5 Under Date Of First Order, click in the Criteria box. Then, type the expression **>=15-Nov-96** and press ENTER.

The expression means "on or after November 15, 1996." After you enter the expression, Microsoft Access puts number signs (#) around the date, indicating that it is a date/time value.

Apply Filter

You can also click Datasheet View on the View menu.

6 On the toolbar, click the Apply Filter button to apply the filter.

The filter is applied, as indicated in the navigation area at the bottom of the form. You can use the navigation buttons to see each of the individual records resulting from the filter, or you can switch to Datasheet view to see all the filtered records at once. You can apply advanced filters in either Form view or Datasheet view.

7 On the toolbar, click the View down arrow, and select Datasheet View to see all the filtered records at once.

8 On the File menu, click Save.

Finish the lesson

1 To continue to the next lesson, on the File menu, click Close.

2 If you are finished using Microsoft Access for now, on the File menu, click Exit.

Lesson Summary

To	Do this	Button
Apply a filter by using Filter By Selection	Select a criteria in Form view or Datasheet view, and then click the Filter By Selection button on the toolbar.	
Apply a filter by using Filter By Form	On the toolbar, click the Filter By Form button. Select criteria in the Filter By Form dialog box, and then click the Apply Filter button on the toolbar.	

To	Do this	Button
Set criteria for an advanced filter	In the criteria grid of the Advanced Filter dialog box, select a field in the Field box, and then type a criteria expression in the Criteria box below the Sort box.	
Sort records in a filter	In Datasheet view, click in a field, and then click the Sort Ascending or Sort Descending button. *or* On the Filter menu, click Advanced Filter/Sort. In the Criteria grid of the Advanced Filter dialog box, select Ascending or Descending in the Sort box below the field on which you want to sort.	
Open and preview a report	In the Database window, click the Reports tab, and then double-click the report you want.	
Switch between a magnified view of a report in Print Preview and a view of the whole page	Click anywhere on the report. *or* On the toolbar, click the Zoom button.	
Print a report	In Print Preview, click Print on the File menu, or click the Print button on the toolbar. *or* To print a report directly from the Database window, select the report. Then, either click Print on the File menu, or click the Print button on the toolbar.	
Create mailing labels	In the Database window, click the Reports tab, and then click New. Select Label Wizard, select the table or query that contains the data for the labels, and then follow the Label Wizard instructions.	

For online information about	On the Help menu, click Contents And Index, click the Index tab, and then type
Specifying criteria	**criteria**
Using expressions	**expression**
Printing reports	**print reports**

Review & Practice

You will review and practice how to:

Estimated time
25 min.

- Open a database and a database form.
- View your data and move between records.
- Find specific records.
- Use a filter to group records.
- Sort records alphabetically and numerically.
- Create a report.

Before you begin to expand your database by working with tables, you can use the steps in this Review & Practice section to practice the skills and techniques you learned in Part 1, "Entering and Viewing Data in Microsoft Access."

Scenario

The Shipping Department has recently been added to Sweet Lil's corporate database. They have created several tables, and you have been asked to help them with some routine data entry tasks.

Step 1: *Open a Database and Examine the Data*

To get a general overview of the data, open the database and view the data using the Orders form. You will use the navigation buttons to view a few records, and then switch to Datasheet view to change a column width.

1 Start Microsoft Access, and open the Sweet Lil's database.

2 In the Database window, open the Orders form, and then use the navigation buttons to browse from the first to the last records.

3 Switch to Datasheet view.

4 Change the width of the City column, and switch back to Form view.

For more information about	See
Opening a database	Lesson 1
Opening a form	Lesson 1
Using the navigation buttons	Lesson 1
Switching between views	Lesson 1
Altering column width	Lesson 1

Step 2: Enter and Edit Data in Forms

Now that you have a general idea of the contents of the Orders table, you are ready to enter some records. The Shipping Department has given you some records to enter.

1 Be sure the Orders form is open, and then enter the following information for a new record.

Customer ID	**5**
Date	**September 5, 1996**
Order ID	**414**
Ship To	**A. Vincente, 123 Burns St., Dallas, Texas 75229 USA**
Credit Card	**World Credit**
Account Number	**123123789**
Expiration Date	**12/31/97**
Order	**Bitt Qty 1**
	Cher Qty 1
	Alls Qty 1

2 The shipping department cancels Order ID 414. Switch to Datasheet view, and delete the record for this order.

3 Switch back to Form view.

4 Go to Order ID 406. Change the number of Bittersweet boxes to 3.

For more information about	See
Entering data in a form	Lesson 1
Moving around in a form	Lesson 2
Deleting records	Lesson 2

Step 3: Find Records

While you are entering data, Bill Nelson calls to say that his order was mistakenly sent to his home address. He wanted the order sent to his cousin in Florida. While the customer is on the phone, you quickly check the order.

1 Switch to Form view of the Orders form.
2 In the Bill To section, select the Last Name field.
3 Use the Find button to locate the first order with Nelson as a last name and Bill as the first name.
4 Close the Find In Field dialog box.

For more information about	See
Finding records	Lesson 2

Step 4: Group Records by Using Filters

One problem with the Orders table is that orders from both 1995 and 1996 are all in the same table, so they all show up on the Orders form. You show the Shipping manager an easy way to view only 1996 orders, and then show her how to view only records in which the person placing the order is the person receiving the order.

1 Switch to the Datasheet view of the Orders form, and select the Order Date field.
2 Use the Filter By Form button to enter the criteria >=#1/1/96#.
3 Use the Apply Filter button to display the datasheet.
4 Switch to Form view, and create an advanced filter/sort.
5 Select the Last Name field as the criteria field for the filter.
6 Enter the criteria =[Ship Last Name].
7 Apply the filter.
8 Scroll through the filtered records.

For more information about	See
Filtering by form	Lesson 3
Creating advanced filters	Lesson 3

Step 5: Sort Records

The Shipping manager is very pleased with the filtered data, but she would also like to be able to place the records in order. You tell her she can order records first to last and last to first. She says she needs to do both, so you show her how.

1 Be sure Orders form is in Form view, and then select the Order Date field.
2 Use the Sort Descending button to place the orders in descending order.
3 Select the Last Name field in the Bill To section.
4 Use the Sort Ascending button to place the orders in ascending order.

For more information about	See
Sorting in ascending order	Lesson 3
Sorting in descending order	Lesson 3

Step 6: Create a Report

You show the Shipping manager how to create a mailing labels report using the Labels Wizard.

1 Close the Orders form.
2 Select the Reports tab.
3 Create a labels report using the Orders table and the Labels Wizard. The fields that should be included on the report are:

Ship First Name Ship Last Name

Ship Street

Ship City

Ship State/Province Ship Postal Code

Ship Country

4 Sort the report by Order ID number, and click Next.
5 When asked for a name, type **Shipping Labels**
6 To save the report, click Finish.

For more information about	See
Creating a labels report	Lesson 3
Sorting a report	Lesson 3

Finish the Review & Practice

1 To continue to the next lesson, on the File menu, click Close.
2 If you are finished using Microsoft Access, on the File menu, click Exit.

Part

2

Expanding and Creating Databases

Controlling Database Growth

Estimated time
55 min.

In this lesson you will learn how to:

- Use a Table Wizard to create a table.
- Add records using a table's datasheet.
- Design a new table.
- Add fields to a table.
- Set field properties.
- Create database relationships.
- Use primary keys to create links.

Organization is the key to a successful database; however, the importance of database organization becomes particularly clear when a database has to be expanded to incorporate new types of data. There are many ways to organize data. Photographs arranged in family albums, for example, are easier to find than those jumbled in a shoe box. A family album can, however, be organized by date or by holiday or even by subject.

In a Microsoft Access database, information is organized in *tables*, which are simply collections of data arranged in rows and columns. You can display database information in a variety of formats, but it's all stored in tables. The form used in Lesson 3, "Viewing Only the Information You Need," is one way of presenting data from one or more tables.

In this lesson, you'll learn how to create a table, define its fields, and add records to the table datasheet. You will also learn how to determine when you need a new database and how to create relationships within that database.

Understanding Tables and Databases

A database table contains data on the same subject or topic. One table might contain data about customers, such as each customer name, address, and phone number. Another table might contain data about candy, such as each bonbon's name, picture, and cost.

A Microsoft Access database is a collection of tables—or is at least one table—that you use to store related information. The tables in the Sweet Lil's database, for example, all contain data relating to different parts of Sweet Lil's business.

An important part of designing a database is deciding how to divide the data into tables and how those tables should be grouped into databases. Sweet Lil's database, for example, is made up of ten tables. Each of these tables describes a distinct entity. Some general guidelines for creating databases and assigning entities to tables are described in Appendix B, "Designing a Database."

Fields are covered in Lesson 1, "Viewing, Entering, and Customizing Data." In this lesson, you'll learn how to define the fields in a table, and you'll see how fields and records are displayed in tables.

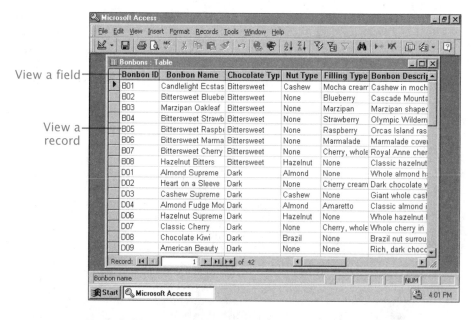

Each field corresponds to a column in a database table, and each field contains one and only one category of information. For example, each field in the Bonbons table contains a different category of information that describes a bonbon, such as the bonbon name, chocolate type, or filling.

Each record appears as a row in the table and contains all the data about each category. Each record in the Bonbons table, for example, contains all the data about a particular bonbon. Each record in the Customers table contains all the data about a particular customer.

Planning for Database Expansion

Sweet Lil's Chocolates is growing rapidly. More and more people are becoming customers, and more and more customers are using the toll-free order number. Most customers now want gift orders to arrive quickly, often overnight. To meet these needs, Sweet Lil's has to increase production and speed up delivery.

Two bottlenecks in producing and shipping the candy are the time it takes to get new supplies and the need for more shipping companies. To expedite communication with suppliers, Sweet Lil's will add supplier information to the corporate database. To meet its customers' requirements for faster delivery, the company will begin using two more shipping carriers so that customers have the option of air delivery.

Expanding Your Database by Using a Table Wizard

Microsoft Access can help you create a table by using a Table Wizard. Using a Table Wizard is a quick way to start a new database or to add a new table to an existing database. The Table Wizard may not capture every aspect of the new table or database, but you can always go back later and edit or change anything in the table.

Start the lesson

➤ If Microsoft Access isn't started yet, start it. Open the Sweet Lil's database. If the Microsoft Access window doesn't fill your screen, maximize the window.

If you need help opening the database, see Lesson 1.

Create a table by applying the Table Wizard

1 In the Database window, be sure that the Tables tab is in the front, and then click New.

The New Table dialog box appears.

2 In the New Table dialog box, select Table Wizard, and then click OK.

The Table Wizard dialog box appears.

3   In the Sample Tables list, scroll down, and then select Suppliers.

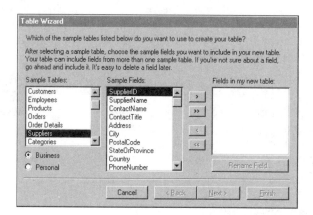

4   In the Sample Fields list, double-click each of the following fields to move the field to the Fields In My New Table list:

SupplierName   FaxNumber

ContactName   E-mailAddress

PhoneNumber

5   Click Next.

Below the What Do You Want To Name Your Table area, the name "Suppliers" appears. You want to name your table Suppliers, so you don't have to make any change.

A primary key is one or more fields that uniquely identify each record in a table. It is usually easiest to let Microsoft Access set the primary key.

6   Be sure the Yes, Set A Primary Key For Me option is selected, and then click Next.

7   The next question you see asks, "Is your new table related to any other tables in your database?" You don't have any tables to relate the Suppliers table to now, so click Next.

8   Select the Enter Data Directly Into The Table option, and then click Finish.

Your new table opens in Datasheet view.

Changing a Table Design in Design View

Tables can be created by using the Table Wizard or when you are in Design view. Regardless of which approach you take, occasionally you will need to change a table design. These changes are always made in Design view.

The Suppliers table you created by using the Table Wizard captures the basic suppliers data that Sweet Lil's wants to store. However, you need to add two additional attributes: delivery time and ingredients. You will add these attributes to the table while it is open in Design view.

Add a field in Design view

View

The graphic on the View button changes to reflect the most recent selection.

1 On the toolbar, click the View down arrow, and select Design View.

2 In the first empty row in the Field Name column, click to position the insertion point.

3 Type **Ingredients** and then press TAB.

The cursor is in the Data Type column. The default data type is Text.

4 Press ENTER to accept Text as the data type. Press ENTER again to move to the next row.

5 Type **Delivery Time**

6 Press TAB to move the insertion point to the Data Type column. Click the Data Type down arrow, and then select Number.

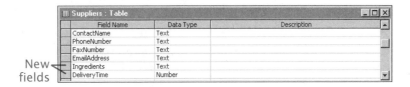

New fields

7 Close the Suppliers Table window.

8 A message appears, asking whether you want to save the changes to the design of the Suppliers table. Click Yes.

Adding Records in Table Datasheet View

The Datasheet view of a table is similar to the Datasheet view of a form. In Datasheet view, you can add to or look at your data. When you switch from Design view to Datasheet view, your records are reordered by the SupplierID field—a special field known as a primary key. A *primary key* is the field or combination of fields that identifies a record as being unique. No two records can have the same value in their primary key field. Primary keys and multiple-field primary keys are discussed in more detail later in this lesson.

You use the View button on the toolbar to toggle between the available views and to select the view you want.

Add records

Because it is a primary key, the SuppliersID field is of the AutoNumber data type. When you open the Suppliers table in Datasheet view, you will see the word "AutoNumber," which lets you know that you don't have to fill in this field. In an AutoNumber-type field, Microsoft Access automatically numbers each new record. AutoNumber guarantees that each record has a unique value for that field. You need to add the other information about the new suppliers to the remaining fields.

NOTE Microsoft Access puts an *input mask*—a control property that, in this case, helps speed up data entry—on the Phone Number field and Fax Number field to fill in the punctuation, so you type only the numbers

1   In the Database window, double-click the new Suppliers table. The table opens in Datasheet view.

2   Press TAB to move to the Supplier Name field, and then type **Chocolate World**

As you begin typing, Microsoft Access gives the record an ID of 1.

3   Press TAB to move to the Contact Name field, and then type **Becky Rheinhart**

4   Press TAB to move to the Phone Number field, and then type **6175555460**

5   Press TAB to move to the Fax Number field, and then type **6175555459**

6   Press TAB to move to the E-mail address field, and then type **BecaR@chocko.com**

7   Press TAB to move to the Ingredients field, and then type **Chocolate**

8   To complete the record, press TAB to move to the Delivery Time field, and then type **5**

Save a record

The record you are working on is saved when you move to a new row. Before you move to another row, look at the record indicator in the field selector to the left of the SuppliersID field. The pencil symbol record indicator shows that you have added or changed data in the record but haven't saved the data yet.

Record Indicator —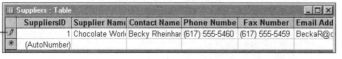

You can move to the next record by clicking in the next row or by using the DOWN ARROW key.

 Press TAB to move to the next record.

When you move to the next record, Microsoft Access automatically saves the data in the previous record. You don't have to do anything else to save the record.

Add more records

1   Press TAB to move to the Supplier Name field, and then add the following two records to the Suppliers table.

When you enter new data, the pencil symbol reappears.

Supplier Name:	**Allfresh Nuts**	**Flavorly Extracts, Inc.**
Contact Name:	**Barney Cutter**	**Beverly Sims**
Phone Number:	**(313) 555-9987**	**(515) 555-9834**
Fax Number:	**(313) 555-9990**	**(515) 555-9888**
Email Address:	**BarneyC@nuts.com**	**BevS@Flavorly.com**
Ingredients	**Walnuts, Pecans**	**Lemon, Mint**
Delivery Time	5	7

2   Close the Suppliers Table window.

Designing and Creating a New Table

The first step in designing a new table is to determine the *key attributes*—what makes each item in the table unique—and what information is required about these items. It is also important to decide whether the new data requires creating a new database, rather than adding a table to the existing database. Creating a new database might be worthwhile if:

■ You have a large number of new records.

■ The information has a unique purpose in the organization.

■ Information gathering or dispersal creates networking or telecommunications issues.

These factors are discussed in Appendix B, "Designing a Database." Creating a database is also discussed in Appendix B.

Develop a new table

Sweet Lil's has decided that the Shipping Department information can be incorporated into the existing database. The information, however, requires adding a new table to accommodate the carriers data. For this table, the following list of attributes has been developed by the Shipping Department.

■ The name of and contact information for the shipping company

■ The type of carrier (air or land)

First, you open a new table.

1   In the Database window, be sure that the Tables tab is selected and the list of tables is in front, and then click the New button.

2   In the New Table dialog box, be sure that Datasheet View is selected, and click OK.

A blank datasheet that has 20 columns and 30 rows is displayed.

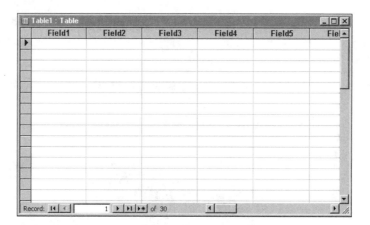

Choosing Appropriate Field Names

Fields are the basic building block of tables. It is important to give your fields appropriate names so that others can understand what the field is describing. You add fields to the new table by renaming the columns with the field names you want to use. Microsoft Access deletes any extra columns after you save the new table.

After you name your fields, you enter your data in the datasheet. Microsoft Access creates an appropriate data type and display format for the data you enter. The *data type* establishes what kind of data a field can hold, and the *display format* specifies how data is displayed and printed. When you create a table by using a Table Wizard, Microsoft Access assigns a data type and display format for all the fields based on the fields you selected from the list.

The following table shows examples of fields that have different data types and the data each field can hold.

Field	Data type	Data you might enter
Last Name	Text	Houlihan
Box Price	Currency	$18.75
Quantity on Hand	Number	500

Data types protect the accuracy of your data by restricting the type of information you can enter in a field. For example, you can't store a picture or a name in a field that has the Currency data type.

Now, you're ready to add the first field to your new table. Later, when you save the new table, Microsoft Access will create a primary key—one or more fields whose values uniquely identify each record in the table. You will use that primary key field to store an ID number for each carrier. To begin building your table, you'll first add data fields.

Name a field

➤ Double-click the default name Field1, and then type **Carrier Name**

A field name can contain up to 64 characters, including spaces. It can include any punctuation mark except a period (.), an exclamation point (!), or brackets ([ ]).

Carrier Name	Field2	Field3	Field4	Field5	Fiel

Table1 : Table

Name more fields

Next, you'll name additional fields.

You can select contiguous columns by dragging across their headers. You can resize all selected columns by double-clicking any header border except the leftmost header border.

1   Double-click the default name Field2, and then type **Air Delivery**

2   Position the pointer over the border between the fields Air Delivery and Field3. When the pointer changes to a two-headed arrow, double-click the border.

The Air Delivery column shortens to best fit the field name.

3   Double-click the default name Field3, and then type **Street Address**

4   Continue adding the following field names:

City Address

State Address

Postal Code

5   Resize column headers if you haven't done so already.

Your table should look like the following illustration.

Carrier Name	Air Delivery	Street Address	City Address	State Address	Postal Co

Table1 : Table

Add records to the table

1   Click in the Carrier Name field for the first record, type **Wild Fargo Carriers** and then press TAB to move to the Air Delivery field.

   Air Delivery is a field that will have a Yes/No data type. Yes will mean Air, and No will mean Surface. No will be the default for the Air Delivery field. Wild Fargo Carriers uses surface as its delivery method, so you type No. After you have entered a few records that have consistent data types, Microsoft Access will assign a data type to the field (which you can change in Design view).

2   Type **No** in the Air Delivery field.

3   Enter the following data for this record:

   Street Address: **410 N.E. 84th St.**

   City Address: **Chicago**

   State Address: **Illinois**

   Postal Code: **45123**

4   Add two more records to the carriers table:

   Carrier Name: **Grey Goose Express**

   Air Delivery: **Yes**

   Street Address: **100 Day St.**

   City Address: **New York**

   State Address: **New York**

   Postal Code: **12378**

   Carrier Name: **Pegasus Overnight**

   Air Delivery: **No**

   Street Address: **45908 Airport Way**

   City: **Dallas**

   State: **Texas**

   Postal Code: **78654**

   Your table should look like the following illustration.

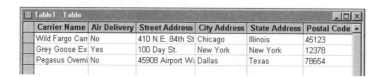

Save the table

Save

1 On the toolbar, click the Save button

2 Name the table **Carriers**, and then click OK.

Microsoft Access asks whether you want to create a primary key for the new table. Every table in your database should have a primary key. The primary key helps Microsoft Access search, find, and combine data efficiently.

3 Click Yes.

Microsoft Access creates a primary key for the table and saves the table as Carriers.

4 Double-click the field name ID at the top of the new primary key field. Type **Carrier ID** and then press ENTER.

The primary key field is named Carriers ID.

5 Close the table.

Create a data entry form

Although it is possible to enter data directly in tables, most data entry is done in forms because appropriately designed forms facilitate data entry and guarantee data validity. If no special formatting or controls are required for a data entry form, you can use Microsoft Access AutoForm to create a basic form.

New Object

1 In the Database window, select the Carriers table.

2 Click the New Object down arrow, and then select AutoForm.

Microsoft Access creates the form.

3 On the File menu, select Save As.

4 Be sure that Carriers is highlighted in the New Name box. Click OK.

5 Close the newly created Carriers form.

Controlling Data Through Field Properties

Properties are used to control how Microsoft Access stores, handles, and displays data in the field. For example, to display numbers in a field as percentages, you would set the field's Format property to Percent.

Each data type is associated with a different set of properties. Fields that have Text and Number data types, for example, have a property called Field Size that sets the maximum size of data you can store in the field. Fields that have the Yes/No data type, on the other hand, don't have a Field Size property, because the values stored in a Yes/No field have a fixed size.

Another property you can set or change for most fields is the default control type. For example, in the Air Delivery field, your entry will always be either Yes or No, and it's easier to click a check box than type.

In the following exercise, you will set the Display Control property for the Air Delivery field to be a check box by changing the Display Control field property.

Set field properties

1 Make sure the Tables tab is selected, and double-click the Carriers Table.

2 On the toolbar, click the View down arrow, and then select Design View.

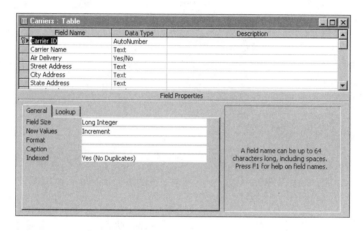

For fast, detailed information about any property, click in its corresponding property box, and press F1.

3 Click anywhere in the row for the Air Delivery field.

The field properties appear in the Field Properties sheet at the bottom of the table.

4 In the Field Properties sheet, click the Lookup tab.

The Display Control property is displayed on the Properties Sheet when the Lookup tab is selected and is set by default to Text Box.

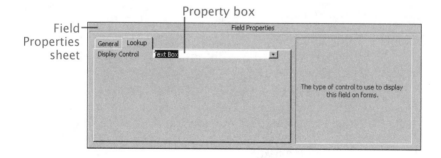

5 Click in the Display Control property box. Then click the down arrow that appears in the box, and select Check Box.

   When you set the Display Control property to Check Box, the default control in the table and in all forms based on the table is a check box.

6 Switch to Datasheet view to see the new check box for the Air Delivery field. When Microsoft Access asks whether you want to save the table, click Yes.

7 Close the Carriers Table window.

Connecting a New Table to a Database

When you are expanding a database, it is important to understand how the new table will interact with existing tables. Creating the table is the first step toward incorporating the new data. To fully integrate the table, you need to build relationships or links to other tables.

There are two main ways of creating relationships: by using a lookup field and by defining relationships in the Relationships window. Relationships built in the Relationships window are generally more permanent and allow the database designer more control over the relationship behavior.

Understanding Relationships

See Lesson 5, "Keeping Database Information Reliable," for a discussion of primary keys.

Microsoft Access is used to create relational databases. Relational databases have become established as the most common form of database because they easily combine data from multiple tables simultaneously. After you create tables in your database and set each table primary key, you can create relationships between the tables. Relationships are used to collect data from several tables and place them in a single form, report, or query.

You can create two types of relationships in Microsoft Access: a *one-to-many relationship* or a *one-to-one relationship*. The most common type by far is the one-to-many relationship. In this type of relationship, one record in one table can have many related records in another table. For example, one customer can place many orders. Similarly, one record in a Customers table (called the primary table in the relationship) can have many matching records in an Orders table (called the *related table*).The *primary table* contains the field on the one side of the one-to-many relationship.

Related fields don't necessarily have to have the same name as the primary key fields to which they are related. However, related fields do have to contain matching data. In addition, related fields must have the same data type, with two exceptions; and if they have the Number data type, they must have the same field size.

 NOTE There are two exceptions to the rule that related fields must have the same data type. The exceptions are (1) that you can match an Increment AutoNumber field with a Long Integer Number field and (2) that you can match a Replication ID number field with a Replication ID AutoNumber field. For example, the Carrier ID field in the Carriers table has the AutoNumber data type, and New Values is set to Increment. The Carrier ID field in the Shipping table has the Number data type, and its Field Size property is set to Long Integer.

Records in the Customers Table (the one side)...

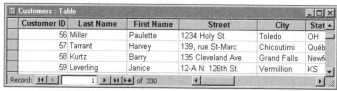

...can have more than one corresponding record in the Orders table (the many side).

In a one-to-one relationship, on the other hand, one record in the primary table can have only one matching record in the related table. The one-to-one type of relationship is less common than the one-to-many relationship; however, some circumstances require the one-to-one relationship. For example, Sweet Lil's might want to create a table of recipes for its bonbons. Each entry in the Bonbons table would have exactly one corresponding entry in the Recipe table.

 NOTE You can also create relationships between your tables to help ensure that the data in the relationship makes sense—for example, that you don't have orders in the Orders table that have no matching customer in the Customers table. For more details, see "Referential integrity" in Microsoft Access online Help.

Making Connections in Complex Relationships

Although the Lookup Wizard easily creates relationships, it is not well suited for creating complex relationships. The Lookup Wizard is not the first choice when:

- Referential integrity is required.
- The primary key relies on more than one field.
- There is no direct link between the two tables.

In these situations, you should create the relationships in the Relationships window. Relationships created in the Relationships window will not contain an automatic Display Control property, such as the combo box the Lookup Wizard created earlier in this lesson. When you create relationships in the Relationships window, you can join fields that have different names, and you can see the big picture" of relationships in your database.

Before you can create a relationship in the Relationships window, the tables must contain matching fields. You relate the primary key field in the primary table (on the "one" side of the relationship) to a field that has a matching value in the related table (on the "many" side). The matching field is sometimes called a *foreign key*. If the related table doesn't contain a field that has data that matches the data in the primary key field in the primary table, you need to add the field to the related table so you can create the relationship.

Primary key 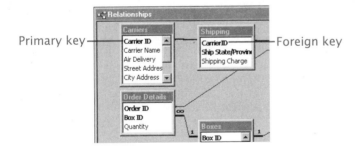 Foreign key

After you create a relationship between two tables, you can't modify or delete the fields on which the relationship is based without deleting the relationship first.

Add tables to the Relationships window

In the relationship between the Carriers and Shipping tables in the Sweet Lil's database, the Carrier ID field is the matching field.

This is a one-to-many relationship. One carrier can have many different shipping charges, depending on the destination of the package, so the Carriers table is the primary table in the relationship. When you create the relationship between these two tables, you'll relate Carrier ID in the Carriers table to Carrier ID in the Shipping table.

Relationships

You can also click Relationships on the Tools menu.

Clear Layout

Show Table

You can also click Show Table on the Relationships menu.

1   On the toolbar, click the Relationships button.

The Relationships window opens.

 NOTE   For this exercise, the Relationships window should be empty. If it is not, on the toolbar, click the Clear Layout button. Or, on the Edit menu, click Clear Layout. Then, click Yes.

2   On the toolbar, click the Show Table button.

The Show Table dialog box appears.

3   On the Tables tab, select the Carriers table, and then click Add.

4   Select the Shipping table, and then click Add.

A window of each table and its list of fields opens in the Relationships window.

5   On the Show Table dialog box, click the Close button.

Create a relationship between tables

1   In the Relationships window, drag the Carrier ID field from the field list in the Carriers table to the Carrier ID field in the Shipping field list.

When you release the mouse button, the Relationships dialog box appears. Be sure that the matching field is listed for both tables. If it is not, you can click in the cell under either the Carriers or the Shippers header, and then click the down arrow to select the proper field.

2   Click the Create button.

3   The Carriers table is now related to the Shipping table. A line links the matching fields in the two tables. This relationship remains intact until you delete it. Your window should look like the following illustration.

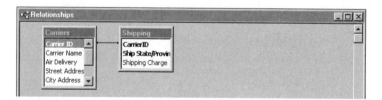

4   Close the Relationships window.

When you close the Relationships window, a message asks whether you want to save changes to the Relationships layout. This decision affects only what is graphically displayed in the Relationships window. Any relationships you have created between tables remain in your database.

5 Click Yes to save the layout of the Relationships window.

The next time you open the Relationships window, you will see the display you just saved.

Delete and restore a relationship between tables

1 On the toolbar, click the Relationships button to see the layout of the Relationships window that you saved.

2 Click the line between the Carriers table and the Shipping table.

The line becomes thicker.

3 Press DELETE to delete the relationship.

A message appears, asking whether you want to delete the relationship.

4 Click Yes.

Microsoft Access erases the line between the two tables. They are no longer related.

5 Drag the Carrier ID field from the Carriers table to the Carrier ID field in the Shipping table, and then click Create in the Relationships dialog box to re-create the relationship.

6 Close the Relationships window.

Creating Links by Using Multiple-Field Primary Keys

For a demonstration of how to create a relationship between tables, double-click The Camcorder Files On The Internet shortcut on your Desktop or connect to the Internet address listed on p. xxvi.

A table primary key can consist of one or more fields. If a table that has a multiple-field primary key is the primary table in a relationship, you must relate *all* the fields in its primary key to matching fields in the related table. To see why, look at the Shipping and Orders tables in the Sweet Lil's database. These two tables have a one-to-many relationship, and Shipping is the primary table.

The primary key for the Shipping table consists of two fields: Carrier ID and Ship State/Province. Before Microsoft Access can correctly relate a shipping charge to an order, it must be able to find matching data for *both* fields because a shipping charge is based on both the carrier that the customer chooses and the destination of the order.

Relate a multiple-field primary key to matching fields

In the following exercise, you will create a relationship between the Shipping and Orders tables so that Microsoft Access can automatically look up an order's shipping charge.

Relationships

Clear Layout

Show Table

1   On the toolbar, click the Relationships button.

The Relationships window opens, showing the layout you last saved.

2   On the toolbar, click the Clear Layout button to give yourself a clean workspace.

The relationships do not change when you clear the layout.

3   Click Yes to proceed.

4   On the toolbar, click the Show Table button to open the Show Table dialog box.

5   In the Show Table dialog box, select and add both the Shipping table and the Orders table to the Relationships window. Then, close the Show Table dialog box.

6   In the Relationships window, drag the Carrier ID field from the Shipping table to the Carrier ID field in the Orders table.

When you release the mouse button, the Relationships dialog box appears. Be sure that the Carrier ID field is listed for both tables. If it is not, you can click the cell under the Shipping heading or the Orders heading, click the down arrow, and then select the proper field.

7   Click the cell under Carrier ID for each table, and then click the list box down arrow to select Ship State/Province.

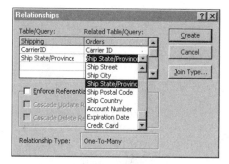

8   Click Create.

The Relationships window displays the relationship between the two tables. To see the relationship more easily, you can drag the Orders table farther away from the Shipping table and drag the border of the Orders table downward to show both fields without having to scroll.

9   Close the Relationships window. When Microsoft Access asks whether you want to save the layout, click Yes.

Because the tables are now related, Microsoft Access can use the values in both tables to find information.

See how your relationships work

You've created one relationship between the Carriers and Shipping tables and another relationship between the Shipping and Orders tables. You can see how the relationships work when you need information that requires data from more than one table.

See Lesson 7, "Getting Answers to Questions About Your Data," for more information about creating queries.

You can use a filter to request information from the Sweet Lil's database; however, when you use a filter, you can only set criteria and display selected data from one table. By using a query, you can take advantage of relationships between tables by drawing on information from two or more tables. In the following exercise, you see how related tables are used in a query by using the Carrier ID and Ship State/Province fields in the Orders table to find the appropriate shipping charge for an order.

1   In the Database window, click the Queries tab to display the list of queries, and then click the New button.

The New Query dialog box appears.

2   In the New Query dialog box, double-click Simple Query Wizard.

The Simple Query Wizard dialog box appears.

3   In the Tables/Queries list, select Table: Orders. Then, in the Available Fields list, double-click Order ID to add it to the Selected Fields list. The Simple Query Wizard dialog box should look like the following illustration.

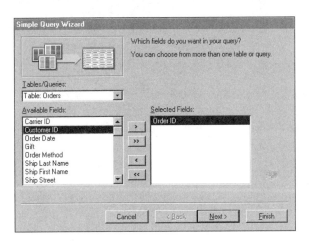

4   From the Carriers table, add the Carrier Name field to your Selected Fields list, and from the Shipping table, add the Shipping Charge field to your Selected Fields list.

Microsoft Access uses the relationships you created to join the tables in the query.

5   Click Next.

6   Be sure the Detail Shows Every Field Of Every Record option is selected, and then click Next.

7   Type **Carriers Query** as the title, make sure the "Open The Query To View Information" option is selected, and then click Finish.

The related data from all three tables appears in the Query window.

8   Close the query.

Microsoft Access has saved the query automatically, and the name Carriers Query appears in the list of queries in the Database window.

One Step Further: Controlling and Filtering Fields

In addition to assigning data types to fields, you can also control how fields behave by setting their properties. Now you will see how field properties are set, and how you can filter a table so that only selected values are displayed in the Datasheet view.

Set a field property

Field properties can be set to enforce business rules or procedures. For example, one of the rules that has been established at Sweet Lil's is that no order can be taken without a customer ID. To enforce this rule, the Required Property of the Customer ID field can be set to Yes.

1   In the Database window, click the Tables tab to display the list of tables.

2   Select the Orders table, and then click Design.

3   Select the Customer ID field.

4   In the Field Properties sheet of the Orders Table window, click in the Property field to select the Required property.

5   Click the Required property field down arrow, and then select Yes.

When the Required property is set to Yes, if you try to leave the field blank, a warning message appears. You cannot add a record until you provide an entry for the Customer # ID field.

Create a filter for a table

Filters can also be used to limit the records displayed in a table Datasheet view. Using a filter can be an easy way to locate selected records in a table. You will now filter the Orders Table to display only those orders placed on February 14, 1996.

1   Click the View down arrow, and then select Datasheet view.

2   Click Yes when asked if you want to save the Orders table, and then click Yes again to have the data tested against the new rule.

Filter By Form

3   Click the Filter By Form button to display the Orders Filter By Form window.

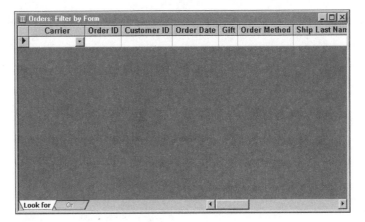

4   Click in the Order Date field, and then click the down arrow to display the list of data values.

     Every value in the Order Date field is displayed.

5   Scroll down the list, and select the date 2/14/96.

     #2/14/96# is entered as the filter criteria.

Apply Filter

6   Click the Apply Filter button.

     Only the orders placed on Feb. 14, 1996, are displayed in the datasheet.

7   On the File menu, click Save.

Finish the lesson

1   To continue to the next lesson, on the File menu, click Close.

2   If you are finished using Microsoft Access for now, on the File menu, click Exit.

Lesson Summary

To	Do this
Create a table	In the Database window, click the Tables tab, and then click New. Select Table Wizard, and follow the prompts.
	or
	In the Database window, click the Tables tab, and then click New. Select Datasheet View. Change the default field names to names you select, enter data for as many records as you choose, and then save the table. You can customize the table in Design view.
Add records to a table	Display the table in Datasheet view, and then type the data in the fields.
Add a field to a table	In the first empty row in Design view, type a field name in the Field Name column. Select a data type from the drop-down list in the Data Type column.
Set properties for a field	In the upper portion of the Design View window, click the row that defines the field in, and then set the property in the Field Properties sheet in the lower portion of the window.
Get Help on any field property	Click in the property box, and then press F1.
Change a field name	Select the table in the Database window, and then switch to Design view. Move to the Field Name column, and then make your changes.
Create a lookup column to relate two tables	Open the table that will contain the lookup column. On the Insert menu, click Lookup Column. Follow the steps in the Lookup Wizard.

To	Do this	Button
Create a relationship between two tables	On the toolbar, click the Relationships button to open the Relationships window, and then click the Show Table button on the toolbar. In the Show Table dialog box, select the primary table on the Tables tab, and click Add. Select the related table, and click Add. Close the Show Table dialog box. In the Relationships window, drag the common field from the primary table to the related table. In the Relationship dialog box, click Create.	
Delete a relationship between tables	Open the Relationships window. Click the line linking the tables, press DELETE, and then click Yes.	
Create a multiple field primary key	Open the table in Design view. Select the fields to be included in the primary key. Click the Primary Key button.	

For online information about	On the Help menu, click Contents And Index, click the Index tab, and then type
Creating a table	**create table**
Adding fields to a table	**add field**
Making changes to a field in a table	**change table**
Adding records to a table	**add records**
Setting or changing a table's primary key	**primary key**
Setting properties for a field	**field properties**
Creating or deleting relationships between tables	**relationships**
Linking tables by creating a lookup column	**lookup**

Keeping Database Information Reliable

Estimated time
45 min.

In this lesson you will learn how to:

- Add a validation rule for a text box control.
- Create a combo box control.
- Change the tab order of controls on a form.
- Set a default value for a control.
- Force data entry of specific fields.
- Ensure related tables always contain the correct data.
- Control data reliability by using a lookup field.
- Detect a many-to-many relationship and use a junction table.

One of the greatest challenges for database designers and administrators is making sure that the data is reliable. Customers, managers, government authorities, and the general public all can be affected by the information contained in an organization's database. In some instances, incorrect or invalid data is a minor irritation; in others, it can have dire consequences.

Database reliability is guaranteed through the use of system controls. Two of the most important system controls are data validation and referential integrity. *Data validation* is the set of procedures and techniques used to ensure that only data that passes a set of tests can be entered into the system. *Referential integrity* is a design technique that is employed to create more reliable databases. Referential integrity uses a system of cross referencing to create a database structure that is more likely to contain reliable data.

In this lesson, you will learn how to use form controls to extend the validation concepts discussed in Lesson 2, "Increasing Efficiency by Using Subforms." You will also learn how to evaluate the relationships discussed in Lesson 4, "Controlling Database Growth," and how to structure your tables so that they are related correctly.

You can also start Microsoft Access and open the Sweet Lil's database in a single step. Click the Start button, point to Documents, and then click Sweet Lil's.

Start the lesson

 If Microsoft Access isn't started yet, start it. Open the Sweet Lil's database. If the Microsoft Access window doesn't fill your screen, maximize the window.

If you need help opening the database, see Lesson 1.

Validating Data by Adding Form Controls

For more information on sections and form design, see Lesson 10, "Streamlining Data Entry."

Any field that contains or accepts data on a form is actually a control. *Controls* are graphical objects that accept, display, or locate data. Microsoft Access is made up of objects; for example, tables, forms, queries, and reports are all objects. Controls are part of the objects that contain them. Controls are labels, text boxes, drop-down boxes, option buttons, toggle buttons, or object controls. In every lesson in this book, you use controls. When you use a wizard to create a form, the controls are created automatically. You can also build validation checks into *sections*, which are the basic parts of the Design window. You can also create new controls or modify existing controls by changing their properties while you are in Design view.

Building Validation Checks by Changing a Form Control Property

A common validation is to check whether data is within a range of acceptable values. For example, a company could have a business rule that limits the amount of credit granted to new customers. This rule could then be transformed into a validation check on a credit purchase field.

For a demonstration of how to add a validation check to a form control, double-click the Camcorder Files On the Internet shortcut or connect to the Internet address listed on p. xxvi.

Add a validation check

Sweet Lil's recently had a complete audit of its data-processing operations. One of the findings of the audit was that the company needs to increase its control over credit purchases. The auditor suggested several additions to the validation procedures to increase credit transaction control. One suggestion was to add a validation check on expiration dates.

You will now add a validation check to the Orders form. The validation check will prevent sales clerks from accepting expired credit cards.

1 In the Database window, click the Forms tab.

The Forms tab moves to the front.

2 Select the Orders form, and click Design.

The Orders form opens in Design view. Your screen should look like the following illustration.

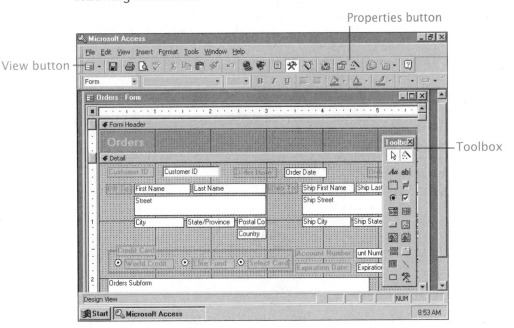

Properties button

View button

Toolbox

3 Select the Expiration Date text box.

4 If the properties sheet is not open, click the Properties button to open it.

Properties

The Text Box: Expiration Date properties sheet opens. The properties sheet displays the properties for the object that is selected. If the form is selected, the properties sheet displays properties that control the behavior of the form. If a control or section on the form is selected, the properties sheet will display the properties for the control or section, respectively.

5 In the Orders Form detail section, select the Expiration Date text box control, and then click the Data tab on the property sheet.

89

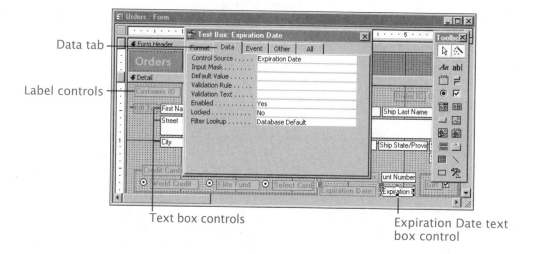

Data tab

Label controls

Text box controls

Expiration Date text box control

6 Click the box next to the Validation Rule property, type **>=now** and press ENTER.

This rule states that the expiration date on the credit card must be after the date indicated by the system date (today's date). The function, now (), which is built into Microsoft Access, returns the current date and time. When you press ENTER, the parentheses are entered automatically.

7 In the Validation Text property of the dialog box, click to position the insertion point, and type:

That is not a valid date. The credit card is either expired, or you have typed the wrong date. Check the date. If it is correct, reject the order.

8 Press ENTER.

9 Close the properties sheet.

Test your validation check

It is always a good idea to make sure any changes to object properties had the intended effect; in other words, you should always check your validation checks. In this exercise, you enter invalid data to see whether your validation rule works.

View

1 Click the View down arrow, and select Form View.

The graphic on the View button changes depending on the current selection.

New Record

2 Click the New Record button to add a record.

Record 407 should be the current record.

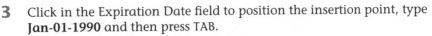

3 Click in the Expiration Date field to position the insertion point, type **Jan-01-1990** and then press TAB.

The validation rule you typed appears as a message.

4 Click OK, change the date to a date after today's date, and then press TAB.

You need to change to a date after today's date to have the record accepted.

Save

5 Click the Save button to save the new version of the form, and then close the form.

A message box appears telling you that Access can't find a record in the table "Customers" with key matching field(s) "Customer ID". This is because you have not completely filled in this test record with data.

6 Click OK.

A message box tells you that your changes to the table will not be saved. This is a built-in control in Access; the control prevents you from entering data that is missing key information.

7 Click Yes.

Increasing Data Validity by Using a Combo Box Control

One way to increase the validity of your data is to allow data entry workers to select possible values from a list. By using value selection instead of typing records, you decrease the chances of typographical errors. One of the best ways to set up value selection is through a combo box. A *combo box* is a field that displays possible values from a drop-down list and lets you select the appropriate value. Combo boxes can be created by placing a combo box control on a form and setting the properties to determine the source for possible data values.

In many cases, the best way to list possible data values is to create a separate query that selects and arranges the data just the way you want it to appear in the list. Then you can use the fields in the query as columns in the list.

Queries are discussed further in Lesson 7 "Getting Answers to Questions About Your Data."

When operators take telephone orders for Sweet Lil's chocolates, speed and accuracy are their top priorities. To make their jobs easier, you plan to make several enhancements to the on-line form they use.

Currently, operators enter the customer ID number in a text box on the Orders form. You're going to replace the text box with a combo box that shows a list of customer names and ID numbers, so the operators can select the ID instead of typing it.

91

Customer ID
text box

 TIP If you want to change the text box into a label, a list box, or a simple combo box, select the control you want to change. Then, on the Format menu, click Change To, and click the control type you want.

Delete a text box

Before you can add the combo box, you need to make room for it by deleting the Customer ID text box and its label.

1 In the Database window, click the Forms tab, and then click Design to open the Orders form in Design view.

2 If the Orders Form window is too small for you to see all the controls, resize the window by selecting a corner of the window and dragging the corner until the window is the appropriate size.

3 Click the Customer ID text box, and then press DELETE.

The Customer ID text box and its label are deleted. If the toolbox is blocking your view, you can move the toolbox by selecting its title bar and dragging the toolbox out of the way. You can also double-click the toolbox title bar. This will dock the toolbox and keep it out of the way.

Create a combo box bound control

One way to increase the validity of data entered through a combo box is by ensuring that the only choices the reader can select are valid ones. If the data selected in the combo box is to be entered into a table, the box must be bound to a field in either a table or a query so that Access can place the data correctly. A *bound control* is a control tied to a field in an underlying table or query. Your combo box on the Orders form should be bound to the Customer ID field in the Customer List query so that when an operator selects a customer from the form's combo box list, Microsoft Access will store the customer ID number in the bound field in the table.

In the following exercise, you use the Combo Box Wizard to create a bound combo box.

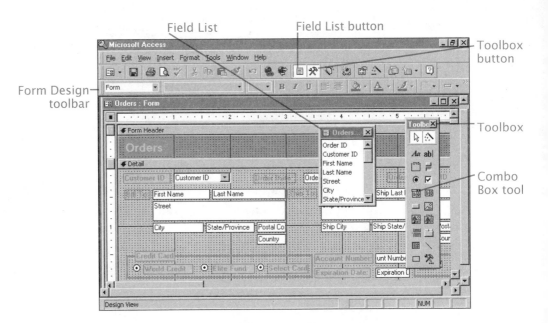

Toolbox

Field List

Combo Box

1 Be sure that the toolbox and the field list are visible. If the toolbox isn't visible, click the Toolbox button on the Form Design toolbar. If the field list isn't visible, click the Field List button on the Form Design toolbar.

2 In the toolbox, click the Combo Box tool.

Now when you drag the Customer ID field from the field list, Microsoft Access creates a combo box that's bound to the field.

3 Drag the Customer ID field from the field list to just above the First Name field on the form.

When you release the mouse button, the Combo Box Wizard appears.

Create a combo box list

The Combo Box Wizard guides you through the creation of the combo box list for your form.

1 In the first Combo Box Wizard dialog box, be sure the I Want The Combo Box To Look Up The Values In A Table Or Query option is selected, and then click Next.

2 In the View area, select the Queries option, and then select the Customer List query. Click Next.

3 On the Available Fields list, double-click the Customer ID field, double-click the Last Name field, and then double-click the First Name field. Click Next.

These will be the columns in your combo box.

4 Double-click the right edge of each column header to adjust the column width to its best fit. Click Next.

5 Select Customer ID as the column that contains the data you want to store in your table. Click Next.

6 Be sure that the Store That Value In This Field option is selected, be sure Customer ID is displayed in the box to the right, and then click Next.

7 Customer ID is the default label for your combo box. This is the label you want, so click Finish.

The Orders form has a combo box bound to the Customer ID field. Your form should look like the following illustration.

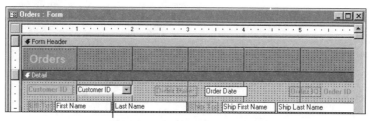

New combo box

8 Close the field list.

Use the combo box

You can see how using the combo box simplifies looking up customer IDs. Now when a new order is taken, all the operator has to do is select the customer's name, and the customer name and address are filled in automatically

1 Click the View down arrow, and then click Form View.

2 Click the Customer ID down arrow, and select the name Arlene Grant.

The customer ID number appears in the Customer ID field.

Improving Data Entry Accuracy by Controlling Tab Order

Good screen design is integral to ensuring valid data. Data entry screens that follow a logical order—or that mirror paper source documents—can increase accuracy and streamline data.

The order form used by the Sweet Lil's sales clerks is an example of good screen design. The fields are well-designated and follow a logical pattern. The customer details are grouped in one area, and the shipping details are grouped in another area. Finally, the credit information is in a separate section. The current process for moving between fields on the online form, however, does not follow this pattern. You will change the tab order of the Orders form so that when the sales clerks use the form, the fields will be presented in a more logical order. The *tab order* of a form is the order in which the insertion point moves through fields when you tab from field to field in Form view.

Change tab order

Now when you open the Orders form in Form view the Order Date is the first field selected. To make the Customer ID field the selected field whenever you open the form, you can change the tab order of the Orders form.

When you create a new control, Microsoft Access puts the new control last in the tab order, regardless of where you placed that control on the form. You'll edit the tab order so that the new Customer ID combo box you just created is first in the tab order, not last.

1 Click the View down arrow, and click Design View.

2 If the Customer ID combo box control is not highlighted, select it by clicking anywhere on the control.

3 On the View menu, click Tab Order.

   The Tab Order dialog box appears.

4 Scroll down in the Customer Order list of controls until you see the Customer ID control at the bottom of the list.

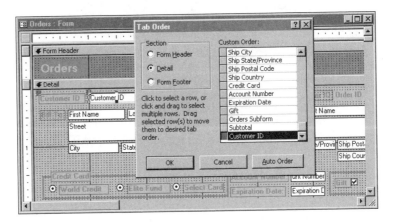

5 Place your mouse pointer in the column to the left of the Customer ID control. When the pointer becomes a right-pointing arrow, click once to select the field.

95

6 Click and drag the Customer ID control to the top of the list.

7 Click OK.

8 Switch to Form view to test the tab order.

The Orders form opens; the Customer ID is selected.

9 Save the Orders form.

Improving Validity by Setting a Default Control Value

Another way to improve the reliability of the data in your database is to set default values. If you know that certain data will always be the same, setting a default will help you avoid incorrect data entry. Default values can be created through the Default Value property of a control. You can set the Default Value property either to an expression or to a constant value, such as text or a number.

Display today's date in a text box

The date a Sweet Lil's order is taken will always be the date on the Order form. You want to give the Order Date box a default value so the operators don't have to type the date themselves. In this case, you'll set the value equal to an expression that includes the Date function. The expression will be entered in the property sheet of the Orders form.

Properties

1 Click the View down arrow, and click Design View.

2 Click the Order Date text box to select it. If the property sheet isn't displayed, on the Form Design toolbar, click the Properties button to display the Order Date control properties.

3 In the Default Value property box on the Data tab, type the expression =**Date( )** and then press ENTER.

4 Close the properties sheet.

5 Switch to Form view.

Because Microsoft Access enters the default value when you start a new record, you need a new record to check your property setting.

New Record

6 Click the New Record button at the bottom of the form to move to a new blank record.

A new record appears; today's date is in the Order Date text box.

7 Close the form. When asked whether you want to save the changes, click Yes.

Improving Validity by Using Field Properties

Although form control properties are an excellent way to improve validity of data, they are not the only tools at your disposal. Another way to increase the reliability of your data is by setting properties for fields in the table. Setting field properties has the advantage of affecting that particular field in each and every form that uses that field. For example, the validation rule you set for the Expiration Date control on the Orders form could have been set for the Expiration Date field in the Orders table. Setting the rule for the field guarantees that the rule is followed by any control based on the Expiration Date field.

Validating Records by Applying the Required Property

One field property that is useful in guaranteeing valid records is the Required property. The *Required property* means that records cannot be accepted without data in that field. A field without any data has a value of *null.* If the Required property is set to Yes, null values are not allowed.

Occasionally you will want to capture a record even though it is missing some information. If the data in a particular field is not crucial to the validity of the record, the Required property for that field should be set to No.

Set a Required property

One field that should be required is the Ship Postal Code field in the Orders form. Without the Ship Postal Code, the order is not valid. In the following exercise, you change the Required property of the Orders table Ship Postal Code field to Yes.

1   In the Database window, click the Tables tab.

2   Click the Orders table to select it, and then click Design to open the table in Design view.

3   Click in the Ship Postal Code field to select it.

4   In the Field Properties sheet, change the Required field to Yes by clicking in the field and selecting Yes from the list

   From now on, you cannot save a record that has a null value in the Ship Postal Code field. Your Orders table should look like the following illustration.

97

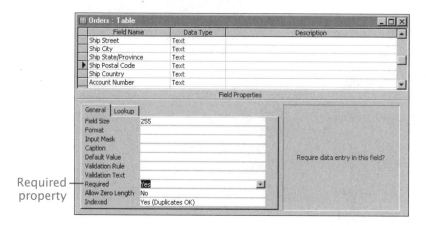

Required
property

5 On the Orders table, click the Close button.

A message appears, asking whether you want to save the changes.

6 Click Yes.

A message appears, asking whether you want to check the existing data to be sure it adheres to the new validation rule. If you don't check the data, you might leave null value records in this field.

7 Click Yes.

If any records violate the rule, another message appears to warn you.

NOTE You shouldn't have any invalid data; however, if you do, the message will ask you if you want to continue checking against the new rule. Answer No to end the test. Then close the table without saving the changes, find the records that are missing the required data, and enter values for the required field. Then complete the above steps again.

Test the Required property

To verify that the Required property has been established, you try to enter an order without a postal code.

1 In the Database window, click the Forms tab, and then double-click the Orders form to open it in Form view.

In the Orders form, the first field selected is Customer ID.

2 Use the New Record button on the navigation bar to start a new record.

3 Select 1 from the Customer ID field list.

Customer 1 is Rita Hanson.

4 Press TAB to move to the Order Date field, and then press TAB a second time to accept the date.

The insertion point moves to the Order ID field.

5 Enter 417 for the Order ID.

6 Press TAB three times to move to the first blank Ship To field. Fill in the following Ship To information. Press TAB to move through the fields.

Field	Value
Ship To First Name	**Orson**
Ship To Last Name	**Jones**
Ship To Street Address	**123 Burnside**
Ship To City	**Chicago**
Ship To State	**Illinois**
Ship To Postal Code	Leave blank
Ship To Country	**USA**

7 Use the following details to fill in the remaining fields.

Field	Value
Credit Card	**World Credit**
Account Number	**123 78429**
Expiration Date	**11/30/98**
Gift	**No**
Box ID	**ALLS**

When you click in the subform to enter the Box ID, a message box indicates that the Ship To Postal Code field cannot have a null value.

8 Click OK, type **32123** in the Ship To Postal Code field, and complete the entry for the Box ID.

9 Close the Orders form.

Validating Records by Creating Referential Integrity

One of the best ways to make sure your data is valid is to use relationships between tables. Database relationships are generally built on rules or policies of the organization. When tables are related to each other, you can guarantee that changes in one table will affect the data in the related table. This is accomplished through referential integrity. Referential integrity is a system of rules

For a demonstration of how to enforce referential integrity, double-click the Camcorder Files On the Internet shortcut on your Desktop or connect to the Internet address listed on p. xxvi.

Linking tables is discussed in Lesson 6, "Getting and Working with External Data."

that ensure that relationships between records in related tables are valid and that you can't accidentally delete or change related data.

Before you can use referential integrity, several conditions must be met. First, the matching field from the primary table must be a primary key or have a unique index. Second, the related fields must have the same data type. Finally, both tables must belong to the same Microsoft Access database. If the tables are linked, they must be in Microsoft Access format. The database in which the linked tables are stored must be open to set referential integrity. Referential integrity can't be enforced for linked tables from databases in other formats; that is, you can't enforce referential integrity for an Access Database when it contains linked tables that are in Microsoft Excel, Paradox, dBase, TXT, or any format other than Microsoft Access.

Referential integrity increases the validity of your data by enforcing the following rules.

- You can't enter a value in the foreign key field of the related table if that value doesn't exist in the primary key of the primary table. However, you can enter a null in the foreign key, specifying that the records are unrelated. For example, you can't assign an order to a customer that doesn't exist, but you can assign to no one by entering a null in the Customer ID field.

- You can't delete a record from a primary table if *matching* or corresponding records exist in a related table. For example, you can't delete a customer record from the Customers table if there are matching orders for that customer in the Orders table.

- You can't change a primary key value in the primary table if that record has related records. For example, you can't change a carrier's ID in the Carriers table if there are shipments assigned to that carrier in the shipping table.

Guarantee validity by creating referential integrity

One standard business rule is that a customer cannot be removed from the database if there are pending orders. Sweet Lil's would like to implement this rule by applying referential integrity to the relationship between the Customers table and the Orders table. In this exercise, you will set referential integrity through the Relationships window.

1 In the Database window, click the Tables tab.

2 On the toolbar, click the Relationships button to open the Relationships window.

Relationships

The Relationships window is a workspace for adding tables and creating relationships. The workspace can be cleared to make it easier to see the relationships you are creating. The relationship you want is the one connecting the Customers and Orders tables.

*Show All
Relationships*

3　Click the Show All Relationships button to display all the database relationships in the Relationships window.

4　Maximize the Relationships window.

5　Double-click the line connecting the Customers table to the Orders table. The Relationships dialog box appears.

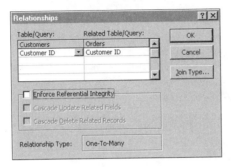

6　Select the Enforce Referential Integrity check box.

7　Click Join Type.

The Join Properties dialog box appears. In the Join Properties dialog box, you can change the type of relationship. In this case, you want to show all records in both tables where the two fields are equal, which is the default selection.

8　Click OK to close the Join Properties dialog box.

9　Click OK to close the Relationships dialog box.

Understanding Cascade Updating and Deleting

After you have established referential integrity, you can use it to increase the validity of your data by using the Cascade Update Related Fields and Cascade Delete Related Fields commands. These commands ensure that changes you make in the primary table will ripple through to the corresponding records in the related tables.

 NOTE　If the primary key in the primary table is an AutoNumber field, setting the Cascade Update Related Fields check box has no effect; you can't change the value in an AutoNumber field.

You can set the Cascade Update And Delete properties when defining a relationship, or you can set these properties later by using the Relationships dialog box. If the Cascade Delete Related Records check box is selected, any time you delete records in the primary table, Microsoft Access automatically deletes related records in the related table. For example, if the Customers table is a primary table, anytime you delete a customer record from the Customers table, all the customer's orders are automatically deleted from the Orders table. In addition, records in the Order Details table, which is related to the Orders records, are also deleted. When you use the Cascade Delete Related Records option, Microsoft Access warns you that related records might also be deleted.

Keep primary keys consistent by using Cascade Update Related Records

The core of Sweet Lil's business is, of course, the boxes of candy. If the business does not focus on identifying the boxes correctly, all the information in the database is at risk. In this exercise, you use the Cascade Update command to ensure that the Box ID fields in the Boxes table, the Box Details table, and the Orders Detail table are consistent.

1   In the Relationships window, click the line connecting the Boxes table and the Box Details table to select it.

    The line thickens.

2   Double-click the line.

    The Relationships dialog box appears.

3   Be sure that the Enforce Referential Integrity check box is selected, and then click the Cascade Update Related Fields check box to select it.

4   Click OK.

    The Relationships dialog box closes, and the Relationships window opens. Both ends of the line between the two tables are thickened. The Boxes table has a 1 next to it, indicating that this is the "one" side of a one-to-many relationship. The Box Details table has the infinity symbol placed next to it, indicating that this is the "many" side of the relationship.

5   Repeat steps 1 through 4 to establish the relationship between the Boxes and Order Details tables.

Ensure data validity by Using Cascade Delete Related Records

Sweet Lil's wants to be sure that when customers are deleted all open orders are removed as well. This will ensure that no orders are open for customers that are no longer valid. You can ensure that the records are deleted by setting the Cascade Delete Related Records property.

1   In the Relationships window, double-click the line between the Customers and Orders tables.

    The Relationships dialog box appears.

2   In the Relationships dialog box, select the Cascade Delete Related Records check box.

When the Cascade Delete Related Records box is selected for this relationship, any changes to the primary table (Customers) will ripple through to the related table (Orders).

3   Click OK to accept the change you have made to the relationship.

4   Close the Relationships window, and click Yes to confirm you want to save changes to the layout of the Relationships window.

Make sure Cascade Delete is working

1   In the Database window, double-click the Customers table to open it.

2   Select record 5.

3   On the toolbar, click the Delete Record button.

A message appears, stating that you are about to delete related records.

Delete Record

4   Click No to continue, and then close the Customers table.

Protecting Data Integrity by Using a Lookup Field

Sweet Lil's has developed a table for carriers. The objective in building the new table was to speed up shipments to customers and from suppliers. To speed up shipping, you will add a field that will keep track of the coverage area for each carrier. There are only three different designations for coverage area: Domestic, International, or Both. To accomplish this, you will create a lookup field that will list each option. This will speed up data entry and protect data integrity by allowing the user to select from a list and limiting the data that is entered in the field to the three available choices.

Create the Lookup field

In the following exercise, you will create a lookup field that lists the coverage options for carriers. The Lookup Wizard will create a combo box control in the Carriers table so that employees can select a name from a list instead of typing it.

1   In the Database window, click the Tables tab, and then double-click the Carriers table.

The Carriers table will contain the lookup field, and the lookup field will display names from a list that you will type.

2   On the Insert menu, click Lookup Column.

The Lookup Wizard starts, and the first dialog box appears. You want the new field (the lookup column) to display values that you will type in, so you select the second option.

3 Click Next.

The Lookup Wizard asks how many columns should be in your lookup field. Leave the default number of columns.

4 Click in the cell below the Col 1 heading, type **Domestic** and press TAB.

The insertion point moves to a new blank cell.

5 Add values for International and Both, and then click Next.

The Lookup Wizard asks what label you would like for your lookup column.

6 Type **Coverage** and then click Finish. Click the Coverage field down arrow. Your screen should look like the following illustration.

Coverage	Carrier ID	Carrier Name	Air Delivery	Street Address	City /
▼	1	Wild Fargo Carriers	☐	410 N.E. 84th St	Chica
Domestic	2	Grey Goose Express	☑	100 Day St.	New Y
International	3	Pegasus Overnight	☐	45908 Airport Wa	Dallas
Both	(AutoNumber)		☐		

A lookup field ensures data integrity
by providing a list of values.

See "Increasing Data Validity by Using a Combo Box Control" earlier in this lesson for a discussion of how to create a combo box control without creating a lookup column.

7 Select Domestic as the coverage for the first record, International for the second record, and Domestic for the last record.

8 Close the Carriers table, and then click Yes to save your changes.

The Carriers table appears in Datasheet view, and the new lookup column is added to the table. Now Sweet Lil's employees can select a coverage value in the table quickly by clicking the down arrow and selecting a name from the list. In addition, when a form is created that uses the Carriers table, the Coverage field will automatically be a combo box on the form.

Understanding Many-to-Many Relationships

One-to-one and one-to-many relationships are discussed in Lesson 4, "Controlling Database Growth."

When you evaluate a relationship between two tables, it's important to look at the relationship from both sides. You might think at first that you have a one-to-many relationship when you actually have a many-to-many relationship. A *many-to-many relationship* occurs when one record in either table can have more than one matching record in the other table. In those cases, because you don't know which table should be the primary table, you need a third table that links the two tables before you can create the relationships.

The Boxes table and Bonbons table are a good example of a many-to-many relationship. At first glance, you might think that boxes and bonbons have a one-to-many relationship because one box can contain many different types of bonbons. But take a look at the relationship from the bonbons side. One type of bonbon can be used in more than one box.

You'd have a problem if you tried to create a one-to-many relationship between the Boxes table and the Bonbons table: which would you make the primary table in the relationship? Suppose you made the Boxes table the primary table. You'd add a Box ID field to the Bonbons table to hold the matching values. But when you got to a record for the Bittersweet Blueberry bonbon, you'd have to enter box IDs for both the All Seasons box and the Alpine Collection box, because the Bittersweet Blueberry bonbon is in both boxes. If you enter two box IDs, Microsoft Access can't match the Bittersweet Blueberry record to the right boxes—you can have only one value in each matching field. The same thing happens if you try putting a Bonbon ID field in the Boxes table.

The solution is to create a *junction table,* a table that acts as a bridge between two other tables and that contains the primary keys of the two tables you want to relate. In a junction table, you can add a field that doesn't exist in either of the original tables but that gives you additional information relevant to both the other tables. In the Sweet Lil's database, the junction table is called Box Details. The primary key of the Box Details table consists of Box ID and Bonbon ID—the primary keys of the two tables you're trying to relate. The Box Details table also contains a Quantity field, which tells you how many of each bonbon are in a box.

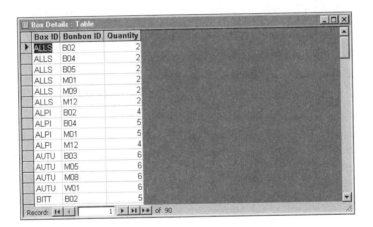

 NOTE   If you'd like to build on the skills that you learned in this lesson, you can do the One Step Further. Otherwise, skip to "Finish the lesson."

One Step Further: Exploring Junction Table Relationships

When you create a junction table, you don't add fields to it that really belong in one of the two related tables. For example, you might be tempted to add the Box Name field to the Box Details table. But that field is already in the Boxes table; it shouldn't be repeated. The only fields that belong in the Box Details table are those needed to define the link (Box ID and Bonbon ID) and any field whose data describes the relationship between the records in the other two tables. The Quantity field qualifies because its data relates to both the other tables—it tells how many of each bonbon are in each box.

View junction table relationships

The Boxes table has a one-to-many relationship with the Box Details table, and so does the Bonbons table. The Box Details table serves as a junction table between the two tables involved in the many-to-many relationship. Use the Relationships window to see how the junction table serves as a bridge between the Boxes table and the Bonbons table.

Relationships

1   In the Database window, click the Tables tab. Then, on the toolbar, click the Relationships button to open the Relationships window.

2   On the toolbar, click the Clear Layout button, and then click Yes.

Clear Layout

Clearing the layout gives you an empty space for working; it has no impact on the relationships.

3   On the toolbar, click the Show Table button.

The Show Table dialog box appears.

Show Table

4   Add the Bonbons table, the Box Details table, and the Boxes table to the Relationships window.

5   Close the Show Table dialog box.

You can see the links between the tables.

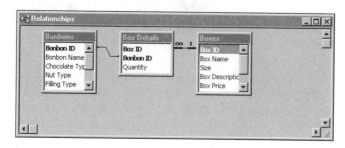

6   On the File menu, click Save.

Finish the lesson

1 To continue to the next lesson, on the File menu, click Close.

2 If you are finished using Microsoft Access for now, on the File menu, click Exit.

Lesson Summary

To	Do this	Button
Change the properties of a form control	Open the form in Design view. Select the control, and use the Properties button to open the properties sheet	
Create a validation rule for a form control	Type the rule in the control's Validation Rule property on the properties sheet.	
Create a combo box control	Open a form in Design view. Select the Combo Box tool in the toolbox. Drag the field from the field list to a place on the form to start the Combo Box Wizard.	
Change the tab order for a form	Open the form in Design view. Select a control, and use the Tab Order command from the View menu to change the order of moving through fields on a form.	
Set the default value for a field	Open the table in Design view, and select a field by clicking its Field Name. In the Field Properties Default Value property, type the value you want as the default for all new records added to the table thereafter.	
Create a Required field	Open the table in Design view, and then select the field you want to require by clicking its Field Name. Click in the Field Properties Required Property field, and select Yes from the drop-down list.	

To	Do this	Button
Enforce referential integrity	In the Database window, click the Relationships button. Double-click the line connecting the two tables. Select the Enforce Referential Integrity check box.	
Establish Cascade Update Related Records	In the Database window, click the Relationships button. Double-click the line connecting the two tables. Select the Enforce Referential Integrity and Cascade Update Related Fields check boxes.	
Establish Cascade Delete Related Records	In the Database window, click the Relationships button. Double-click the line connecting the two tables. Select the Enforce Referential Integrity and Cascade Delete Related Fields check boxes.	
Insert a lookup field	Open a table in Design view. On the Insert menu, select Lookup Column to start the Lookup Wizard. Select values from a table or query, or add your own. Follow the wizard prompts, and then click Finish when done.	

For online information about	On the Help menu, click Contents And Index, click the Index tab, and then type
Creating validation rules	**validating data**
Changing tab order	**tab order in forms**
Establishing default values	**default field value**
Establishing referential integrity	**referential integrity**
Using cascade update	**referential**
Creating or deleting relationships between tables	**relationships**

Getting and Working with External Data

Lesson

6

Estimated time

35 min.

In this lesson you will learn how to:

- Link your database to a table created in another database management program.
- Work with data in a linked table.
- Import a file from a different database.
- Use a hyperlink to connect a form to a table.

In ideal conditions, a database is constructed quite logically using a single tool or a set of related tools, such as those offered by Microsoft Office. In the real world of business computing, however, systems are often constructed using a variety of tools, and data is usually stored in a variety of formats. This is particularly true in organizations that have a long history of computer use.

To accommodate this variety of formats, Microsoft Access databases can incorporate data from many different software packages. For example, Microsoft Access can use data stored in Microsoft Excel, Lotus 1-2-3, dBASE, Microsoft FoxPro, Paradox, Btrieve, Microsoft SQL Server, or a text file.

In this lesson, you'll learn how to attach a table from a different database format to your Microsoft Access database and how to use Microsoft Access to work with data in a table. You'll also learn how to share data between your Microsoft Access database and outside sources, such as an external database.

Gathering Data from External Sources

When you *import,* or pull in, data into your Microsoft Access database, Microsoft Access copies the data from its source into a table in your database. You can import data from these file formats:

- A spreadsheet file, such as a Microsoft Excel or a Lotus 1-2-3 file

- A text file, such as a file you might create in a word-processing program or a text editor

- A file in another database format, such as a Microsoft FoxPro file, a Paradox version 3.*x* or later file, a dBASE III or later file, a Btrieve file (that has an Xtrieve dictionary file), a Microsoft SQL Server file, or another Microsoft Access database file, just to mention a few

You also have the choice of linking to files in any of these formats. A *link* is a connection between the place where the file was created, the *source,* and the place to which the file has been linked, the *destination.* You create a link between your Microsoft Access database and the external table, which can also be another Microsoft Access table. A linked table isn't copied into your Microsoft Access database; the table stays in its original file format. That way, you can use Microsoft Access to work with the data, and someone else can still use the table in its original program.

In this lesson, you'll start by linking a table to the Sweet Lil's database, which is stored in a common database format known as a DBF (the Database File format used by dBASE, FoxPro, and other programs) file. Later, you'll import the same data.

You can also start Microsoft Access and open the Sweet Lil's database simultaneously. Click the Start button, point to Documents, and then click Sweet Lil's.

Start the lesson

➤ If Microsoft Access isn't started yet, start it. Open the Sweet Lil's database. If the Microsoft Access window doesn't fill your screen, maximize the window.

If you need help opening the database, see Lesson 1.

Getting Connected Through an External Table

If you link an external table to your Microsoft Access database, you can view and update the data even if others are using the data in the table's source program. You can create Microsoft Access forms and reports based on the external table. You can even use a query to combine external data with the data in your Microsoft Access tables. See Lesson 7, "Getting Answers to Questions About Your Data," for information about using queries to combine data from different tables.

One of the first business functions Sweet Lil's converted to electronic processing was a simple database of fixed assets. Most processes in the organization have been converted to the new systems; however, the company still maintains a fixed assets register table in an older file format. The Assets table was created using dBASE IV, a database management program. The data is stored in a file format known as DBF. The Accounting Department is anxious to have the table incorporated into the larger database; however, the data must remain in DBF format because other systems are still using DBF.

Link an external table

To integrate the table of shipping rates without changing the file format, you will link the data to Sweet Lil's database.

1   On the File menu, point to Get External Data, and then click Link Tables.

The Link dialog box appears.

Look In
Favorites

2   Click the Look In Favorites button, and then double-click the Access SBS Practice folder.

3   In the Files Of Type list, select dBASE IV.

The dBASE IV file, Assets.dbf, appears in the list of files. Assets.dbf was copied to your Access SBS Practice folder when you copied the practice files to your hard disk.

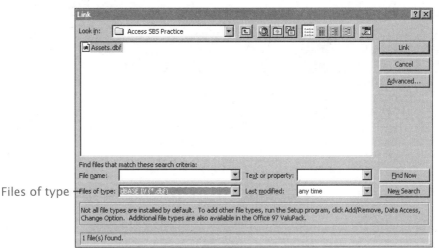

Files of type

4   Click Link.

Microsoft Access links the table to your database, and then the Select Index Files dialog box appears. An index file indicates the order for displaying records in a DBF file. This file does not have an associated index file, so you cannot include one in the link.

111

5 Click Cancel.

A message indicates that the table was successfully linked.

6 Click OK, and then close the Link dialog box.

The Assets table is listed in the Database window along with the other tables in the Sweet Lil's database. The symbol identifies the table as a linked dBASE table.

dBase table symbol —

Incorporating a Linked Table

Now that the external table is linked to your Microsoft Access database, you can use it much as you would a regular Microsoft Access table. You can't change the structure of a linked table (that is, you can't add, delete, or re-arrange fields), but you can reset the field properties in Design view to control the way Microsoft Access displays the data. You can also use field properties to give a field a default value or to check new data entered in a field. You can edit data in the linked table, and if the linked table is edited by another program, the changes will appear in your database.

Open a linked table

➤ In the Database window, double-click the Assets table.

The table opens in Datasheet view. The table should look like the following illustration.

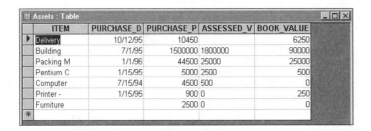

Change a field property

You decide you would like to see the data in the Book Value field displayed as currency.

View

The graphic on the face of the View button changes according to the current selection.

1 On the toolbar, click the View down arrow, and click Design View.

A message indicates that you can't modify some properties of a linked table, and asks whether you want to open the table anyway.

2 Click Yes.

The Assets table opens in Design view.

3 Click in the selection column next to the Book_Value field.

The properties of the Book_Value appear in the Field Properties sheet in the lower pane of the window. The Hint box beside the Field Properties listing says that the Data Type property can't be modified in linked tables. But you can still modify how Microsoft Access displays the data by setting the field's Format property.

4 In the Field Properties sheet, click in the Format property box.

The Hint box displays information about how to set the Format property.

5 Click the Format property down arrow, and then select Currency.

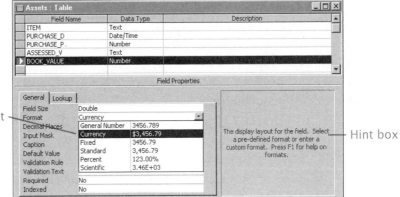

6 Switch to Datasheet view. In the message box, click Yes.

The data is reformatted.

7 Close the Assets table.

Importing a Table

The Accounting Department has decided to convert all its old files to Microsoft Access files. One of the files used by the Accounting Department is a spreadsheet that keeps track of employee payroll deductions. This file was created in Microsoft Excel. The Accounting Department is going to update these records in Microsoft Access; the file can be imported into Sweet Lil's database. Remember that when you link a table, the data retains its original file format. When you import a table, the data is converted to Microsoft Access format.

Import a table

1 On the File menu, point to Get External Data, and then click Import.

The Import dialog box appears.

2 In the Files Of Type list box, select Microsoft Excel.

The Payroll.xls file is displayed in the list of files.

3 Double-click the Payroll.xls file.

The Import Spreadsheet Wizard opens.

4 Click the First Row Contains Column Headings check box indicating that you want to use the column headings as field names, and then click the Next button.

5 Click the In A New Table option indicating that you want to save the data in a new table, and then click the Next button.

6 This dialog box allows you to specify whether fields are indexed. You do not need to make any changes to the suggestions made by Microsoft Access, so simply click the Next button to continue.

7 Select the Choose My Own Primary Key option.

The Employee ID field will be selected as the primary key.

8 Click Next to go to the last dialog box.

9 Press DELETE to erase the default name, and type **Payroll**

10 Click Finish, and then click OK to close the successful importing acknowledgment message box.

In the Database window, the imported Payroll table is added to the list of tables.

Working with Data in the Imported Table

The data in the imported table is now part of your Microsoft Access database, but you want to change some aspects of the table. You can customize the table's design, just as you can customize a table you created yourself.

Change properties

In this exercise, you customize the tables.

1 In the Database window, click the Design button to open the Payroll table in Design view.

2 In the YTD Insurance field, click the Data Type down arrow, and then select Currency.

3 On the toolbar, click the View down arrow, and then select Datasheet View.

A message indicates that you need to save the table.

4 Click Yes.

A message box indicates that you might lose some data and ask whether you want to continue.

5 Click Yes.

Your table should look like the following illustration.

Payroll : Table			
Employee ID	**First Name**	**Last Name**	**YTD Insurance**
1	Mary	Culvert	$722.55
2	Jerome	Woods	$542.36
3	Nora	Bromsler	$450.25
4	Frederick	Mallon	$893.52
5	Adrienne	Snyder	$542.36

6 Close the Payroll table.

Adding Hyperlinks to Your Database

For a demonstration of how to add a hyperlink to your database, double-click the Camcorder Files On The Internet shortcut on your Desktop or connect to the Internet address listed on p. xxvi.

One of the most important recent changes in computing is the growth of the Internet or, more specifically, the World Wide Web. The *Internet* is a complex system of interconnected networks that spans the globe. Many organizations share information with their suppliers, consumers, and the general public by creating a permanent presence on the Internet. Anyone interested in the company or its products can view the site by using a type of software known as a *browser.*

In Microsoft Access, it is very easy to connect your database to other resources, including the Internet. Access now includes hyperlinks as a data type that can be stored in a table. A *hyperlink* is a way of "jumping" from one object to another. You can think of a hyperlink as a trail that leads from your database to data stored in another location. The trail's destination can be another object in your database, another Office document, or an Internet site. In this lesson, you will learn how to create a hyperlink to another object in the database.

115

Microsoft Office and Intranets

Using hyperlinks to connect Microsoft Office documents is an excellent way to develop a corporate intranet. An *intranet* is an internal communications system that makes use of the World Wide Web protocol to exchange information from desk-to-desk or across the world.

Sweet Lil's is in the process of improving internal office communications. The company is establishing links to make it easier to move between the forms in its database. For example, the Human Resources manager would like to be able to quickly move between the Employees form and the Payroll table. This type of link is established by inserting a hyperlink in the form in Design view.

Connect two forms by using a hyperlink

The Human Resources manager wants to be able to check an employee's payroll deductions while she is viewing the employee's other records. Although she is aware that you can create a form that ties the data together, she believes that this would create an overly complex form. You decide to insert a hyperlink in the Employees form to tie the two forms together.

In this exercise, you will insert a hyperlink that can open the Payroll table from within the Employees form.

1   Select the Employees form in the Database window. Click Design to open the form in Design view.

    The form opens in Design view.

2   On the toolbar, click the Insert Hyperlink button.

    The Insert Hyperlink dialog box appears.

Insert Hyperlink

The Link To File Or URL box creates hyperlinks to other documents or to the Web.

The Named Location In File box creates hyperlinks to locations within your database.

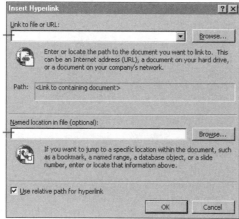

The Insert Hyperlink dialog box is used to create hyperlinks within or external to your database.

Connecting a Microsoft Access Table to the World Wide Web

Connecting a form or report to the World Wide Web (WWW) is very similar to connecting to an object in the database. Both use hyperlinks to make their connections. The only real differences are the type of address that is inserted in the hyperlink, and how the insertion is made. Although Microsoft Office hyperlinks can use either a Universal Naming Convention path or a Universal Resource Locator (URL) path, hyperlinks to the WWW must be made through a URL.

The location a hyperlink leads to can be either a Universal Naming Convention Path (UNC) or a Universal Resource Locator (URL). UNCs are written \\server\share\path\filename, and are used more frequently for communications within an organization. URLs generally start with a protocol (which is like an area code), such as http, for accessing the site. The protocol is then followed by the identifier (which is like a phone number) for the organization that maintains the Internet site. For example, http://www.msn.com opens the Microsoft Network site.

With the development of the intranet as a new medium for conducting internal business, many organizations have begun allowing people outside the organization to have limited access to the organization database through "firewalls" that segregate data made available to the public World Wide Web from data available only to members of the organization. Microsoft Access is well-designed to accommodate presentation of data through the Internet.

World Wide Web documents are viewed using a browser such as the Microsoft Internet Explorer. Browsers display documents that include commands for a special programming language called the *Hypertext Markup Language* (HTML). HTML documents can be created by using such programs as Microsoft Word Internet Assistant or Microsoft FrontPage. HTML files can be read by any word-processing package, but they are filled with commands that Web browsers use for displaying graphics and managing hyperlinks.

When a customer anywhere in the world fills in a field on Sweet Lil's Candy Order page, a command is sent through the World Wide Web to Sweet Lil's. When Microsoft Access receives the command, it is processed just as if a sales clerk had issued it in Sweet Lil's home office. In effect, Sweet Lil's Web page allows customers to place orders just as they once could by mail or by calling on the phone. The advantage is that they can do it from anywhere in the world, and any time of the day or night. Sweet Lil's is now open 24 hours a day, worldwide!

117

3 Next to the Named Location In File box, click Browse.

The Select Location dialog box appears. This is where you select the object to which the hyperlink will lead.

4 Be sure the Tables tab is selected, and then scroll through the list of tables until Payroll is displayed.

5 Click the Payroll table to select it, and then click OK.

The table name appears in the Insert Hyperlink dialog box.

6 Click OK.

A Table Payroll label is added to the form. If the label is too small, resize it by dragging the handles to the right until the full text is displayed. You can also reposition the field.

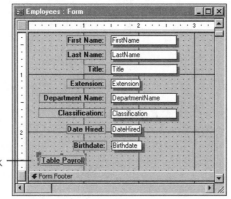

The new hyperlink ──┐

Test your new hyperlink

In this exercise, you test the hyperlink.

View

1 Click the View down arrow, and then click Form View.

2 Click the new Payroll Table hyperlink.

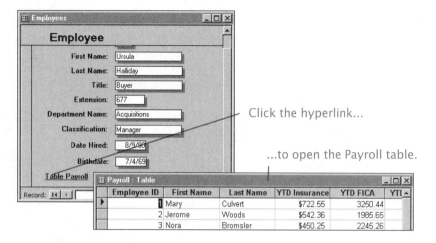

Click the hyperlink...

...to open the Payroll table.

The Payroll table opens in Datasheet view.

3 Close the Payroll table.

4 Close the Employees form.

5 When the dialog box asks if you want to save your changes, click Yes.

NOTE If you'd like to build on the skills that you learned in this lesson, you can do the One Step Further. Otherwise, skip to "Finish the lesson."

One Step Further: Hyperlinking to an Office Document

IMPORTANT You must have Microsoft Office installed to complete this exercise. If you do not have Office installed, skip to "Finish the lesson."

Sweet Lil's has adopted Microsoft Office as its standard set of tools for creating applications and has chosen to use Office documents to build the corporate intranet. Every month, the Credit Department uses Microsoft Word to write letters to credit customers who are late in making payments. The Accounting Department wants to view those letters in the Credit Customer form for accuracy.

NOTE In the Insert Hyperlink dialog box, you can create a hyperlink to any file you can browse to. Whether you are on a network, an intranet, or the WWW, you can make a connection just as easily as you are connecting to your local hard drive in these exercises.

In the following exercises, you will modify the design of the Credit Customer form to include a command button that hyperlinks to the Microsoft Word file containing the credit letter.

Add the command button

Control Wizards

1   In the Database window, select the Credit Customer form, and click Design to open the form in Design view.

2   In the toolbox, make sure the Control Wizards tool is not selected, and then click the Command Button tool.

3   Drag a rectangle on the form below the current fields to create the command button.

Command Button

   A new command button appears on the form.

4   If the property sheet is not already open, on the toolbar, click the Properties button.

5   Click the All Tab option, and type **View Credit Letter** for the Caption property.

Properties

Establish the hyperlink

Builder

1   Click in the Hyperlink Address property. Click the Builder button.

   The Insert Hyperlink dialog box appears.

2   Click the Browse button next to the Link To File Or URL combo box, and then in the Access SBS Practice folder, select the Credit Letter.doc file. (Hint: Change the Files Of Type to Microsoft Word.) Click OK.

   The path to Credit Letter.doc appears in the Insert Hyperlink dialog box.

3   Click OK to return to Design view.

4   Close the properties sheet.

Open the credit letter

1   On the Form Design toolbar, click the View down arrow, and click Form View.

   The Credit Customer form opens in Form view.

2 Click the View Credit Letter command button.

Microsoft Word opens, and the credit letter is displayed.

3 Close Microsoft Word, and then close the Credit Customer form and save your changes.

Finish the lesson

1 To continue to the next lesson, on the File menu, click Close.

2 If you are finished using Microsoft Access for now, on the File menu, click Exit.

Lesson Summary

To	Do this
Link an external table	Open the database. On the File menu, point to Get External Data, and then click Link Tables. Navigate to the file you want to link, and then click the Link button.
Change field properties of a linked table	In Design view, click the field name and then click the property you want to change in the Field Properties sheet in the lower half of the window. The Hint box text will let you know whether the property can be changed.
Import a table	Open the database. On the File menu, point to Get External Data, and then click Import. Select the file type, double-click the file-name, and then click OK. Follow the instructions of the Import Spreadsheet Wizard for Excel and text files.
Insert a hyperlink from a form to another Microsoft Access object in the current database	Open the form in Design View. Click the Insert Hyperlink button to open the Insert Hyperlink dialog box. Click Browse next to the Named Location In File box. Select the object by opening the appropriate sheet (table, query, form, report, macro, or module), and double-clicking the object's name. Click OK in the Insert Hyperlink dialog box.

For online information about	On the Help menu, click Contents And Index, click the Index tab, and then type
Linking an external table	**linked table**
Importing a table	**import tables, importing and exporting**
Inserting hyperlinks	**hyperlinks, creating**

Part

2

Review & Practice

Estimated time
25 min.

You will review and practice how to:

- Create a table and establish a hyperlink.
- Build and identify relationships between tables.
- Change a field property.
- Use Autoform to create a form.
- Create a combo box.

In Part 3, you will learn how to turn the data you've been managing and entering into meaningful information. Before you take that step, however, you should solidify the skills you learned in Part 2, "Expanding and Creating Databases."

Scenario

For the next quarter, the Marketing Department is planning advertising promotions for selected boxes of bonbons. They have also created a Web page to advertise the promotions. You create and relate tables to track the promotional information. When you're finished, you will delete the table from the database.

Step 1: Create a Table and Set a Hyperlink Data Type

The Marketing Department wants to use Microsoft Access to keep track of advertising promotions for different boxes of bonbons and the employee who is responsible for each promotion. Marketing would like employees to be able to create forms that link to the appropriate Web page. The promotion name will be unique to each project.

If you are using the Table Wizard, a good sample table to use is Projects.

1 Create a new table that has fields for Promotion Name, Employee ID, Start Date, Box ID, and Web Link.

2 Save the table with the name **Promotions**

Allow Microsoft Access to create a primary key for you.

3 Select Hyperlink as the data type for Web Link.

4 Close and save the table, and verify that the Promotions table is listed in the Database window.

For more information about	See
Creating a table	Lesson 4
Selecting a data type	Lesson 4
Setting a primary key	Lesson 4
Setting a hyperlink data type	Lesson 6

Step 2:   *Relate Tables with a One-to-Many Relationship*

Each promotion will be assigned to one employee, but one employee might handle more than one promotion. Create a one-to-many relationship between the Employees table and the Promotions table, using the Employee ID field as the matching field.

1 Find and clear the relationships in the Relationships window, and use the Show Tables dialog box to add the new tables.

2 Determine which table is the primary table and which is the related table.

3 Use the Relationships window to create a relationship between the Employees table and the Promotions table.

4 Do not save the layout of the Relationships window when you close the window.

For more information about	See
Understanding relationships between tables	Lesson 4
Displaying relationships in the Relationships window	Lesson 4

Step 3:   *Relate Tables with a Many-to-Many Relationship*

The Marketing Department wants to track the dates and locations of orders for certain boxes. The Orders table contains a record for each order, with information about when the order was placed, where it should be shipped, and how the customer paid. The Boxes table contains a record for each box in the product line, with information such as the box name, size, description, and price. An order can include more than one kind of box, and a box can appear in more than one order.

Relate the Orders and Boxes tables so that you can easily find the names of all the boxes in an order.

1   Analyze the relationship between the Orders and Boxes tables from both sides.

2   Open the Order Details table, which is a junction table between the Orders and Boxes tables based on their primary keys. It also contains a Quantity field.

3   Close the Order Details table, and view the relationship between the Orders, Boxes, and Order Details tables in the Relationships window.

For more information about	See
Identifying a many-to-many relationship	Lesson 5
Using junction tables	Lesson 5

Step 4:   *Change a Field Property*

To be sure that every promotion is assigned to an employee, you decide to give the Promotion name field in the Promotions table the Required property of Yes. You also decide to create a Promotions form for assigning employees to promotions. You want to include a combo box control for choosing the appropriate employee.

1   Open the Promotions table in Design view, and set the Required property of the Promotion Name field to Yes.

2   Create an Autoform based on the Promotions table. Save it as Promotions.

3   Open the Promotions form in Design view. Delete the text box control for Employee ID, and create a combo box control to replace the text box.

4   Close and save the Promotions form.

For more information about	See
Working with Field properties	Lesson 5
Using Autoforms	Lesson 4
Creating a combo box control	Lesson 5

Step 5: Delete Objects from a Database

The Marketing Department has notified you that, for the next quarter, they will use an outside consultant for their promotions. Therefore, they do not need to track promotions in the Sweet Lil's database.

1   In the Relationships window, delete the relationship between the Employees table and the Promotions table.

2   In the Database window, delete the Promotions table from the database.

3   In the Database window, delete the Promotions form.

For more information about	See
Deleting a table from a database	Lesson 4

Finish the Review & Practice

1   To continue to the next lesson, on the File menu, click Close.

2   If you are finished using Microsoft Access for now, on the File menu, click Exit.

Turning Data into Meaningful Information

Getting Answers to Questions About Your Data

Estimated time
45 min.

In this lesson you will learn how to:

■ Create a query based on a table or on another query.

■ Set criteria to extract a set of related records.

■ Sort data and hide a field in a query.

■ Create a query that shows related data.

■ Join tables in a query.

■ Relate tables in a query.

The raw data stored in a database is factual. When organizations first begin using a database, they generally focus on creating systems that will accurately and quickly retrieve this data. A more sophisticated use of databases moves beyond retrieving data to converting that data into information. *Information* is processed data.

The power of database systems is their ability to respond quickly to day-to-day business changes. Frequently, organizations need to look at their data from different angles. Before calling your customers about a marketing campaign, you might want to create a list of selected names and phone numbers. To review sales trends, you might want to find out how many orders you received in a specific month. To facilitate express orders of supplies, you might want to quickly locate the name and phone number of a business contact.

Relational databases are commonly used for developing business systems because they are so adaptable. A well-designed database contains a table for each key section of the organization. The result is a system that provides extraordinary flexibility in making data into information.

In Microsoft Access, you can find the information you want by creating a fundamental database analysis tool: the query. A *query* is a tool that brings together data from multiple tables to answer a question or perform an action on the data. In this lesson, you will create a variety of queries that select the data you want. You'll also calculate total values using a query, and you'll use a query to answer a "what if" question.

Customer	State/Province	Gift	Order Date
Adams, Cathy	CA	Yes	23-Dec-95
Fogerty, Sam	CA	Yes	09-Dec-95
Harkin, Rory	CA	Yes	03-Dec-95
Kennedy, Brian	CA	Yes	10-Dec-95
Kimball, Mary	CA	Yes	23-Dec-95
Kimball, Mary	CA	Yes	02-Dec-95
Kumar, Andrew	CA	Yes	19-Dec-95
Lopez, Maria	CA	Yes	10-Dec-95
Olembo, Julia	CA	Yes	15-Dec-95
Pence, Stephen	CA	Yes	23-Dec-95

In Lesson 4, "Controlling Database Growth," queries were previewed when relationships were created between tables. In this lesson, you learn to create queries and refine your requests for more specific data.

Understanding Queries

A query is a way to define a particular group of records. A query can also manipulate records and show you the results. Think of a query as a request for a particular collection of data, such as "Show me the names and phone numbers for our carriers, and show me their shipping charges." A query is made up of records that were created from fields from various tables.

You use queries in much the same way that you use tables. You can open a query and see its results in a datasheet. Queries can be the basis for forms or reports. You can also use a query to update tables; that is, you can update the data in the query results, and then save the updated data to the originating table.

Because queries are so flexible, you might find that you use them more often than tables in day-to-day operations. You can use a query to sort data or to view a subset of the data in your database. You can also use the query to perform analysis. For example, instead of wading through all the customers in the Customers table, a regional sales manager could look at only the customers in his region and see information about their purchases at the same time. He could then manipulate the records to see what effect a 10 percent increase in purchases would have on his commissions.

Datasheet of the Ingredient Source query

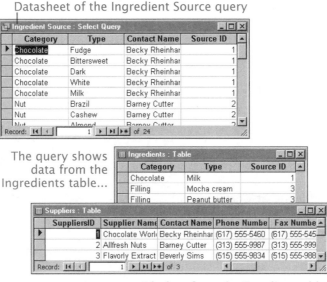

The query shows data from the Ingredients table...

...with data from the Suppliers table.

For more information about using filters, see Lesson 3, "Viewing Only the Information You Need."

Queries are similar to filters in that both can be used to select data. Queries, however, are more powerful than filters. Filters select data from one table; queries can extract data from many different tables. You can also save a query and use it again, and you can use an existing query to build a new query.

Using queries, you can approach the same information in many different ways. For example, you can use the same tables to create one query that shows which customers bought which products, another query that shows which products sell best in Europe, and another that shows product sales sorted according to postal codes. You don't have to store the product information three times for the three different queries—each piece of information is stored in its table only once.

Creating Queries

In Microsoft Access, you can create a query by using the Simple Query Wizard. When you first start creating queries, using a wizard is the best approach, because a wizard will guide you through the process. After you have selected the data you want to examine, you can modify the query to focus on the particular information you want. You should plan your query—that is, decide what data you want to use— before you begin using the Simple Query Wizard, because you want to select only the data you need to answer your question.

Start the lesson

▶ If Microsoft Access isn't started yet, start it. Open the Sweet Lil's data-base. If the Microsoft Access window doesn't fill your screen, maximize the window.

If you need help opening the database, see Lesson 1.

Generating a List by Creating a Query

You're in charge of a telephone survey of Sweet Lil's customers in your sales re-gion. Your region is New York State, so you'll use a query to get a list of the names and phone numbers of the New York customers. The information you need is stored in the Customers table.

Create a query

In the following exercise, you create a query for the New York customers.

1 In the Database window, click the Queries tab.

2 Click New.

The New Query dialog box appears.

3 In the New Query dialog box, double-click Simple Query Wizard.

The Simple Query Wizard appears.

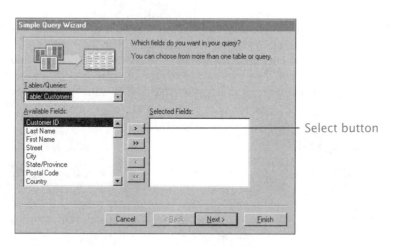

4 Click the Tables/Queries down arrow, scroll up, and then select Table: Customers.

The Customers table fields are displayed in the Available Fields list. You use this list to select the fields you want your query to display.

You can also select the Customer ID field and use the Select button (>) to move the field to the Selected Fields column.

5 Double-click the Customer ID field.

The Customer ID field moves to the Selected Fields list.

6 Select the Last Name, First Name, State/Province, and Phone fields, and then click the Select button to move them to the Selected Fields box.

The Selected Fields list now has five fields displayed. You have defined the query; now you just need to save it before you put it to work.

Name and save a query

In this exercise, you name and save the query.

1 In the Simple Query Wizard, click Next.

A dialog box in which you define the query's name appears.

2 In the What Title Do You Want For Your Query box, type **NY Customers** and then click Finish.

The results of the query are displayed in Datasheet view so you can see whether the query is correctly defined. The name of the query appears in the title bar. Microsoft Access automatically saves the query and adds it to the list of queries in the Database window.

Modifying Queries in Design View

For more information about setting query criteria, see Appendix C, "Using Expressions."

After you have created the basic structure to select the data you want to work with, you can make the modifications by opening the query in Design view and dragging fields from the upper portion of the Query window to the design grid in the lower portion. You place the fields in the design grid in the order you want them to appear in the datasheet. Microsoft Access then assembles the SQL commands required to perform your query.

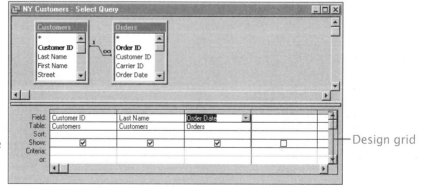

Design grid

You can also use the Query window to create a query, but it is faster to use the Simple Query Wizard.

The Query window can help you build on an existing query. Often, one question leads to another, and you will find that you want to keep changing a query. For example, you might start by finding all your customers from California. Then, by making small changes in the query design grid, you can find all the California customers who ordered gifts, and finally, all the California customers who ordered gifts in December. And you can keep refining the query until you get it just right.

Setting Criteria to Focus Your Queries

The current query displays records for all customers in the Customers table. But you're interested only in the customers from New York State, so you'll set criteria to limit the query to records for customers in New York State.

Expressions in queries are discussed in Lesson 4; expressions in filters are discussed in Lesson 3.

You set criteria for a query using an *expression*, a formula that specifies which records Microsoft Access should retrieve. For example, to find fields with a value greater than 5, you'd use the expression >5. The symbol > means "greater than." You use an expression in a query the same way you use an expression in a filter.

In these exercises, you'll specify criteria to limit the query, and then you'll run the query.

Specify criteria

View

The graphic on the View button changes to reflect the current selection.

1   Click the View down arrow, and then click Design View.

2   In the State/Province column in the design grid, click in the Criteria row.

3   Type **NY** and press ENTER.

When you press ENTER, Microsoft Access automatically places quotation marks around what you typed. The quotation marks indicate text. If your criteria is a number, it is not enclosed in quotation marks.

Run your query

▶   Click the View down arrow, and click Datasheet View to check the query results. Your query should look like the following illustration.

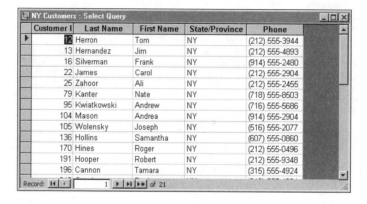

Microsoft Access displays a list of the customers in New York State and their phone numbers; these are the fields that you specified in the Simple Query Wizard.

Add more criteria

Now you have a list of customers in your sales region. But you want to call only your most recent customers: those who have customer IDs greater than 200. In this exercise, you'll add another criterion to the query to find these customers.

1 Click the View down arrow, and click Design View.

2 In the Criteria row in the Customer ID column, type the expression >**200** and press ENTER.

By adding this criterion, you're telling Microsoft Access, "Find customers who have customer IDs greater than 200 and who live in New York State." Your query should look like the following illustration.

For a demonstration of how to set the criteria for a query, double-click the Camcorder Files On The Internet shortcut or connect to the Internet address listed on p. xxvi.

Find customers who have Customer IDs greater than 200...

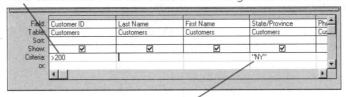

...and who live in New York.

3 Click the View down arrow, and click Datasheet View to switch to Datasheet view and see the list of the customers you're going to call.

Improving the Appearance of a Query

You can make your query more effective and easier to use, you can arrange records in a more convenient order, and you can modify the query results so that the selected fields are hidden.

Sorting Records

For more sorting examples, see Lesson 3, "Viewing Only the Information You Need."

Sorting the records makes it easier to find specific information in your query. For example, to find a phone number for a specific customer, you can list the customers in alphabetical order.

Sort records alphabetically

1 Click anywhere in the Last Name column.

Sort Ascending

2   On the toolbar, click the Sort Ascending button.

All the records in the query results are sorted according to customer last name. Your query should look like the following illustration.

Customer I	Last Name	First Name	State/Province	Phone
310	Brownlee	Jason	NY	(914) 555-0931
249	Gunther	Paul	NY	(212) 555-4934
298	Hendricks	Louise	NY	(516) 555-2067
280	Kahn	Juliet	NY	(212) 555-9424
374	Knutson	Jean	NY	(518) 555-6207
343	Mitchell	Sandy	NY	(607) 555-9679

Record: 1 of 8

Hiding Fields

Occasionally, you have to include a field for the query to generate the correct information, but you don't want to include that field in the query results. For example, in the NY Customers query, you don't want the State/Province field in the datasheet because all the records have the same value, NY. This field must be included in the Design view of the query, because you use the field to set the criteria, but you can use the Show check box in the design grid to hide this field so it doesn't appear in the datasheet.

Hide a field

1   Click the View down arrow, and click Design View.

2   In the Show row in the State/Province column, click the check box to clear it. Your query should look like the following illustration.

Clear the State/Province Show
check box to hide the column.

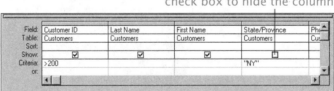

The query will use any criteria or sort information in this field, but it will not show the field in the datasheet.

3   Click the View down arrow, and click Datasheet View.

The State/Province field no longer appears in the query results.

4   Close the NY Customers query window. If prompted to save your changes, click Yes.

Bringing Data Together by Using a Query

When you create a query that gathers information from more than one table, Microsoft Access needs a way to determine which records are related. Microsoft Access uses matching values in equivalent fields in two tables to correctly associate data in different tables. To create a relationship between two tables, you draw a join line between two matching fields in the Relationships window. The *join line* is a graphic image that indicates the database has issued the commands needed to create a relationship. In most cases, the primary key from one table is joined to a field in another table that contains the matching values.

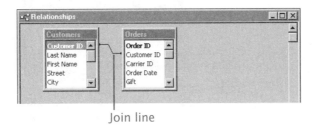

Join line

Creating relationships between tables is discussed in Lesson 4, "Controlling Database Growth."

You can use the relationships you've already developed to create queries that draw data from throughout your database.

Create a query using related tables, and add a field to the query

Lillian Farber, the president of Sweet Lil's, is analyzing the company's orders for November, and she wants a list of all orders placed in that month. She wants to know the order IDs, the customer names, and the dates of the orders. The information that Lillian Farber needs is contained in two different tables: the Orders table and the Customers table. In this exercise, you create a new query by using these tables in the query design grid.

1   In the Database window, click the Queries tab if it is not already in front, and then click New.

The New Query dialog box appears.

2   In the New Query dialog box, double-click Design View.

The Query window opens, and the Show Table dialog box appears.

3   On the Tables tab in the Show Table dialog box, double-click the Orders table, and then double-click the Customers table.

4   On the Show Table dialog box, click Close.

Field lists for the Orders table and the Customers table are shown in the Query window. A join line automatically appears between the Customer ID fields in the two tables. This is because a relationship was created in the database that was included on the Microsoft Access SBS Practice disk. Your query should look like the following illustration.

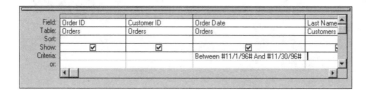

5   In the Orders table field list, double-click the Order ID, Customer ID, and Order Date fields.

The three fields appear in the design grid.

6   In the Customers table field list, double-click the Last Name field.

The Last Name field appears in the design grid.

7   On the File menu, click Save.

8   Name the query Order Information, and then click OK.

Fine-tune and test the query

In this exercise, you use an expression to select records for the month of November. This expression includes the Between...And operator.

1   In the Criteria row in the Order Date column, type **Between 1-Nov-96 And 30-Nov-96** and then press ENTER.

The format of the date changes, and number symbols (#) automatically appear around the dates.

2   To size the column to its best fit, double-click the right border at the top of the Order Date column in the design grid.

The column is resized to show the complete expression, as shown in the following illustration.

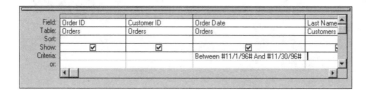

3 Click the View down arrow, and click Datasheet View to see the orders for November. Your query should look like the following illustration.

4 Save the query again, and then close the Order Information window.

Relating Tables by Applying a Query

It is impossible to anticipate all the possible information requirements when designing tables and relationships. Fortunately, queries can draw data from tables that do not have predefined relationships.

If you build a query from tables that do not have a relationship but do have a field with the same name and data type, a temporary relationship is developed between the tables. In this temporary relationship, at least one of the join fields must be a primary key. This relationship exists solely for the purposes of the query. The Query window will automatically display a join line between the tables, indicating that the matching fields will relate the data for the query.

If no relationship exists between the tables you want to use, and they do not have fields with the same name and data type, Microsoft Access will not create a relationship when you add the tables to a query. You can still use related data by joining the tables in the Query window when you create the query. Relationships built in the Query window, however, are not permanent. The reason: relationships require memory for storage. Microsoft Access was designed to allow temporary relationships to be built for query purposes without requiring that the relationship be saved. Just as with any relationship, for the join to work in a temporary relationship, the tables must contain fields with matching data in the primary and foreign keys.

NOTE When you draw a join line between two tables in the Query window, the join applies to that query only. If you want to use the same two tables in another query, you'll need to join them again in the new query.

Join two tables in a query

The Ingredients table lists categories and types of ingredients that bonbons are made of, and it contains a field called Source ID that identifies where the ingredient is purchased. The Suppliers table has information about Sweet Lil's ingredient suppliers, and the table contains a field called Suppliers ID. You can join these two fields in a query because they contain matching data.

In this exercise, you create a quick way to look up the contact names for Sweet Lil's suppliers.

The Suppliers table was added in Lesson 4, "Controlling Database Growth."

1   In the Database window, click the Queries tab, and then click New.

2   Double-click Design View, add the Ingredients table and the Suppliers table to the query by selecting them and clicking Add, and then close the Show Table dialog box.

3   From the Ingredients table, drag the Category field to the Suppliers ID field in the Suppliers table.

A join line indicates a relationship between the two fields that associates the data correctly between the two tables. Your query should look like the following illustration.

You realize that the tables should be linked on the Source ID field rather than the Category field, so you need to delete the join line and re-make the join linking on the Source ID field.

4   Click on the line between the Ingredients and Suppliers tables in the QBE (query by example) grid, and, after the line thickens, press DELETE.

The join line is removed.

5   Drag the Source ID field from the Ingredients table to the Suppliers ID field in the Suppliers table.

The line connects the two fields.

6   In the Ingredients table field list, double-click the Category and Type fields to add them to the design grid.

7   In the Suppliers table field list, double-click Contact Name to add it to the grid.

8   In the Ingredients table field list, double-click Source ID to add it to the grid.

9   In the Source ID column, click in the Sort box, click the down arrow, and then select Ascending.

You have sorted the fields in the order you want them to appear in the query results.

Check the query datasheet

1   Click the View down arrow, and click Datasheet View to view the results.

Your query should look like the following illustration.

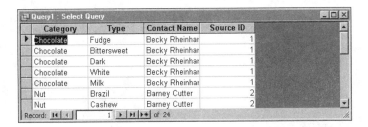

2   Scroll through the records to see the information in the Contact Name field change according to which supplier (Source ID) is used.

3   Close the query. When Microsoft Access asks whether you want to save changes, click Yes.

The Save As dialog box appears.

4   In the File Name box, type **Supplier Contacts** and then click OK.

Print the query datasheet

You decide it would be useful to have a paper copy of the query results. In this exercise, you use the Print command to print the datasheet.

1   In the Database window, double-click the Supplier Contacts query.

The Supplier Contacts query opens in Datasheet view.

2   On the File menu, select Print.

The Print dialog box appears. You can select to print multiple copies or to set up your printer if it is not properly configured.

3   Click OK to print the datasheet to your printer.

4   Close the query.

 NOTE   If you'd like to build on the skills you learned in this lesson, you can do the One Step Further. Otherwise, skip to "Finish the lesson."

One Step Further: Refining Queries

You can also display the bottom values for a field by sorting the field in descending order or see only a percentage of the returned values by selecting one of the percentage values from the Top Values list.

A well-designed query is both specific enough to contain all relevant information and flexible enough to be applied to a variety of situations. Two easy ways to add value to a query are to add a field caption, which helps ensure that data is described completely, and to use the Show Top filter, which limits the information that is returned. If the query is used as the basis for a form, the field caption is used to label the data. If a field caption is not available, the name of the field from which the query extracted data is used as a label. For example, consider the NY Customers query. The query does not locate just any customers, it locates customers who are in New York. However, if this query is used to build a form, the data would be labeled Customer ID, because the field does not have a caption.

Set properties for a field

You want to be certain that your NY Customers query accurately describes exactly what is being displayed. You decide to include a caption for the Customer ID field, so that any form using the query will accurately describe the data in its default caption property. In the following exercise, you will set the Field Caption property to New York Customers.

1 Open the NY Customers query in Design view.
2 Select the Customer ID field by clicking inside the Field row of the first column.
3 On the toolbar, click the Properties button to open the Field Properties sheet.

Properties

4 To add a caption to the Customer ID field, click in the Caption field.
5 Type **New York Customers**
6 Close the Field Properties sheet.

Display only the top five values

You also decide that this query would be more useful if it limited the values displayed to five customers at a time. In the following exercise, you will use the Top Values property to limit the query.

All ▼

Top Values

1 Click the Top Values down arrow, and then click 5.
2 Switch to Datasheet view to see the changes.

   Only the records with the five highest Customer ID numbers are displayed.

3 Close the query, and when Microsoft Access asks if you would like to save changes, click Yes.

Finish the lesson

1   To continue to the next lesson, on the File menu, click Close.
2   If you are finished using Microsoft Access for now, on the File menu, click Exit.

Lesson Summary

To	Do this	Button
Create a query	In the Database window, click the Queries tab. Click New, and then double-click Design View or Simple Query Wizard.	
Add a field to a query in the Query Design view	Double-click the field in the upper portion of the Query window.	
Save and name a new query	On the File menu, click Save. In the Save As dialog box, type a name, and then click OK.	
Set criteria	In the query design grid, enter criteria in the Criteria box for any field in the query.	
Sort the records in a query	In the design grid, click the Sort box of the field you want to sort, click the down arrow, and then select Ascending or Descending. *or* In Datasheet view, click in the column you want to sort, and then click the Sort Ascending or Sort Descending button on the toolbar.	
Hide a field in a query	In the design grid, clear the Show check box under the field you want to hide.	
Find a range of data	In the design grid, enter criteria using the Between...And operator.	
Join tables in a query	Use the Show Table dialog box to add the tables to the design grid. The two tables must contain fields with matching data. Drag the matching field from one table, and then drop it on the matching field in the other table.	

For online information about	On the Help menu, click Contents And Index, click the Index tab, and then type
Creating queries	**queries**
Adding or deleting fields and tables in a query	**queries**
Joining tables in a query	**joins**
Database operators	**operators, logical**
Setting criteria in a query	**criteria**
Changing field properties	**field properties**

Analyzing Your Data

Estimated time
40 min.

In this lesson you will learn how to:

- Summarize information and show calculations in a field.
- Change column headings.
- Use calculating queries.
- Use crosstab queries.
- Present the results of a query in a chart.

Queries are tools used in Microsoft Access to retrieve and analyze data. The queries we have seen so far have been useful; however, they have merely demonstrated faster ways of completing tasks that can be handled using other database tools. Queries are special because they can also be used to create new data. The new data is formed by applying an analytical process to the original data. The newly created data can then be summarized to produce additional reports or forms, just as if the new data were stored in tables. The new data, however, can be created from one or from several tables and will change as its source tables change.

One approach to data analysis is to use a query that performs some sort of calculation. For example, if you needed to find the total sales of a particular product you would use a calculating query. Another type of analytical query summarizes and groups data from selected fields; for example, you might create a query that shows sales for a particular product, grouped by regions. Finally, queries can be used to both calculate and summarize data. This latter type of query is known as a *crosstab query*. A crosstab query can be created to both group sales by product and show total sales values for those products. In this lesson, you will use all three types of analytical queries.

Start the lesson

➤ If Microsoft Access isn't started yet, start it. Open the Sweet Lil's database. If the Microsoft Access window doesn't fill your screen, maximize the window.

If you need help opening the database, see Lesson 1.

Creating Information by Summarizing

When you design a query, you can specify which fields to use for grouping records and which fields to use for totals (calculations). For example, you might specify that a field containing the number of bonbons would be used to create a total. The records could then be grouped according to the values contained in their box description field.

One of the primary ways of transforming raw data into meaningful information is to create a summary of the data. A list of every sales transaction for a particular product is important data; however, it might not be terribly useful, particularly if there are hundreds or thousands of sales transactions. On the other hand, an average sales value for a product or an average amount sold for a particular salesperson is useful information for market planning.

Example of a query

Data is taken from the Orders table...

...and totaled in the Total Orders By Country query.

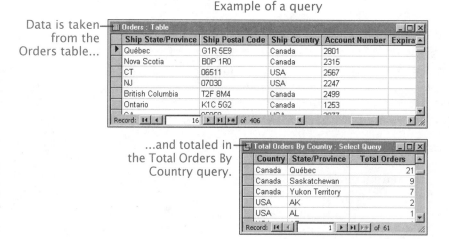

The Sweet Lil's database already contains an Order Information query that generates a list of orders by customer. Frequently, however, you'll want more than just a listing of your data. For example, you might want to know the total number of orders placed by country or the total value of all boxes within one order. To get this information, you could begin a new query, but in this case you can use an existing query as the foundation of your new query.

In the following exercises, you'll create a new summary query by modifying the existing Order Information query. The new query will find the total number of orders by country. Then, you'll find the totals of each state or province in each country. You use Microsoft Access queries to perform these calculations.

Use an existing query to create a summary query

1 In the Database window, click the Queries tab, and then select the Order Information query.

2 In the Database window, click Design.

    The Orders Information query opens in Design view.

3 On the File menu, click Save As/Export.

    The Save As dialog box appears.

4 Be sure the With The Current Database As option is selected. In the New Name box, type **Total Orders By Country**, and then click OK.

    The name of the query appears on the title bar of the query and also in the list of queries in the Database window. Your screen should look like the following illustration.

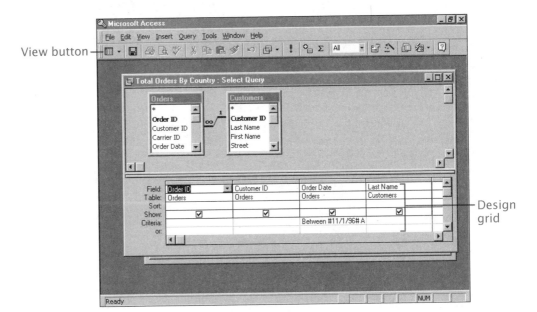

Add and delete fields in a query

The query has been given a new name, and you now need to specify the fields which will extract the data you need.

The Design grid is also known as the Query By Example (QBE) grid.

1 In the Design grid, click at the top of the Last Name column to highlight it, and then press DELETE.

The Last Name column is deleted.

2 Delete the Customer ID field and the Order Date field from the query.

You can select both fields by selecting the Customer ID field and then dragging the mouse to the right to select the Order Date field.

3 In the Customers field list, drag the Country field to the top of the query Order ID field.

The Country field is the first field listed in the query grid, and the Order ID field moves to the right.

Design grid ——

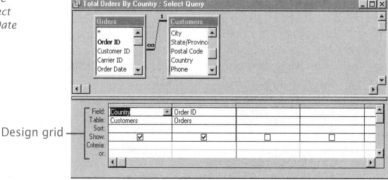

Perform calculations and group the query results

Now that the query contains the fields that will extract the appropriate data, you need to add expressions to perform the necessary calculations and place the data in the required groups, so that you can find the total number of orders placed. The data will be grouped by country.

Σ

Totals

1 On the toolbar, click the Totals button.

Total row ——

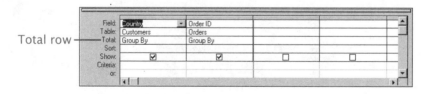

A row called Total appears in the Design grid. Each cell contains the designation "Group By."

2　Click the Total cell in the Order ID column, and then click the down arrow.

3　On the drop-down list, select Count.

Because there is one order ID for each order, you are counting the number of orders. You have decided to group by country, so you want to count the total number of orders for each country.

View

The graphic on the View button changes according to the current selection.

4　Click the View down arrow, and click Datasheet.

The datasheet displays the results of the query.

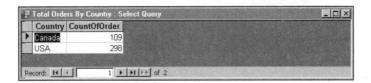

The datasheet shows the total number of orders for each country. The second column automatically displays the name CountOfOrder ID. If you cannot see the full column header, size the column to its best fit by double-clicking the right border at the top of the column. The "best fit" is the width that completely displays the data.

Group totals by two fields

This is a very useful query, but you decide to investigate further. So far, you have grouped the results of your query by country. But you also want to know how many orders you've received from each state or province within each country. You can group by a second field.

1　Click the View down arrow, and click Design View.

2　From the Customers table, drag the State/Province field to the QBE grid and drop it on top of the Order ID cell. The State/Province field is added between the Country and Order ID fields.

The "Group By" label appears in the Total row.

3   Click the View down arrow, and then select Datasheet View to see your changes.

Microsoft Access groups first by country (because this is the first Group By field in the Design grid) and then by state or province. The totals are calculated, not by country, but for each state or province within each country.

Providing Meaningful Names for Datasheet Columns

It is very important that the names given to fields fully describe the contents of the fields. It is just as important that the columns in a query datasheet are correctly named. Columns in a query are similar to fields in a table in that query columns can provide the basis for creating forms, reports, or other queries. By changing the name of a field in a query, you can ensure that the datasheet shows a relevant column heading.

Change a column heading

CountOfOrder ID is a generic field name assigned by Microsoft Access. You can easily change it to a more meaningful name, such as Total Orders.

1   Click View down arrow, and click Design View.

2   In the Design grid, click just to the left of the Order ID field name to position the insertion point. Type **Total Orders:** (include the colon).

   TIP   The space after the colon in a column header (for example, following Total Orders) is optional. The space has no affect on the appearance of the name when the field is used in other views and objects. However, it does help the query designer more easily see the changes.

---

3 Click the View down arrow, and click Datasheet View to view your results.

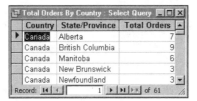

4 Close the query, and when prompted to save your changes, click the Yes button.

Analyzing Data by Using Calculating Queries

When you're running a business, your most common questions begin "What if." Sweet Lil's is no exception. The bonbons are selling so well that the sales manager wants to know, "What will the new prices for our products be if I raise prices on our boxes by 5 percent?"

The tables in the Sweet Lil's database don't contain a field that shows prices raised by 5 percent. You could build that information into a table, but it would be very inefficient, because one day you might want to change the percentage to 6 percent or to 10 percent. When a percentage is fixed in a table field, it is cumbersome to change the value every time you want to adjust the variable. Queries are better suited to perform this type of analysis.

Create the query

You'll use a query that has a calculated field to answer the sales manager's question. The new query is based on the Boxes table.

1 Be sure the Query tab is selected, and then click New.

2 Select Design View in the New Query dialog box, and then click OK.

3 Select the Boxes table in the Show Table dialog box, and then click Add to use the table as the source of the query's data.

4 Close the Show Table window.

5 Drag the Box Name field and the Box Price field to the Design grid.

The query will display the current price for each box. The Box Name field is included to identify the box.

6 Click the View down arrow, and then click Datasheet View to examine the query.

The query displays the current price for each box, as shown in the following illustration.

7 Save the query, and name it Raise Prices.

Add a calculated field

Now you'll add a calculated field that will show what prices would be if you raised them by 5 percent.

1 Switch to Design view, and then click in the empty cell to the right of the Box Price column in the Field row to position the insertion point.

In an expression, the square brackets indicate a field name. Brackets automatically appear around a single-word field, but if the field name contains a space, you must type the brackets.

2 Type **[Box Price]*1.05** and then press ENTER.

Multiplying by 1.05 is the same as raising the price by 5 percent. After you press ENTER, Microsoft Access names the field Expr1. This is the name that will appear as the heading for this column in the datasheet.

3 To see the whole expression, double-click the right border of the Expr1: [Box Price]*1.05 field selector.

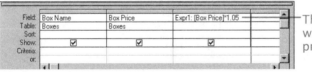

The Expr1 expression will show the box price raised by 5%.

4 Switch to Datasheet view to see your results.

Your query should look like the following illustration.

Customize the calculated field

Expr1 is a generic field name that doesn't describe your data very well. You decide to change the name of this field to "New Price." You also want to show the new price information formatted as currency, and you want a description that readily explains what the new prices represent. In this exercise, you use the Properties sheet to customize the characteristics of your query.

1 Switch to Design view, and then double-click the field name Expr1 to select it.

2 Type **New Price**

The field name changes from Expr1 to New Price.

3 Click the Properties button.

The Field Properties dialog box appears.

Properties

4 To change the display of the new price information, click in the Format box, and then click the down arrow to display the list of formats.

5 Select Currency to format the prices with dollar signs and decimals.

6 Click in the Description box, and then type **Shows prices raised by 5 percent**

7 Close the Field Properties box.

8 Switch to Datasheet view to see the new prices with the properties you specified.

The new prices are formatted with dollar signs and decimals, and the New Price caption is at the top of the column.

9 Click in the New Price field.

The description appears on the status bar at the bottom of the Microsoft Access window.

10 Close the query, and when prompted to save your changes, click Yes.

Summarizing and Calculating by Using a Crosstab Query

It is possible to combine the summarizing and calculating forms of analysis in a single query. The crosstab query, which uses a row and column format, is structured like a table; you can think of each row as a separate record, and each column as a field describing that record. Unlike a table, however, the crosstab query includes a column that performs a calculation on the data, a calculating column. For example, if you create a crosstab query based on a table of Sales Orders, you might select a Products field for the rows and an Order Date field for the columns. You could then create a *calculating column* (a column in which any necessary calculations takes place) to sum the values in an Order Value field. Such a query would give you a list of the orders taken for a particular product on a particular day. The calculating column would provide a total value for that product.

Use a crosstab query to analyze data

Sweet Lil's is debating whether to consolidate its product line. The business is doing well, but the Accounting Department believes that cutting down on the number of different ways the products are packaged would increase efficiency. The Marketing Department opposes this view, and contends that the product line meets the diverse tastes of the customer base. They contend that there might be short-term reductions in sales of a particular box, but that, over the long term, the entire product line does very well. To defend this position, the Marketing Department needs a query that will create a list of how many boxes of each product have been sold over time. In this exercise, you create the query for the Marketing Department.

1 In the Database window, make sure the Queries tab is selected, and click the New button to create a new query.

2 Select the Crosstab Query Wizard, and click OK.

The Crosstab Query Wizard opens and gives you a choice of basing the crosstab query on tables, queries, or both. The Crosstab Query Wizard allows you to choose the fields that will be the source of the data in the queries rows, and columns. The wizard also allows you to specify the data that will be placed at the intersection of the rows and columns, and whether you want that data to be used to perform a calculation. As you respond to the wizard, a diagram of the building query appears in the wizard. This diagram allows you to visualize the query as you are building it.

3 Select the Queries option.

You will base this query on a previous query.

4 Select the Sales By Box query from the list, and click Next.

5 Select the Box Name field and then click the Select button to move Box Name from the Available Fields list to the Selected Fields list. Click Next.

Select

The Box Name field is selected as the row heading for the crosstab query. The Crosstab Query Wizard should look like the following illustration.

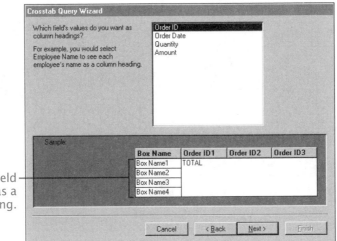

Box Name field is selected as a row heading.

6 Select Order Date from the list of fields, and then click Next.

Order Date is the column header in the diagram of the new crosstab query.

7 On the list of possible intervals, select Date, intervals, and then click Next.

The Order Date field is grouped by date.

8 Select Amount as the Field to be included in the calculation and Sum as the type of calculation to perform. Click Next.

9 Click Finish to accept the default name Sales By Box_Crosstab.

Group by dates

The query is grouping the data according to dates. To use dates as the criteria for selecting data, you must specify a range of dates to be included in the query. The Marketing Department is arguing that the product line sells well over the course of a year, but you need to see the data.

1 Specify the starting date as Jan-1-96 and the ending date as Dec-31-96.

Box Name	Total Of Amou	1/2/96	1/4/96	1/6/96	
All Seasons	$315.00				
Alpine Collection	$1,867.50	$20.75			
Autumn Collection	$2,752.00		$43.00	$86.00	
Bittersweets	$5,688.75		$55.50	$55.50	
Cherry Classics	$1,365.00	$32.50			
Fudge Mocha Fanta	$2,376.00			$18.00	
Heavenly Hazelnuts	$1,858.50				
International	$2,278.00				
Island Collection	$2,170.00			$35.00	
Lover's Hearts	$3,797.50	$35.00			
Marzipan Marvels	$1,354.50				
Northwind Collectio	$7,148.75	$33.25			
Pacific Opulence	$1,428.00		$21.00		

Record: 1 of 18

The query shows the total sales for each box sorted by date. The Totals column shows the total sales for each type of box during 1996. The sales volumes vary from a low of $315 for All Seasons to a high of $7,148.75 for the Northwind Collection. It appears that the Accounting Department might have a point, as there is a fairly large variation in sales volumes. Determining whether the product lines are all profitable, however, would require further analysis.

2   Close the query.

Displaying Data in a Chart

So far in this lesson you have seen that queries are an excellent way to take raw data and convert it into meaningful information. Another excellent way to create meaningful information is by presenting data in a graphical format. The adage "a picture is worth a thousand words" is particularly apt when applied to numerical analysis. Few of us are able to look at a column of numbers and immediately spot trends. When that data is presented in a graph, however, such realizations often become obvious.

In this exercise, you will convert the data collected by the Sales By Box query into a chart to see if the product line has peaks and valleys in its monthly sales totals. If there are any such trends, they should be immediately obvious in a line chart of the monthly sales volume.

Create a chart based on a query

To further explore the analysis you started with the crosstab query you created in the last exercise, you decide to create a chart that will visually depict the data returned by the Sales By Box query. You believe this will help you determine if sales of the product line are even throughout the year or if there are periods of high and low sales volumes. You decide that the best form of chart for this analysis is a simple line chart. You will use the Chart Wizard to quickly create the kind of chart you need.

IMPORTANT To complete this exercise, you must have Microsoft Graph installed. Microsoft Graph is not included in the default installation. You can run the Microsoft Access Setup program or the Microsoft Office Professional Setup program again and specify that you want to install the Graph feature only.

1   In the Database window, make sure the Reports tab is selected, and click New to create a new report.

2   Select the Chart Wizard, and click the Tables And Queries down arrow to display the list of tables and queries that can be used as the basis for the chart.

3   On the list, select the Sales By Box query, and click OK.

The Chart Wizard opens.

4   Select the Order Date, Box Name, and Quantity fields by selecting them and clicking on the Select button to move them from the Available Fields column to the Fields For Chart column. Click Next.

The Chart Wizard displays a page for selecting the type of chart you want.

Line Chart

5   Click the Line Chart button, and then click Next.

The next sheet of the Chart Wizard displays a page for selecting how you want the data displayed. This page also allows you to preview the chart. The default setting is to show the sum of any selected numeric, which in this case is the Quantity field. Rather than having the sum of the values displayed, you decide to use the Count function to show the actual values.

6   Double-click the SumofQuantity field to open the Summarize dialog box, and then select Count. Click OK to return to the Chart Wizard.

The field displayed on the vertical axis changes to CountofQuantity.

Preview Chart

7   Click the Preview Chart button to examine the basic layout of the chart.

An Enter Parameter Value dialog box opens. Because the query is based on a series of dates, Access needs to know which dates to select.

8   Type **1-Jan-96** and then click OK. Type **31-Dec-96** and then click OK.

The chart opens in Chart preview. You decide after examining the chart that it is difficult to read, so you decide to summarize the data by quarter.

157

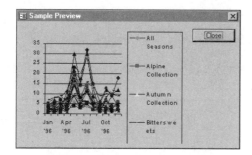

9 Click the Close button to return to the Chart Wizard. Double-click the Order Date By Month field, and select the Quarter Option in the Group dialog box. Click OK.

10 Click Next.

The next page of the wizard helps you create a title for your report.

11 Make sure the Yes, Display A Legend option and the Open The Report With The Chart Displayed On It option are selected, and then click Finish.

12 Type **1-Jan-96** and then click OK. Type **31-Dec-96** and then click OK.

A new report, which includes the chart, opens.

13 Click Close, and when prompted to save your changes, click Yes and name the report Sales By Box Chart.

NOTE If you'd like to build on the skills that you learned in this lesson, you can do the One Step Further. Otherwise, skip to "Finish the lesson."

One Step Further: Setting a Parameter to Limit a Crosstab Query

Sometimes you want a query for a very limited set of data. For example, Orders table queries might return an unwieldy list because the Orders table is extremely long. You can limit the items selected by a crosstab query by setting parameters for selecting the records to return. A *parameter* is a criteria used to limit the records selected by a query. You have already seen how parameters work: the Sales By Box_Crosstab query asks for a parameter value when it is opened. The parameter value in that instance selected data falling within a range of dates. This parameter was set automatically, as the selection criteria for this query is a date. Whenever data is selected on the basis of date, Microsoft Access automatically prompts the user for a range of valid dates. This range is the parameter.

Set a parameter

Sweet Lil's would like to be able to view the Sales By Box_Crosstab query for specific boxes. To limit the query, you will add a parameter to the Box Names column of the crosstab. Adding the parameter allows the user to select which box to view.

1   In the Database window, be sure the Sales By Box_Crosstab query is selected, and then click Design.

2   In the Criteria row of the Box Name column, type **[Enter the Box Name]** to specify the parameter.

3   On the Query menu, select Parameters.

4   In the top row of the Parameter column, type **Enter the Box Name**

5   In the Data Type column, click in the first cell to select the type of data the Parameter dialog box will accept.

    By default, the Text data type appears.

6   Click OK.

7   Switch to Datasheet view, and when prompted, type **Alpine Collection** in the Box Name column, and then click OK.

8   When prompted, enter the dates Jan-1-96 and Dec-31-96.

    The sales for the Alpine Collection box are displayed for the dates you specified in the dialog box for the date parameter.

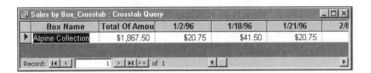

9   On the File menu, click Save As/Export. In the File Name box, type **Sales By Selected Box** and then click OK.

Finish the lesson

1   To continue to the next lesson, on the File menu, click Close.

2   If you are finished using Microsoft Access for now, on the File menu, click Exit.

Lesson Summary

To	Do this	Button
Create a new query by modifying an existing query	Click Design in the Database window to open the query in Design view. Make any desired changes to the query, and use the Save As command on the File menu to rename the query.	
Add a field to a query	Open the query in Design view, and drag the field from the field list to the Field row in the query grid.	
Delete a field from a query	Open the query in Design view. At the top of the column, click the field selector to select it. Press DELETE.	
Group a query's results	Open the query in Design view. Click the Totals button on the toolbar, and then click the Total cell for any field you want to group by. Click the cell down arrow, and select the basis for the grouping.	Σ
Change a column name in a datasheet	Open the query in Design view. Edit the column name in the top row of the query grid by clicking in the row and typing a new name to the left of the original field name, followed by a colon.	
Add a calculated field to a query	Open the query in Design view. Type the calculated field expression in the Field row of the query grid. In the expression, enclose any references to fields or other query results in [ ].	

To	Do this
Create a crosstab query	In the Design window, click the Query tab, and click New. Select the Crosstab Query Wizard. Add row and column headers as prompted by the wizard. Add the fields whose data will be placed at the intersection of the rows and columns. Select a calculating method for the summary column.
Create a chart based on a query	On the Reports tab in the Database window, click New, select Chart Wizard, and then click the Tables And Queries down arrow. Select the table or query you want to chart, and then follow the instructions in the Chart Wizard.
Delete a field from a query	Click the field selector in the design grid to select the field, and then press DELETE.
Give a field a custom name	In the design grid, position the insertion point to the left of the field name. Then, type a custom field name and a colon.

For online information about	On the Help menu, click Contents And Index, click the Index tab, and then type
Summarizing queries	**queries**, and then display Bringing data together from multiple tables
	criteria, and then display Selecting records in queries
Calculations in queries	**queries**
	calculations and queries
	calculated fields
Crosstab queries	**Crosstab queries**
	Crosstab Query Wizard
Parameters	**queries**, and then display Prompting for criteria

Merging Data from Two Tables onto One Form

Estimated time
35 min.

In this lesson you will learn how to:

- Create a form with the Form Wizard.
- Use a query as the basis for a form.
- Add a command control to a form.
- Run a macro from a command control.

Queries and relationships are used to extract and summarize data from multiple tables. Using queries and relationships is the most flexible way to focus data from distinct tables. By combining queries and relationships, you can produce forms that span multiple tables. Combining is accomplished by using the form structure and the subform structure, which was introduced in Lesson 2, "Increasing Efficiency by Using Subforms." A *subform* is a form that is inserted into another form. This nested structure makes it easy for you to simultaneously view or enter data in two different tables or queries.

Queries are powerful tools in Microsoft Access. In this lesson you will learn how to use queries that can bring together related records from two or more tables in your database, and you will create a multiple-table form. You also learn how to add a command button to a form. The command button will launch a *macro*: a special combination of Microsoft Access commands. You will learn how to create your own macros in the next lesson.

Start the lesson

➤ If Microsoft Access isn't started yet, start it. Open the Sweet Lil's database. If the Microsoft Access window doesn't fill your screen, maximize the window.

If you need help opening the database, see Lesson 1.

Focusing Data Through Forms

The database design principles outlined in Lesson 4, "Controlling Database Growth," require that unique information be described in distinct tables. In many instances, however, you will want to either update or extract data about several different entities at the same time. This is because distinct entities are frequently brought together to meet a particular need. For example, when new types of boxes are added to the Sweet Lil's database, both the Boxes table and the Box Details table must be updated. Even though boxes and box details are distinct entities, both are needed to create new box descriptions.

Create a multiple form by using Form Wizard

Sweet Lil's is overwhelmed with customer orders. The sales clerks want a form that quickly shows all orders for a particular customer. They've asked you to create this form, and you decide to use the Form Wizard. Using the Form Wizard is the easiest and quickest way of producing a form that meets the requirements. The form will draw data both from the Customers table and from a query named Orders.

1   In the Database window, click the Forms tab, and then click New.

2   Select Form Wizard.

Using the Form Wizard, you can select the tables and queries you want to use in the form. Your screen should look like the following illustration.

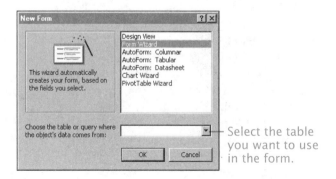

Select the table you want to use in the form.

3   Click the Tables/Queries down arrow, select the Customers table, and then click OK.

The fields contained within the Customers table appear in the Available Fields list box.

4   In the Available Fields list, click Customer ID, and then click the Select button between the Available Fields and Selected Fields list boxes.

The Customer ID field moves to the Selected Fields list.

5   Move the First Name and Last Name fields from the Available Fields list to the Selected Fields list by clicking the field and clicking the Select button. The wizard should look like the following illustration.

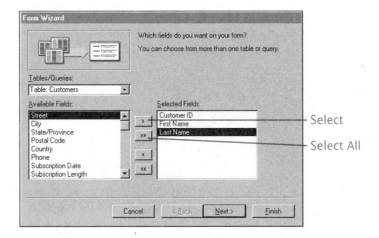

6   Click the Tables/Queries down arrow, and then select the Orders Form query.

7   In the Available Fields list, move the Customer ID, Order ID, and Order Date fields to the Selected Fields list one at a time by selecting each field and clicking the Select button.

8   Click Next.

The next Form Wizard dialog box asks, "How do you want to view your data?"

9   Select the By Customers option, be sure the Form With Subform(s) option is selected, and then click Next.

A Form Wizard dialog box appears, offering a tabular or datasheet layout for the subform.

10 Select Datasheet as the layout, and then click Next.

A Form Wizard dialog box appears; there are several form layout options available. An example of each style appears in the Sample area when that style is selected. The Standard style will meet most of your formatting requirements.

11 Select the Standard style for the form, and then click Next.

The final Form Wizard dialog box appears. This is where you name the form and subform, and choose whether you want to open the form or modify its design.

12 Accept the suggested names for the form and subform. Make sure the Open The Form To View Or Enter Information option is selected, and then click Finish.

The form and subform open in Form view. Your forms should look like the following illustration.

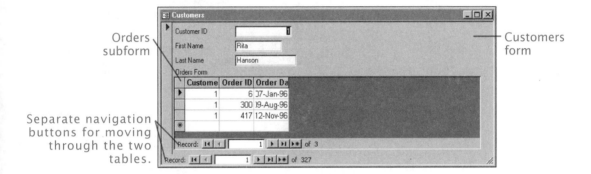

Orders subform

Customers form

Separate navigation buttons for moving through the two tables.

Examine the records

You check some records to make sure the Customers table and Orders Form query are linked.

1 On the Customers form, click the Next Record button on the navigation bar at the bottom of the window.

The second customer, Stephen Pence, should be displayed in the Customers form, and his associated orders should be in the Orders subform.

2 On the Orders subform, click the Next Record button on its navigation bar to move to the next Order record for Stephen Pence.

The second order for Stephen Pence is selected.

3 Close the form and subform.

The forms were saved by the Form Wizard, so there is no need to save again.

Automating Processes by Adding Command Buttons

For a demonstration of how to add a command button, double-click the Camcorder Files On The Internet shortcut on your Desktop or connect to the Internet address listed on p. xxvi.

In Microsoft Access, when you use a wizard to create a table, form, report, or query, many processes are handled for you. The Form Wizard automates these processes when creating a form. In the last exercise, for example, the Form Wizard used a special database language to create a command to link the form and subform to the appropriate table and query.

You can create your own automated processes in two ways. First, you can create a macro. A *macro* is a list of one or more Microsoft Access commands that are executed in sequence. Macros can be very powerful and can greatly enhance how you or other users interact with your database. In Lesson 2, a macro was used to make a command button open a view of box sales. That command button executed the macro called Show Box Sales.

The second way to automate a process is by writing programs with Visual Basic for Applications (VBA). VBA, a powerful programming language that's sometimes used to customize databases, is part of the Microsoft Access program. Programming with VBA is not covered in this book. A good resource for getting started using VBA is *Microsoft Visual Basic 5 Step by Step*.

Creating a Lookup Button on the Customers Form

Now that the Customers form has been established, the sales clerks realize that it would be helpful to be able to look up the details of a particular order when a customer calls with an inquiry. A macro, View Order, is available to quickly accomplish this task; what the sales clerks want is a quick way to run the macro. In this exercise, you will add a command button to the Customers form.

View the macro

In this exercise, you familiarize yourself with the View Order macro.

1 In the Database window, click the Macros tab.

2 Select the View Order macro, and then click Design.

The macro commands are listed in the View Order macro window. Some macros need special values to function properly. These special values, known as *action arguments*, are established in the lower half of the Macro window. The View Order macro uses the OpenForm command to open the Order Details form. The OpenForm command can have up to six different action arguments. The Where action argument specifies which Order Details to retrieve. Macros are covered in greater detail in Lesson 10, "Streamlining Data Entry."

Macro commands —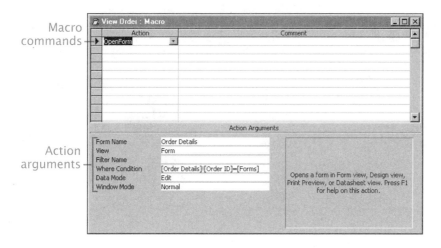

Action arguments —

3 Close the View Order macro window.

Add a command button to the Customers form

1 In the Database window, click the Forms tab.

2 Select the Customers form, and then click Design.

The form opens in Design view.

Toolbox — 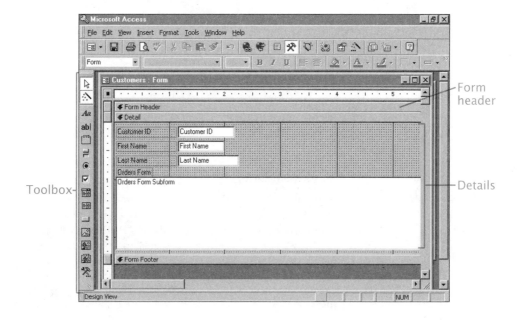 — Form header

— Details

Command Button

3   On the toolbox, select the Command Button tool, and then just to the right of the Customer ID field, click the form.

The Command Button Wizard opens. This wizard can be used to specify a macro to run or to build a VBA program. You want to use it to specify a macro.

4   Select Miscellaneous from the Categories column and Run Macro from the Actions column, and then click Next.

The Command Button Wizard displays all the macros in the database.

5   Select View Order from the list, and then click Next.

The Command Button Wizard opens a sheet to allow you to specify either a picture or text to appear on the button.

6   Select the Text Option, click in the blank field, and then type **View Order**

7   Click Next.

The Command Button Wizard opens the final screen, which allows you to specify a name for the new command button.

8   Type the button name **View Order** and then click Finish. Your form should look like the following illustration.

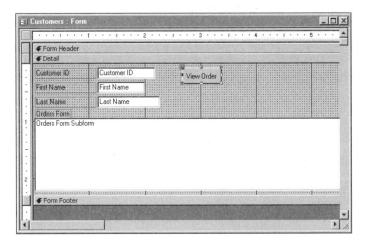

Test the command button

Whenever you add a new feature to your database, you should test that feature to make sure it works as intended.

1   Switch to Form view.

The first record is displayed.

2 Click the View Order command button.

The Order Details form opens for the order that's selected in the Order Form subform. You can use the navigation bar on the form to view all the order details.

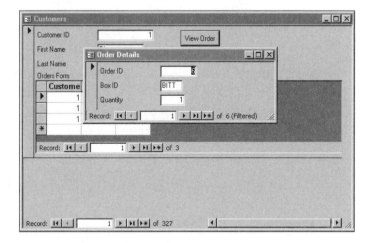

For a discussion of the Expression Builder, see Appendix C, "Using Expressions."

3 Close the Order Details form, and move to the next order for Customer 1 by clicking the Next Record button on the subform navigation bar.

4 Click the View Order command button.

The Order Details form opens for the next order.

5 Save and close the form.

NOTE If you'd like to build on the skills you learned in this lesson, you can do the One Step Further. Otherwise, skip to "Finish the lesson."

One Step Further: Adding a Calculated Control to a Form

Controls can augment the uses of a form in many ways. In addition to displaying summarizing information, controls can be used to perform calculations on a form. Calculations can be done by using the functions built into Microsoft Access or by creating complex formulas using standard mathematical operations (addition, subtraction, multiplication, division, etc.).

The *control source* is the formula that calculates the value displayed in the control. You can either type a formula in the Control Source field or use the Expression Builder tool to create the calculation. The Expression Builder lets you assemble expressions that make use of built-in Microsoft Access functions.

A text box can contain a formula, but a label can only contain text.

The Marketing manager for Sweet Lil's wants the Box Sales form to calculate the average sales value for each type of box. Currently, the Box Sales form includes a field for total sales, which the manager says is very helpful. She would also like to know whether some boxes tend to be ordered in larger quantities than other boxes. Using the Expression Builder, you will add a calculation control to the Box Sales form that will use the built-in Average function to find the Average Extended Price for Box Sales.

Text Box

Properties

1   Select the Box Sales form, and then click the Design button.

2   Click the Text Box control in the toolbox, and then just below the Total Sales control, click on the form.

A text box and label appear on the form.

3   On the Form Design toolbar, click the Properties button to open the Properties sheet.

4   Select the Data tab, and click in the Control Source field. Your form should look like the following illustration.

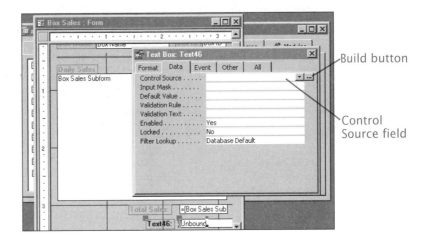

Build

5   Click the Build button to open the Expression Builder.

The Expression Builder dialog box appears.

The Expression Builder window includes an Expression box, operator buttons, and a list box containing folders that access all the objects in your database. Your screen should look like the following illustration.

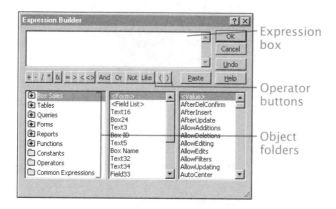

Expression box

Operator buttons

Object folders

6 In the row of operator buttons below the Expression box, click the = button

The equals sign is placed in the Expression box.

7 Double-click on the Forms folder in the leftmost list box to display two subfolders: Loaded Forms and All Forms. The dialog box should look like the following illustration.

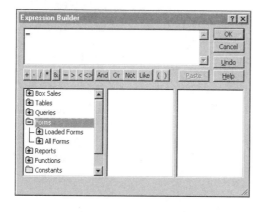

In the picture of the Expression Builder dialog box on the next page, the second reference to Box Sales is selected. The complete title of the selected subform is actually Box Sales subform, although the word subform is not visible.

8 Double-click on the Loaded Forms subfolder, and then double-click the Box Sales Subform subfolder.

All the objects in the Box Sales subform are listed in the middle list box.

9 Scroll down to the Average Sales field, and select it.

10 Click Paste to place the field in the Expression box.

The complete description of the field
=[Box Sales Subform].Form![Average Sales]
is placed in the Expression box. The dialog box should look like the following illustration.

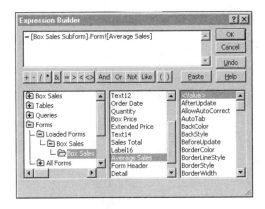

11   Click OK, and then press ENTER.

The formula is placed in the Control Source property field for your new control.

Edit control properties

1   Click the Text control to the left of the control you've been working with. You might have to move the Properties sheet.

2   In the Properties sheet, make sure the Format tab is active, and in the Caption property, type **Average Sales**, and then press ENTER.

3   Close the Properties sheet, and adjust the size of the Average Sales text control if necessary.

4   Close the form.

If a message asks whether you want to save changes to the form, click Yes.

5   Open the Boxes form, and then click the Sales button at the top of form.

The Box Sales form opens. The Average Sales control is displayed at the bottom of the Box Sales subform.

6   Close the form.

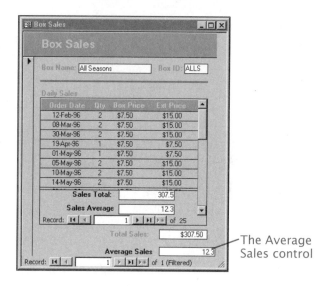

The Average
Sales control

Finish the lesson

1 To continue to the next lesson, on the File menu click Close.

2 If you are finished using Microsoft Access for now, on the File menu click Exit.

Lesson Summary

To	Do this
Create a form with the Form Wizard	In the Database window, select the Forms tab. Click the New button. Select Form Wizard, and then follow the Wizard's instructions.
Use a query as the basis for a form	When prompted by the Form Wizard, select the query from the Tables/Queries drop-down list. Select the query fields that you want included on the form by moving them from the Available Fields list box to the Selected Fields list box. Complete the remainder of the Form Wizard.

To	Do this	Button
Add a command control to a form.	In the Database window, select the form in the Forms tab, and click the Design button to open the form in Design view. In the toolbox, click the Command Button tool, and then click the form where you want to place the control. Follow the instructions in the Command Button Wizard, and as needed, click the Properties button to set the command button properties.	

For online information about	On the Help menu, click Contents And Index, click the Index tab, and then type
Using command buttons	**command buttons**
Creating macros	**macro window, macros**
Calculating fields	**calculated controls**

Review & Practice

Estimated time
25 min.

You will review and practice how to:

- Create a query and set criteria.
- Sort information and find a range of data in a query.
- Create a query that includes related tables.
- Summarize data in a query.
- Create a form based on a query.
- Add a command button to a form.

Queries are one of the most important tools for converting raw data into useful information. This Review & Practice lets you apply some of the techniques you learned in Part 3 about querying for information. It also reviews how to use queries to build forms and how to use your forms more effectively by adding command buttons.

Scenario

Each department in Sweet Lil's is researching a plan for increasing production while lowering costs. The Marketing Department wants to find out which products would be appropriate for customers who want candy that is high-quality, yet inexpensive. The Shipping Department is investigating whether it is using the most appropriate carriers and shipping methods. Both departments need your help in designing queries for the information they want.

Step 1: *Create a Query and Set Criteria*

The Marketing Department wants to focus on increasing the orders from customers who request boxes of candy in a certain price range. You will create a query that identifies those boxes weighing more than 8 ounces that cost less than 30 dollars.

1   Create a new query using the Boxes table.

2   Add fields to the query to see the names, sizes, and prices of the possible boxes.

3   Create an expression that will find boxes weighing more than 8 ounces.

4   Create an expression that will find boxes costing less than 30 dollars. You don't need to enter the dollar sign in the expression.

5   Run the query.

6   Close the query without saving it.

For more information about	See
Creating a query and setting criteria	Lesson 7
Using an expression in a query	Lesson 8

Step 2: *Sort and Find a Range of Data in a Query*

To move existing merchandise quickly, the company is planning a large-scale campaign to promote medium-priced assortments of bonbons ("Quality Everyone Can Afford"). You want to advertise only those boxes that cost between 17 and 25 dollars inclusive and for which Sweet Lil's has more than 200 boxes in stock. You'd like to list the boxes in alphabetical order.

1   Create a new query based on the Boxes table.

2   Add fields to the query to show the names, prices, and quantities of the boxes on hand.

3   Sort the query alphabetically by the names of the boxes.

4   Use an expression that has comparison operators to find prices between 17 and 25 dollars, but do not include dollar signs. (Hint: Type **>=17 and <=25**)

5   Create an expression that shows only those selections that have more than 200 boxes in stock.

6   Run the query.

7   Save the query as Mid-Priced Boxes, and then close the query.

For more information about	See
Sorting data in a query	Lesson 7
Using an expression in a query	Lesson 8
Naming and saving a query	Lesson 7

Step 3: *Create a Query That Includes Related Tables*

The Marketing Department also wants to identify customers who buy candies for the winter holidays. The department wants you to help compile a list of customers who have placed more than one order between December 12 and December 25. Create a query that shows the last name of all customers who meet the criteria.

1 Create a new query, and add the tables for Orders and Customers.

2 Add a field to the query that shows the order identification numbers.

3 Add a field and criteria to the query that shows the order date as between December 12, 1996, and December 25, 1996.

4 Add a field to the query that shows the customer's last name.

5 Run the query.

6 Save the query as Holiday Orders, and then close it.

For more information about	See
Creating a query that includes related tables	Lesson 7

Step 4: *Summarize Data in a Query*

The Marketing Department now wants to know how much revenue was generated by these holiday orders. Modify the Holiday Orders query to show the total value for all orders that meet the criteria specified in step 3.

1 Add the Order Details and Boxes tables to the Holiday Orders query.

2 Add the Quantity field from the Order Details table and the Box Price field from the boxes table to the query.

3 Add a new field called Order Total that uses the formula Quantity * Box Price.

4 From the View menu, choose Totals to add the Total row to the query grid, and then select Sum from the list for the Orders Total field.

5 Hide the Quantity column and the Box Price column for a better view of the relevant data.

6 Run the query.

7 Close the query, and save your changes.

For more information about	See
Summarizing data in a query	Lesson 8

Step 5: *Create a Form Based on a Query*

The Marketing department wants you to create a form to speed up order entry during the holiday rush. This Holiday Orders form will be abbreviated, but will capture enough information to allow the Marketing department to fill in the details later.

1 Add the Ship Last Name and Ship First Name to fields from the Order table to the Holiday Orders query.

2 Use the Form Wizard to automatically build a form for you, based on the Holiday Orders query.

3 Save your form, and name it Quick Orders.

For more information about	See
Creating a form based on a query	Lesson 9

Step 6: *Add a Command Button to Your Form*

During the holiday season, it is important that orders be taken only if there is quantity on hand. A macro, Check Quantity, has been written to open the On Hand query. The macro uses boxes in the current order as the criteria for checking the On Hand fields. You will now add a command button to the Holiday Orders form to run this macro.

1 Add the CheckQuantity macro as the OnClick event property.

2 Save and test your form.

For more information about	See
Creating a command button	Lesson 9
Running macros	Lesson 9

Finish the Review & Practice

1 On the File menu, click Save.

2 To continue to the next lesson, on the File menu, click Close.

3 If you are finished using Microsoft Access for now, on the File menu, click Exit.

Part

4

Refining Your Database

Streamlining Data Entry

Estimated time
45 min.

In this lesson you will learn how to:

- Format titles and add logos to forms.
- Add a toggle button to a form.
- Copy formatting.
- Fine-tune your forms.

Using Microsoft Access makes creating a database relatively simple. The next three lessons focus on putting the finishing touches on your database. These refinements will give your database the polished, professional look that is the hallmark of good database design.

In this lesson, you'll learn how to make your forms easier to use by adding pictures and other features. You will also learn how to design forms efficiently by working with a group of controls.

Start the lesson

➤ If Microsoft Access isn't started yet, start it. Open the Sweet Lil's database. If the Microsoft Access window doesn't fill your screen, maximize the window.

If you need help opening the database, see Lesson 1.

Enhancing a Form Wizard Form

The wizards in Microsoft Access help you create standard objects, such as forms, tables, queries, and reports. One approach to developing professional-looking forms is to create an initial form by using the Form Wizard and then adding special features or controls. The next two exercises use this approach to creating a professional form for tracking employee withholding information.

Create a draft form using the Form Wizard

When new employees begin work at Sweet Lil's, they must fill out a W-4 form. The W-4 form is used to tell the Personnel Department how much federal income tax to withhold from the employee's paycheck. The Payroll table created in Lesson 6 stores this data. The Human Relations Department has asked you to create a form to gather this information.

1   In the Database window, click the Forms tab.

2   Click New, and select Form Wizard from the list displayed in the New Form dialog box.

3   Select the Payroll table from the drop-down list of tables or queries that supply the form's data, and then click OK.

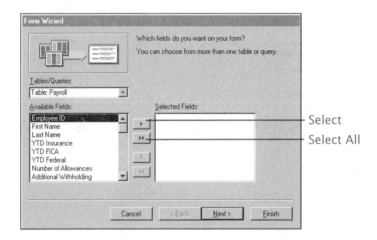

4   In the first Form Wizard dialog box, click the Select All button to move all the fields from the Available Fields list to the Selected Fields list, and then click Next.

The second Form Wizard dialog box appears.

5   Be sure the Columnar option is selected, and click Next.

6   Select Standard from the list of available styles, and click Next.

7 Select the Modify The Form's Design option, and click Finish.

Clicking Finish accepts Payroll as the title of the form. The new form opens in Design view.

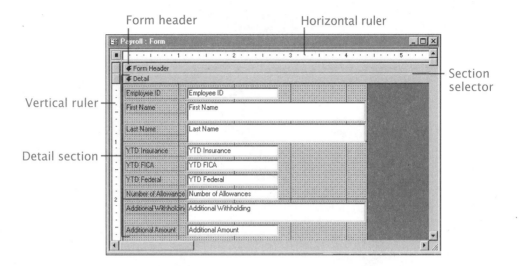

Form header Horizontal ruler

Section selector

Vertical ruler

Detail section

Adding Titles

For a demonstration of how to add and modify titles, double-click the Camcorder Files On The Internet shortcut on your Desktop or connect to the Internet address listed on p. xxvi.

All forms include three basic areas: a header section, a detail section, and a footer section. *Controls*—objects that accept, display, or locate data—were introduced in Lesson 5. Controls in the header and footer sections are included at the top and bottom of every record. Controls in the Detail section display data about each unique record.

When you used the Form Wizard to create the Payroll form, nine text box controls (one for each of the selected fields) and nine corresponding label controls were inserted in the Detail section. Nothing was added to the Header section or the Footer section.

Add a title

In this exercise, you'll add a title to the form to make it easy to identify.

IMPORTANT If the toolbox and property sheet aren't displayed, on the View menu, click the Toolbox and Properties commands.

185

Maximize the form if it's too small.

1 Place the mouse pointer on the line separating the Header section from the Detail section. When the mouse pointer changes to a double-headed arrow, drag the double-headed arrow down to the 1-inch mark on the vertical ruler.

The Header section expands. Now you can add controls to the Header section to identify the form.

Label

2 In the toolbox, click the Label button.

The mouse pointer changes to the letter A.

3 In the Header section, click in the third column from the left.

A new Label control is added to the form.

4 Type Employee Withholding Form, and then press ENTER.

The text might wrap to the next line if there is not enough room to fit the label on the form. It doesn't matter; you will change the label format in a later exercise.

5 On the toolbar, click the Font Size button, and select 14.

6 On the right edge of the control, place the mouse pointer on the middle sizing handle. When the mouse pointer changes to a double-headed arrow, double-click.

7 Save the form.

Reformat the title

You can also select a section by clicking the section selector. This is the method of choice for particularly busy forms.

The title you have created does the basic job of describing the form. All titles on Sweet Lil's forms, however, have a blue background. In this exercise, you will change your title formatting to match that of Sweet Lil's other forms.

1 To select the Header, click anywhere in the form header except on the Label control. On the toolbar, click the Properties button.

The description at the top of the property sheet is Section: Form Header. The Form Header section bar darkens, to indicate that the Form Header section is selected.

Fill/Back Color

2 Click the Fill/Back Color property field.

The Builder button appears. The Builder button opens a *builder*, which is a tool Access uses to simplify tasks. In this case, the Builder button opens the Color dialog box.

Builder

3 Click the Builder button. In the Color dialog box, select one of the bright blue boxes.

> NOTE You can also set the value for the background color by typing a number in the Back Color field on the property sheet. The number correlates to the amount of red, green, and blue color used and must be one of the Windows 95 pre-set color values or a color value that you have defined in the Color dialog box.

4 Click OK, and press ENTER. Close the Properties sheet.

The back color of the Form Header is blue.

5 Click anywhere inside the Label control to select it.

6 On the toolbar, click the Font/Fore Color down arrow, and select a color that will contrast with the bright blue you selected for the background color.

Font/Fore Color

7 On the Formatting toolbar, click the Bold button.

The text in the Label control becomes thicker. You might need to resize the control to accommodate the larger size of the characters.

Bold

You can also change a font to bold by selecting the Font Weight field in the Properties sheet, clicking the down arrow, and then selecting Bold.

8 Click the View down arrow, and select Form View.

You switch to Form view. Your form should look like the following illustration.

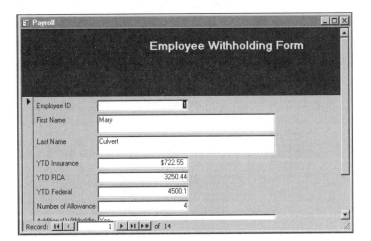

9 Save the form.

Customize the form with a logo

The Sweet Lil's logo is in a Microsoft Paint file named Sweet Lil's Logo. The Sweet Lil's Logo file was copied to your Access SBS Practice folder when you copied the practice files to your hard disk. You'll add an image control to the header of the Presenting Bonbons form, and then insert the logo in the control frame.

View

1   Click the View button arrow, and select Design View.

2   In the toolbox, click the Unbound Object frame tool to create an image control on the form.

3   To the left of the title "Employee Withholding Form," click in the form Header section.

The Insert Object dialog box appears.

Unbound Object

4   In the Insert Object dialog box, click Create From File, click Browse, and then scroll through the files listed on your hard disk until you see the Access SBS Practice folder.

5   Click on the Access SBS Practice folder, and then double click on the Sweet Lil's logo.bmp file. In the Insert Object dialog box, click OK.

The logo is inserted in the Header section of the form. If you need to re-position the control, place the mouse pointer over the control, and when the pointer changes to a hand, drag the control to the desired position.

TIP If you want to resize the image, you can drag the sizing handles on the image control frame and then use the image control property sheet to fit the picture into the new frame margins. Double-click the image. On the property sheet, click in the Size Mode property box, and select Clip, Stretch, or Zoom. Clip displays the picture at actual size. Stretch sizes the picture to fit within the margins (and might distort the image). Zoom sizes the picture to fit within the height or width of the margins without distorting the picture.

For a demonstration of how to add a logo to a form, double-click the Camcorder Files On The Internet shortcut on your Desktop or connect to the Internet address listed on p. xxvi.

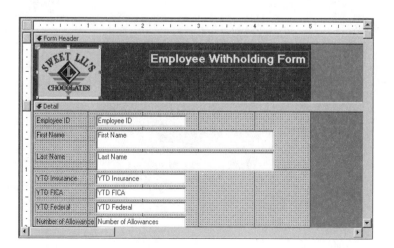

Editing Images

The logo you inserted is an example of an OLE object. An *OLE object* is any piece of information created by a program that will link or embed data. If an object is *embedded*, any changes made to the original object are not reflected in the copy of the object. If an object is *linked*, however, any changes made to the original object will be reflected in the copy of the object in your database.

Access can store sound files, media clips, Microsoft Excel charts, and many other file types. If a program capable of editing the OLE object is installed on your computer, you can start that program while viewing the object, and then edit the object—and the changes will be immediately reflected in Access. In this exercise, you use Windows Paint to edit a logo you inserted in the Payroll Form.

Edit an image

For help using Paint, press F1, or click Help Topics on the Help menu.

You decide that the light gray background in the logo doesn't look good with the blue header in the form. You open the logo file and use Windows Paint to change the logo background to a light blue.

1 Double-click anywhere inside the logo.

   The logo opens in Windows Paint. Although the file name is Sweet Lil's Logo.bmp, in Paint it is called Bitmap Image In Payroll Form—Paint.

2 To change the background to light blue, click the light blue color in the palette at the bottom of the window, and then click the Fill With Color tool to select the tool. Your screen should look like the following illustration.

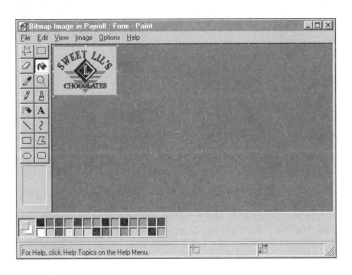

3   Click the gray background of the logo. If you click in the wrong area, on the Edit menu, click the Undo command.

4   When you are satisfied with your changes, on the File menu, click Exit & Return To Payroll Form—Paint.

5   If you are prompted to save your changes, click Yes.

Adding Toggle Buttons to Assist the User

Sometimes employees want more tax withheld than is required. For example, employees who have a second source of taxable income might want to have an additional amount withheld. The Payroll table includes an Additional Withholding field that indicates whether the employee would like an additional amount withheld. The Additional Withholding field is of the Yes/No data type.

Add a toggle button control to the form

In the following exercise, you will add a toggle button control to the Employee Withholding Form to make it easier to select the correct value for the field.

Toggle Button

1   In the toolbox, click the Toggle Button tool.

2   Click the Field List button on the Form Design toolbar to display the field list. Select the Additional Withholding field from the field list, and drag the field to the empty area immediately to the right of the Additional Withholding field. Close the Field List.

When a control is bound to a field in a table, the control will always display the contents of that field.

After you have selected the toolbox Toggle Button control, when you move the mouse pointer across the work area, the pointer changes to the Toggle Button tool. When you release the mouse button, a square box is added to the form. The control has been *bound* to the Additional Withholding field. You can confirm this by selecting the Data tab in the Toggle Button property sheet and viewing the value in the Control Source property field.

Properties

3   On the toolbar, click the Properties button. In the Toggle Button property sheet, make sure the Format tab is selected.

4   Type **Click Here For Additional Withholding** and then press ENTER. Close the Properties sheet.

The new caption appears on the Toggle Button control.

5   Select the Additional Withholding text control, and then press DELETE.

6   On the right edge of the toggle button, place the mouse pointer on the middle sizing handle. When the pointer changes to a double-headed arrow, double-click. Drag to position the toggle button so it is aligned to the left of the form.

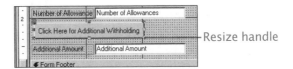
—Resize handle

View your changes in Form view

You have greatly improved the look of the Payroll Form. You should now check and see that all your changes are as you intended them to be.

1   Click the View down arrow, and select Form View.

Your form should look like the following illustration.

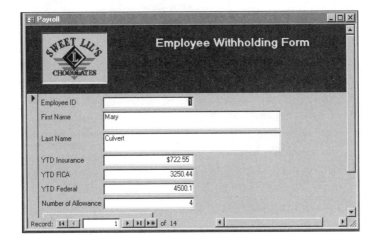

2   Move from record to record on the form to see how the form looks with the new formatting.

Because the logo and title have been placed in the header section of the form, they appear on the form background for every record.

3   Save your changes.

Creating Controls That Have the Same Format

When you create a form with the Form Wizard, the controls all have the same format properties. This guarantees that the controls all have same look. However, when you make changes to one of those controls, you lose that common look. You can use the Format Painter restore the consistent formatting. The *Format Painter* is a tool you use to copy formatting properties from one control to another.

The following list describes the properties that the Format Painter will copy between fields:

BackColor	BorderWidth	FontSize	LabelY
BackStyle	DisplayWhen	FontWeight	SpecialEffect
BorderColor	FontItalic	ForeColor	TextAlign
BorderStyle	FontName	LabelX	

Copy the control formatting

Sweet Lil's forms should all have two things in common: the field labels should be blue, and the font weight should be bold. In the following exercise, you'll change the label in one field to match this standard, and use the Format Painter to copy the change to the other fields.

1 Click on the View button down arrow, and select Design View.

You need to be in Design view to make formatting changes.

2 Double-click the Employee ID label control to select it and open its property sheet.

3 In the property sheet, make sure the Format tab is still selected, and then click on the Fore Color label to select the field's current value.

The value is highlighted

4 Press DELETE, type **8388608** and press ENTER.

5 Click in the Font Weight property box. Click the down arrow, and then select Bold. Close the Properties sheet.

6 Click the View down arrow, and then select Form View.

The label for the Employee ID field has the new properties. Your form should look like the following illustration.

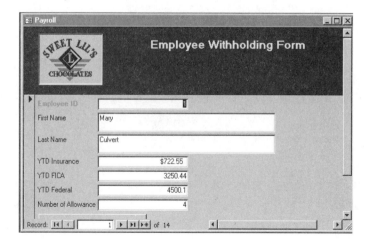

Copy the format with the Format Painter

The Format Painter can be used to copy formatting properties between different types of controls. For example, you can copy formatting characteristics from a text box to a combo control.

Format Painter

Because you are going to copy the format properties to more than one control, you double-click the Format Painter to lock it down. If you are copying to only one control, you single-click the Format Painter.

1   Click the View down arrow, and click Design View.
2   Click in the Employee ID label control to select it.
3   On the Form Design toolbar, double-click the Format Painter tool.
4   Click each of the label controls, including the toggle button, to copy the formatting properties. When you are through, press ESC to turn off the Format Painter.
5   Resize the toggle button as necessary.
6   Click the View down arrow, and click Design View.

Your form should look like the following illustration.

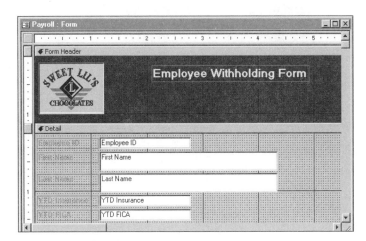

Fine-Tuning Your Forms

As is true with most forms, the form you have created can be used as is, but its appearance can be improved. The final step in formatting a form is to fine-tune the form, adjusting the controls for the best position and checking to be sure that the formatting is appropriate for the form.

Fine-tune the form

First, the form is not balanced, so you will move the controls more toward the middle of the form. Second, you'll improve the form by adding a colored line above the Employee ID field.

1   Select the Employee ID control by clicking anywhere in either the control itself or the label control.

2   Hold down the SHIFT key, and then click each of the eight controls below the Employee ID control.

Holding down the SHIFT key allows to you select a group of controls. As each control is selected, handles appear around the control to indicate that the control is selected. The mouse pointer changes to a small hand when it is positioned over any of the selected controls. The controls can now be repositioned as a group.

3   Move the controls to the right by placing the mouse pointer inside any one of the selected controls and dragging the control until its label edge is lined up with the 1-inch mark on the horizontal ruler.

4   Select the bottom nine controls as a group, and drag them down to the ½-inch mark on the vertical ruler.

5   Click the Format menu, and if Snap To Grid is not already selected, click it.

The Snap To Grid command ensures that the line you draw will be straight.

Line Tool

6   On the Form Design toolbar, click the Line tool, and then place the mouse pointer on the left edge of the form even with the ½-inch mark on the vertical ruler.

Move the Form Design toolbar as necessary to view the Line tool. Be sure to align with the vertical ruler, not the horizontal ruler.

7   Drag the Line tool across to the far right edge of the form.

When you release the mouse button, a horizontal line appears on the form.

Line/Border Color

8   On the Formatting toolbar, click the Line/Border Color down arrow, and select a blue box.

9   On the Formatting toolbar, click the Line/Border Width down arrow, and select width 3.

Line Width

10   Click the View down arrow, and select Form View.

The form is now easy to use and looks professional.

Your form should look like the following illustration.

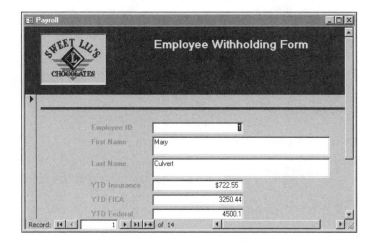

Print the form

Now that the form is finished, you decide to print a hard copy.

1 On the File menu, click Print.

2 Click the Select Record field, and click OK.

The form prints.

Adding custom pages to a form

You can create custom pages for forms in Design view. These custom pages are defined by adding a tab control and setting control properties that determine the page format. Using custom pages, you can create several different versions of a form that can be used in different applications. In this exercise, you will add a custom control to the Payroll form that calculates the total year-to-date withholding for an employee.

View

1 Click the View down arrow, and click Design View.

2 In the Toolbox, click the Tab Control tool, and then, just below the Additional Amount field, click the form.

Two new custom pages are added to the form. The custom pages should look like the following illustration.

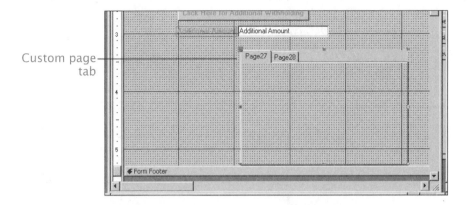

Custom page tab

3 Select the second custom page, and then press DELETE.

4 Drag a Text Box control onto the custom page. On the toolbar, click the Properties button.

Properties

5 Click the Data Properties tab. Click in the Control Source Property, type **=[YTD Insurance]+[YTD FICA]+[YTD Federal]** and then press ENTER.

6 At the top of the Custom page, click the tab.

7 In Format Properties, click in the Caption Property, and then type **YTD Total**

8 Close the Properties sheet.

9 Select the text control label, and then press DELETE. Resize the custom page.

10 Click the View down arrow, and then select Form View.

The Payroll form appears with the custom page attached. The form should look like the following illustration.

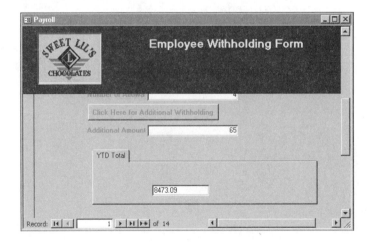

11 Close the form and when prompted to save the changes to the form, click Yes.

 NOTE If you'd like to build on the skills that you learned in this lesson, you can do the One Step Further. Otherwise, skip to "Finish the lesson."

One Step Further: Creating a Macro

Macros are introduced in Lesson 2, "Increasing Efficiency by Using Subforms," as a collection of commands which are executed in sequence. In that lesson, a command button is used to execute a macro. Lesson 9, "Merging Data from Two Tables onto One Form," explains how to attach a macro to a command button. In this One Step Further, you will use the Macro window to create a macro.

Macro commands are sometimes needed to ensure that the data is presented correctly. For example, one finishing touch that you can add to the Employee Withholding form is a macro that will allow you to apply a filter when the form is opened. When the filter is applied, only the records that have a value of Yes in the Additional Withholding field will be displayed.

Appendix C, "Using Expressions," discusses expressions, how they are used, and how they are built.

The pieces of data required to create a macro are known as *arguments*, and to build a macro, you must specify which arguments to include and you must specify which commands to include. Macros are created in the Macro window, which is divided into two parts. The top part is used to specify the macro commands, and the bottom part to specify the arguments. Some arguments contain mathematically based expressions.

In these exercises, you will create a macro and add it to the On Open property of the Payroll form. The macro will open a form that will allow you to apply the filter to the records in the Payroll form. Since you won't always need the filter, the form uses two different macros to make applying the filter optional.

Create a macro to open a form that will filter the payroll records

1 In the database window, select the Macros tab, and click New.

The Macro window opens. The first cell in the action column is blank.

2 In the first cell in the Action column, click the down arrow, and select OpenForm. Press ENTER.

In the Action Arguments portion of the window, the six arguments required for this action open.

The Ask About form and the macros Yes Button and No Button are hidden objects in the database. To see them, click Options on the Tools menu and select the option to view the hidden objects.

3 In the Comments cell type **This macro opens the Ask About form when the Payroll form is opened.**

The Comments should explain the purpose of and possible uses for the macro. When you use this macro, the Ask About form will give you the option of viewing all the records in the Payroll form or only those where there is additional withholding.

4 Click in the Form Name condition field, and then type **Ask About**

5 Press ENTER.

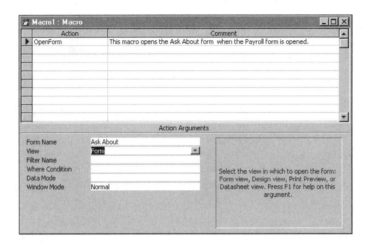

6 Close the Macro window, and when a message box asks whether you want to save changes, click Yes.

The Save dialog box appears.

7 In the Macro Name box, type **Ask About Additional**

The Ask About form will open when this macro runs.

Add the macro to the Payroll form

You are ready to add the Ask About Additional macro to the Payroll form. There are two command button controls on the Ask About form. When the Payroll form opens, the Ask About form asks you whether or not you want to display only records with additional withholding. If you click Yes, the Payroll form opens with the filtered records displayed. If you click No, the Payroll form opens with all records displayed.

Controls can have macros associated with certain events. For example, a macro can execute when the control is clicked. Forms can have macros associated with their events as well. You will set the Ask About Additional macro to be the On Open event on the Payroll form. This means that the Ask About Additional macro will run every time the form is opened in Form view.

1   In the Database window, click the Forms tab. Click the Payroll form to select it.

2   Click Design.

3   Open the Properties sheet, and click the Event tab on the Form property sheet.

4   Click the On Open property, click the down arrow, and then click Ask About Additional.

5   Click the View down arrow, and select Form View.

    A message asks whether you want to see only the employees with additional withholding amounts.

6   Click the Yes box.

    The Payroll form opens. The navigation bar indicates that you are looking at filtered data.

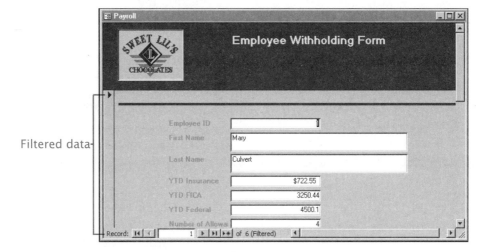

7   Close the form, and when a message asks if you want to save changes, click Yes.

Finish the lesson

1   To continue to the next lesson, on the File menu, click Close.

2   If you are finished using Microsoft Access for now, on the File menu, click Exit.

199

Lesson Summary

To	Do this	Button
Add a title to a form	Open the form in Design view. Select the Form Header section. Add a label control that contains the form title.	
Edit an OLE object	Open the form or table that contains the object. Double-click the object, and use the appropriate software tool to make any changes. Save the embedded object and return to the form or table.	
Add a toggle button to a form	Open the form in Design view. In the toolbox, click the Toggle Button tool. Drag the field to be bound to the toggle control from the field list onto the form. Add a caption to the control by typing the text in the control Caption field on the property sheet.	
Add an image to a form	In Design view, select the Unbound Object tool in the toolbox. Click where you want to position the image on the form. In the Insert Object dialog box, double-click the picture file you want.	
Work with a group of fields	In Design view, select the first field in the group. Hold down the SHIFT key, and click any other fields to be included in the group.	
Give your forms a standard appearance	Set the appearance for one control. Click the Format Painter—or double-click if copying to more than one control—and click the controls that you want to have the new format.	

To	Do this	Button
Change the background color of a form's section	Open the form in Design view. Click in the Form Header, Detail, or Form Footer section to select it. In the section's property sheet, click the Fill/Back Color down arrow, and select the desired color from the available choices.	
Change the color of the text in a label control	In Design view, select the Label control. On the toolbar, click the Font/Fore Color down arrow, and select the desired color from the available choices.	
Add a line to a form	In Design view, click the Line tool, and drag from the desired starting point to the desired ending point.	
Change a line color	In Design view, select the line. On the toolbar, click the Line/Border Color down arrow, and select the desired color.	
Change a line width	In Design view, select the line. On the toolbar, click the Line/Border Width down arrow, and select the desired width.	
Add a custom page or tab control	Open the form in Design View. In the toolbox, click the Tab Control tool. Click on the form where you want to position the tab control. Edit the tab control as necessary.	

For online information about	On the Help menu, click Contents And Index, click the Index tab, and then type
Formatting controls	**formatting controls** **Controls, properties**
OLE objects	**OLE objects** **OLE object fields**
Toggle Button controls	**toggle buttons**
Inserting lines	**lines, drawing**

For online information about	On the Help menu, click Contents And Index, click the Index tab, and then type
Working with a group of controls	**controls, moving and positioning**
Creating a standard control format	**Format Painter**
Custom pages	**tab controls**
Creating macros	**macros, creating**

Customizing a Report

Estimated time

35 min.

In this lesson you will learn how to:

- Use a report wizard to create a detail report.
- Preview and print a report.
- Understand and change the design of a report.
- Create a report that performs calculations.
- Show groups of records by hiding duplicates.

One of the most important functions of a database is, of course, producing useful information. This information is the only aspect of the database that some members of the organization ever see. It is vital, therefore, that this finished product be timely and have a professional appearance. There is no value in a report that is produced two weeks after it's required or that is so poorly prepared that other users cannot understand it.

Reports are introduced in Lesson 3, "Viewing Only the Information You Need." In this lesson, you will learn to quickly produce professional reports that draw information from multiple sources. Most of the work will be accomplished with the help of a report wizard. As do other wizards, a report wizard asks you a series of questions to help you build a professional-looking report. You can use the report as it is, or you can customize it. You'll also learn how to create a simple detail report with a report wizard. You'll preview the report and then switch to Design view to make a few changes.

Summarizing Data by Creating a Detail Report

Tables and queries can be printed as they are; this output is often useful when you need a listing of only the raw data in the database. In most circumstances, however, you will want a report that presents your information in a more professional-looking format that's easy to read. A *detail report* displays the same information as a table or query, but a detail report includes report headers, page headers, and page footers.

The query locates the raw data...

but the report presents the data attractively.

The fastest way to create a report is by using a report wizard. A report wizard places fields on the report and displays the data in one of several presentation styles. After you've created the report, you can customize it.

Start the lesson

> If Microsoft Access isn't started yet, start it and open the Sweet Lil's database. If the Microsoft Access window doesn't fill your screen, maximize the window.
>
> If you need help opening the database, see Lesson 1.

Create a detail report

Sweet Lil's is preparing a marketing plan for next year. They want to create advertisements that promote the most popular boxes of bonbons. At a Marketing Department meeting, you plan to hand out a report that shows sales by state or province. You don't need anything elaborate—just an easy-to-create, easy-to-read report.

The two reports in the following illustration show the differences between a single-column and a tabular report. The single-column report displays the data in one long column, while the tabular report is more compact and presents the data in a table.

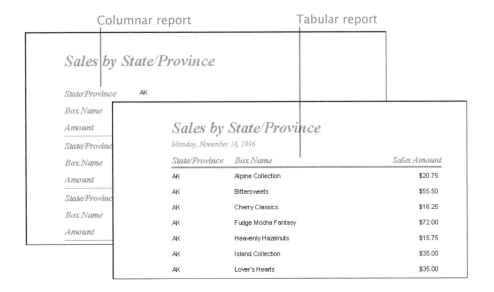

Begin a new report

The Sales By State/Province query in the Sweet Lil's database contains the records you need for this report.

1   In the Database window, click the Reports tab, and then click New.

   The New Report dialog box appears.

2   In the list of wizards, select AutoReport Tabular.

3   In the Choose The Table Or Query Where The Object's Data Comes From box, select the Sales By State/Province query.

4   Click OK.

   The AutoReport Wizard creates a tabular report for you. The report opens in Print Preview. Your screen should look like the following illustration.

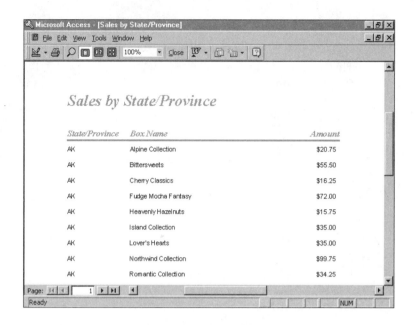

 NOTE The text in your report might look different from the text in the illustration, depending on your printer and your current default AutoFormat for reports. Later in this lesson, you'll learn how to change the default AutoFormat.

5 On the File menu, click Save.

6 In the Save As box, be sure Sales By State/Province appears in the Report Name box. Click OK.

Change the picture size in Print Preview

In this exercise, you use the magnifying-glass pointer to switch between viewing data in a magnified view and seeing the layout of the entire page.

1 To see the whole page, click anywhere on the report.

A reduced view of the whole page appears.

2 To return to a magnified view, click the report again.

In magnified view, the spot where you click the magnifying-glass pointer will be in the center of the screen.

3   Use the navigation buttons at the bottom of the window to page through your report in Print Preview.

Print the report

Because this is a long report, you will print only a sample page to view the report.

IMPORTANT   You must have a printer installed on your computer to print reports. If you don't have a printer installed, skip this exercise.

---

1   On the File menu, click Print.

2   In the Print Range area, click the Pages option.

3   To print only the first page, type **1** in the From box, and type **1** again in the To box.

4   Click OK.

Exploring the Design of the Report

As you preview the report, you can see how Microsoft Access displays the records from your query and adds information that makes the report easier to read. As you page through this report, you'll see:

■ A *report header* at the top of the first page of the report. The report header displays the title of the report.

■ A *page header* at the top of every page of the report. The page header displays the heading for each column of data.

■ The *detail* section, between the page header and the page footer. The detail section displays the records you selected; in this case, the data is from the Sales By State/Province query, which you selected as the report's underlying query when you created the report.

■ A *page footer* at the bottom of every page of the report. In this case, the page footer shows the page number, total pages, and the date the report was printed.

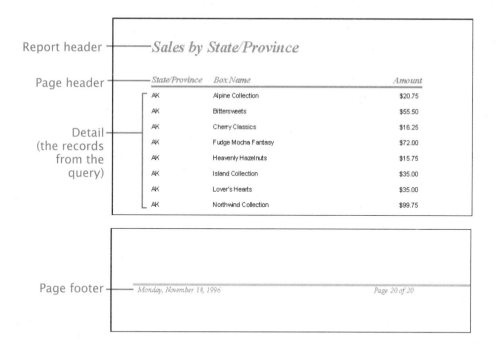

Report header ———— *Sales by State/Province*

Page header ————

State/Province	Box Name	Amount
AK	Alpine Collection	$20.75
AK	Bittersweets	$55.50
AK	Cherry Classics	$16.25
AK	Fudge Mocha Fantasy	$72.00
AK	Heavenly Hazelnuts	$15.75
AK	Island Collection	$35.00
AK	Lover's Hearts	$35.00
AK	Northwind Collection	$99.75

Detail (the records from the query) ————

Page footer ———— *Monday, November 18, 1996* ———— *Page 20 of 20*

Selecting the Correct View and Identifying Screen Elements

Up to this point, you've used Design view to modify forms. You can also use Design view to modify reports.

In Design view, the different sections of a report represent the elements you saw in Print Preview. For example, there is a Report Header section in Design view that corresponds to the first page title you saw in Print Preview. When you view the report in Design view, you can see how each element will be displayed when you preview or print the report. In Design view, the detail section shows how the records from the underlying table or query will look.

Switch to Design view

View

The graphic on the View button changes according to the current selection.

1   On the toolbar, click the View down arrow, and then click Design View.

The report opens in Design view. Your report should look like the following illustration.

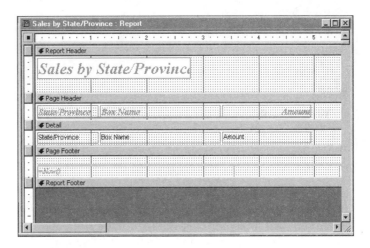

2 If the Report window is too small for you to see all the controls, resize the window to make it larger.

> **TIP** When you have the report open in Design view, you can print by clicking Print on the File menu. You can also print a report from the Database window without opening the report. First, select the report from the list on the Reports tab, and then click the Print button.

Move the design tools

When you switch to Design view, the toolbox might cover up part of the report. You use the toolbox to customize your report. In this exercise, however, you'll move the toolbox so you can see the report better.

➤ If the toolbox is not visible, click Toolbox on the View menu.

Drag the toolbox title bar to move the toolbox to a more convenient location.

Identify the elements created by a report wizard

A report wizard will:

- Create the sections on your report.
- Place the data and other information in the appropriate sections.
- Align the columns and add some decorative lines to create an attractive report.
- Select fonts and font sizes for all the text on the report.
- Add the date to the page header or footer, depending on the default style.

You can build a report from scratch that contains all these elements—but you can often save hours if you use a report wizard and then customize the report after the report wizard creates it.

When you created the Sales By State/Province report, the AutoReport Wizard did a lot of work behind the scenes.

➤ Using the above list, find each item on your report that the AutoReport Wizard created for you automatically.

Customizing the Design of a Report

It took only a short time to create this report, which attractively presents the data you need for your meeting. But you'd like to change a few things. Working in Design view, you'll:

- Change the text in the Amount label so it's more descriptive, and move the date text box into the report header.
- Add some information, including a grand total, to the page footer and report footer.

Change the label in the page header

1 In the Page Header section, select the Amount label.

2 Move the mouse pointer to the left of the word "Amount" until the pointer appears as a vertical line, and then click to position the insertion point.

3 Type **Sales**, type a space, and then press ENTER.

Move labels

1   In the Page Footer section, select the label =Now(), and drag it to the Report Header section, just below the Sales By State/Province report title.

Layout Preview displays the first page of a report so you can quickly preview your Design view layout.

2   Click the View down arrow, and click Layout Preview.

The report printing date appears in the Report Header on the first page.

> **Sales by State/Province**   `_ □ ×`
>
> *Sales by State/Province*
>
> *Friday, November 15, 1996*
>
> *State/Province   Box Name*   *Sales Amount*

Add more information to the page footer

To help other Marketing personnel understand the purpose of the report, you'll add a footer to each page of the report.

1   Click the View down arrow, and then click Design View.

2   In the toolbox, click the Label tool.

Label

3   Click the left side of the Page Footer section.

A label is added to the section.

4   Type **Data for Marketing Quarterly Meeting** and then press ENTER.

5   Place the mouse pointer on the left edge of the label control. When the pointer changes to the shape of a hand, drag the control to the center of the page footer. The left edge of the control should align with the 3-inch mark on the horizontal rule.

Format the report footer

You want the new text to match the text that appears in the other footer controls. You will copy the formatting by using the Format Painter, and then you reposition the text.

Format Painter

1   Select the text box that contains the page numbers. Click the Format Painter button, and then click the new label.

Align Left

2   Select the new label, and on the Formatting toolbar, click the Align Left button to make the text left-align.

Add a grand total to the report footer

In this exercise, you'll add a grand total to the Report Footer, which will appear on the last page.

Text Box

1   In the toolbox, click the Text Box tool, and then click the right side of the Report Footer.

    A new text box and label are pasted in the Report Footer, and a grid area appears in the Report Footer area to encompass the new text box.

2   Select the default label text in the text box, type **Grand Total** and then press ENTER.

3   Double-click the new text box.

    The property sheet for the text box appears.

4   Click the Data tab, and then in the Control Source box, type **=sum([amount])**

5   Click the Format tab, and then click the Format property. Click the down arrow, select Currency, and then press ENTER.

6   Close the property sheet.

Bold

7   Make sure the text box is selected, and on the Formatting toolbar, click the Bold button.

    The grand total expression is in bold type.

8   On the Report Design toolbar, click the Print Preview button to view the report.

    The page footer is at the bottom of every page, and the new grand total is at the bottom of the last page.

Summarize Data by Grouping Records

The report you have created does a good job; but it can be improved. For example, when you look down the left side, you see the name of the state or province repeated over and over. Each name should be shown once for each group. Lesson 12, "Sharing Summarized and Grouped Data," discusses how to create a grouped report, which will solve this problem. But for the report you're working on now, there's another quick way to fix this.

As the report is now, Microsoft Access displays data for the State/Province field even though this field contains duplicate values. You can change the Hide Duplicates property for the State/Province text box so that duplicate values are shown only once.

Hide the duplicate values

1   Click the View down arrow, and then select Design View.

2   In the Detail section, double-click the State/Province text box.

    The property sheet appears.

3   In the property sheet, click the Hide Duplicates property, click the down arrow, and then select Yes. Close the property sheet.

Print Preview

4 On the Report Design toolbar, click the Print Preview button to switch to Print Preview.

Each state or province appears only once on the report. Your report should look like the following illustration.

Sales by State/Province
Friday, November 15, 1996

State/Province	Box Name	Sales Amount
AK	Alpine Collection	$20.75
	Bittersweets	$55.50
	Cherry Classics	$16.25
	Fudge Mocha Fantasy	$72.00
	Heavenly Hazelnuts	$15.75
	Island Collection	$35.00
	Lover's Hearts	$35.00
	Northwind Collection	$99.75
	Romantic Collection	$34.25
	Sweet and Bitter	$27.75

Page: |◄ ◄ 1 ► ►| ◄

5 Save and close the report.

NOTE If you'd like to build on the skills that you learned in this lesson, you can do the One Step Further. Otherwise, skip to "Finish the lesson."

One Step Further: Creating a Custom AutoReport

An international gourmet food company wants to order large quantities of individual bonbons from Sweet Lil's. The representative for the international company wants a report that shows all Sweet Lil's bonbons categorized by chocolate type. Because the representative wants the report immediately, you want to create a report as quickly as possible.

You can create this new report by using the AutoReport button on the toolbar, and then you can customize the AutoReport feature to create the type of report you use most often.

Create a report by using the AutoReport feature

1 In the Database window, select the Chocolate Types query.

New Object

2   On the toolbar, click the New Object down arrow, and then click AutoReport.

A report based on the Chocolate Types query is created automatically and opens in Print Preview.

3   Click the report to see a whole page at once.

The report style is inappropriate for distribution outside the company. You would like a slightly different look for the report.

4   Click the View down arrow, and click Design View so that you can change the format using AutoFormat.

Change the default format of an AutoReport

You can change the default format so that the AutoReport is in the style you want.

AutoFormat

1   On the Report Design toolbar, click the AutoFormat button.

The AutoFormat dialog box appears.

2   In the Report AutoFormats list, select Bold, and then click OK.

The report is formatted in the Bold style.

3   Switch to Print Preview.

Your report appears in Bold style. From now on, all reports you create with AutoReport will be in the Bold style unless you change the default AutoFormat again.

4   On the File menu, click Save, type **Chocolate Types** and then click OK.

Customize your report

To further improve the appearance of the report, you adjust the report so that each type of chocolate appears only once.

1   Click the View down arrow, and click Design View.

2   In the Detail section, double-click the Chocolate Type text box.

3   In the property sheet, change the setting of the Hide Duplicates property to Yes, and then close the property sheet.

4   Switch to Print Preview to see your changes.

5   Save the report.

Finish the lesson

1   To continue to the next lesson, on the File menu, click Close.

2   If you are finished using Microsoft Access for now, on the File menu, click Exit.

Lesson Summary

To	Do this	Button
Create a quick detail report using the AutoReport Wizard	In the Database window, click the Reports tab, and then click New. Select the table or query that will provide the data for the report, and then click the AutoReport: Tabular Wizard or the AutoReport: Columnar Wizard.	
Preview a report	In the Database window, double-click the report, or click the Preview button. *or* In Design view, click the View button down arrow on the toolbar, and select Print Preview or Layout Preview.	![Preview button]
View the design of a report	In the Database window, click the report, and then click Design.	
Print a report	In the Database window, select the report, and click the Print button on the toolbar or click Print on the File menu. *or* In Design view, Print Preview, or Layout Preview, click the Print button on the toolbar or click Print on the File menu.	![Print button]
Hide duplicate values in the Detail section	In Design view, select the control for which you want to hide duplicates. In the property sheet for this control, set the Hide Duplicates property to Yes.	

For online information about	On the Help menu, click Contents And Index, click the Index tab, and then type
Creating a report	**creating report**
Customizing a report	**customizing reports**
Hiding duplicate records	**hiding duplicate data, reports**
Laying out a report	**reports, examples**
Using AutoReport	**AutoReport**

Sharing Summarized and Grouped Data

Estimated time
40 min.

In this lesson you will learn how to:

- Create a grouped report.
- Customize the group header.
- Change the sort order.
- Keep related groups of data on the same page.
- Add customized page numbering.
- Prepare reports for publication on the Internet or an intranet.

When you look at a list of data, it's difficult to see the overall picture. Lessons 7 through 9 discuss how analyzing and grouping data can turn it into meaningful information. Reports are another tool you can use to group and summarize your data. When you're looking at regional sales patterns, for example, you don't want to see just a long list of sales data—you'd rather see a list of sales for each region. Even better would be a list of sales that has a subtotal for each region so you can pinpoint your strongest sales at a glance.

Using report wizards, you can design grouped reports that make data easier to understand. In this lesson, you'll create a report that groups your data and automatically calculates subtotals for each group. Then, you'll create another grouped report that calculates a percentage, and you'll change the sort order of that report and add customized page numbering. Finally, you will learn to share your Microsoft Access reports through either the Internet or your organization's intranet.

Creating Groups and Totals

Similar records are gathered together in groups. A *group* is a collection of records that share a common value. A grouped report can often improve your reader's understanding of the data. That's because a grouped report not only displays similar records together, but also shows introductory and summary information for each group.

In the report shown in the following illustration, the records are grouped by state or province. The records for the state of Alaska (AK) make up the first group.

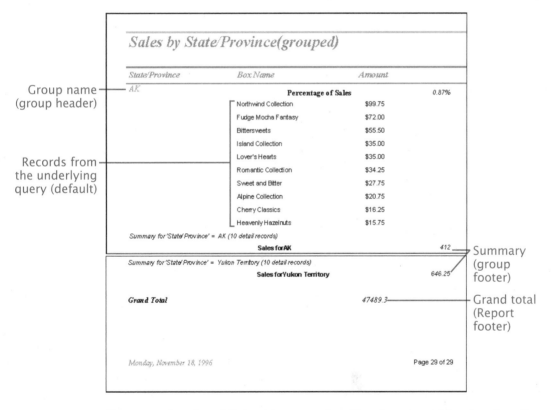

Group name (group header)

Records from the underlying query (default)

Summary (group footer)

Grand total (Report footer)

The group header—AK, in this case—identifies the group. The detail section, which is the body of the group report, displays the appropriate records from the selected query. The group footer summarizes the data for the group, showing the total sales for Alaska. The report footer at the very end of the report includes the grand total for all the sales from all the groups

For more information about expressions, see Appendix C, "Using Expressions."

In this lesson, you'll use the Groups/Totals Report Wizard to create grouped reports. This Report Wizard is a real time-saver. It asks how you want to group records in your report, and then it adds the group header and group footer sections for you. It even adds the mathematical expressions that perform the subtotal and total calculations.

Start the lesson

➤ If Microsoft Access isn't started yet, start it and open the Sweet Lil's database. If the Microsoft Access window doesn't fill your screen, maximize the window.

If you need help opening the database, see Lesson 1.

Summarizing Data by Creating a Grouped Report

Sweet Lil's new Marketing manager plans to expand sales through a mail order campaign and needs your help. He wants to send a mail order advertisement to people in the states and provinces where your products have been most successful. To do this, you need a report that shows the total sales for each state and province so the Marketing manager can decide where to send the advertisement.

To get the report you want, you'll create a new report using the Report Wizard. In this report, you want to see sales totals for each state and province, so you'll group the report by the State/Province field. You'll choose options that calculate both a sum total and a percentage of the total for each state or province. The Sales By State/Province query in the Sweet Lil's database provides the records you need.

Create a new report based on a query

You can ensure that both the Formatting and Report Design toolbars are fully displayed. On the View menu, click Toolbars, and select the toolbars.

In this exercise, you open the Report Wizard and begin creating the report.

1 In the Database window, click the Reports tab, and then click New.

2 In the list of wizards, select Report Wizard.

3 Click the Chose The Table Or Query Where The Object's Data Comes From down arrow, select Sales By State/Province, and then click OK.

Enter information in the Report Wizard

Now that you've selected the Report Wizard, you'll go through a series of dialog boxes. In this exercise, you'll enter information in the dialog boxes.

1 Click the Select All button between the two list boxes to add all three available fields to the report, and then click Next.

2 In the second dialog box, double-click the State/Province field in the left panel, and then click Next.

The third dialog box, in which you establish sort order and summary information, appears.

3 In the first combo box, click the down arrow, and select Box Name. The

If you wanted to sort box names from Z to A, you would click the Sort button again.

Sort button next to the combo box shows that the box names will be sorted in ascending alphabetical order, from A to Z.

4 At the bottom of the dialog box, click Summary Options.

The Summary Options dialog box appears, showing data fields that can be summarized. In this report, only the Amount field can be summarized.

5 Click the Sum check box for the Amount field to select it, and then click the check box for Calculate Percent Of Total For Sums to select it.

6 Be sure that the Detail And Summary option is selected. Click OK, and then click Next on the Report Wizard dialog box.

The fourth Report Wizard dialog box opens and offers several layout and orientation options.

7 Be sure that the Stepped option is selected, and be sure that the Portrait option is selected as the orientation. Click Next.

The fifth dialog box shows how your report will appear in several preformatted styles.

8 Select Corporate, and then click Next.

The final Report Wizard dialog box appears.

9 In the What Title Do You Want For Your Report box, type **Sales by State/Province (grouped)** and then click Finish.

The Report Wizard creates your grouped report and displays it in Print Preview.

10 Review the report.

Check the report in Design view

In this exercise, you switch to Design view to compare the two views.

1 Click the View down arrow, and click Design View.

Your report should look like the following illustration.

View

The graphic on the View button changes to reflect the current selection.

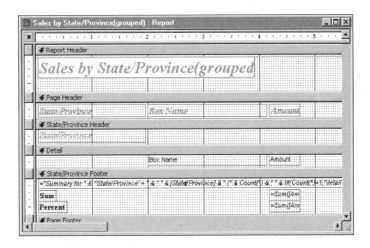

2   Maximize the Report window to see more of the controls on the report. You might need to move the toolbox or property sheet out of the way.

The Report Wizard has added the following elements to your report:

An expression that displays the current date At the bottom of each page, the date appears in the page footer.

A group header and a group footer The Report Wizard has added a group header and a group footer for the State/Province group. In Design view, they're identified as the State/Province Header and the State/Province Footer. In more complex reports, you might have several group headers that have different names.

Expressions that calculate totals The expression for totals in the State/Province footer is exactly the same as the expression in the report footer: =Sum([Amount]). When you place an expression in the State/Province footer or the State/Province header, the expression performs calculations for the records in each State/Province group. When you place an expression in the report footer or the report header, the expression calculates a value for all records in the report.

An expression that adds percentages In the State/Province Footer, the Report Wizard has added the expression =Sum([Amount])/ ([Amount Grand Total Sum]), which calculates the percentage of the grand total for each State/Province group. You might need to increase the size of the two text boxes in the State/Province Footer to read the complete expression.

An expression that adds page numbers At the bottom of each page, the current page number and total number of pages appear automatically in the page footer.

Describing the Group by Creating an Appropriate Header

Now you can easily skim through your report and find the figures you need. For your mail order campaign, you'll choose only those states and provinces that have the highest percentages of sales.

You'd like to see at a glance what percentage of total sales is brought in by each state and province, and you'd like to display this information next to the name of the state or province.

Move a text box

In this exercise, you'll move the percentage expression to the group header.

1 Drag the Percent text box that contains the expression =Sum([Amount])/ ([Amount Grand Total Sum]) from the State/Province Footer section into the State/Province header, and place it above the Amount text box of the Detail section.

2 Drag the Percent label from the State/Province Footer to the State/Province Header, and place it to the left of the percentage text box you just moved. Then click to the right of the word "Percent" and type **age of Sales**

3 Press ENTER.

You might need to move the label to the left if the added characters overlap the text box. If so, hold your pointer on the upper-left selection handle until the pointer becomes a pointing hand, and then drag to move the label separately.

4 On the Report Design toolbar, click Print Preview to review your work in Print Preview.

Your report should look like the following illustration.

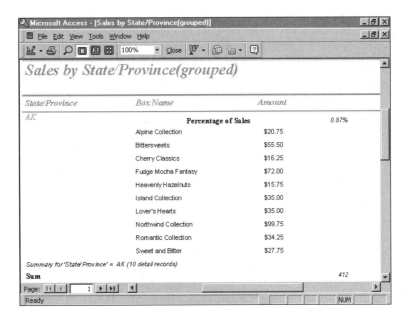

Editing the Group Footer

You'd like to make it easier to skim the report and find the total sales figure for each state or province, so you'll add some text to identify each sales total. For example, to the left of the Alaska total, you'd like to see "Sales for AK" instead of "Sum." To add this text, you'll use a text box that has an expression so that the appropriate name for each state or province is filled in automatically.

Because you're adding descriptive text, you might think you'd use the toolbox Label tool. But a label can contain only words. If you use the toolbox Text Box tool, you can add an expression that performs a task for you.

Add a text box in the State/Province footer

Text Box

1   On the toolbar, click the View down arrow, and select Design View.

2   In the toolbox, click the Text Box tool.

3   Click near the middle of the State/Province footer to add the text box.

4   Click in the text box to place the insertion point, and then type the following expression: =**"Sales for "** & [State/Province]

IMPORTANT Be sure to start the expression with the equals sign (=) and to leave a space before the second quotation mark. If you don't leave a space, your label will contain text like this: Sales forAK.

The words in the quotation marks will appear on your report exactly as you type them. The & symbol means "followed by." The information in brackets is taken from the State/Province field and will change for each location.

5 Press ENTER.

6 Select and delete the original Sum label and the label attached to the new text box.

7 Drag the text box sizing handles to make the text box wide enough to accommodate long state or province names, and move the text box so that it's roughly in the position shown in the following illustration.

Change the format of the text box

The footer captures the information you want; however, it needs to stand out. In this exercise, you will change the text to bold in order to emphasize it.

Bold

1 Select the text box, and on the Formatting toolbar, click the Bold button.

2 On the toolbar, click the View down arrow, and then click Layout Preview to look at the changes you made.

3 On the File menu, click Save.

Displaying Data in an Appropriate Order

When you use a report wizard to create reports, you're asked how you want to group and sort your data. If you decide to change sorting or grouping after you've created a report, you don't have to start from scratch and run the report wizard again. Instead, you can use the Sorting And Grouping box to make the changes.

When you originally created your report, you grouped by the State/Province field and then sorted by the Box Name field. Now you'd like to change the sort order. Within each state or province, you'd like to see a list that starts with the type of box that brought in the most money and ends with the type of box that brought in the least. In other words, you want to sort by the Amount field rather than by the Box Name field, and you want to sort in descending order (for numerical material, ascending order is from least to most; descending order is from most to least).

Open the Sorting And Grouping dialog box

Sorting And Grouping

1 Click the View down arrow, and then click Design View.

2 On the Report Design toolbar, click the Sorting And Grouping button.

The Sorting And Grouping dialog box appears; its settings were established when you answered the Report Wizard questions.

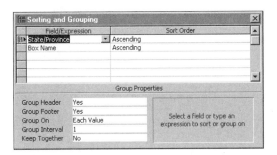

The Field/Expression column shows fields that are used either for grouping and sorting or for sorting only. To the left of the State/Province field is the Grouping icon, which tells you that this field is used for grouping and sorting. The Box Name field doesn't have this icon, so you can tell it is used solely for sorting.

Change the sort order

In this exercise, you'll specify Amount instead of Box Name as the second field to sort.

1 In the Field/Expression column, click the Box Name cell, and then click the down arrow to display a list of fields.

2 Select the Amount field from the list.

The Amount field replaces the Box Name field.

3 Click the Sort Order cell to the right of the Amount field, and then click the down arrow.

4 Select Descending from the list.

By selecting Descending, you're asking Microsoft Access to display the box sales for each state or province, starting with the highest amount and working down to the lowest.

5   Close the Sorting And Grouping dialog box. Click the View down arrow, and then click Layout Preview.

Your report now shows the boxes listed in descending order of sales.

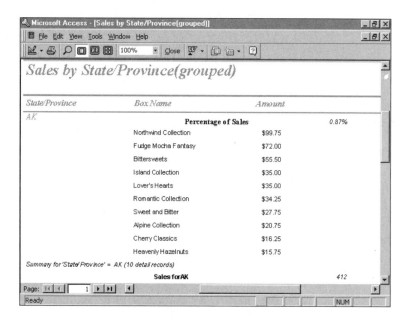

Keeping Related Groups on the Same Page

Some of the groups in the report begin on one page and finish on another. You can avoid a page break in the middle of a group by setting the Keep Together property in the Sorting And Grouping box.

NOTE   When you use the Keep Together property, a consecutive short report will be placed at the end of a report that is longer than one page. Two consecutive short reports will be placed on the same page. However, the reports will always be presented in the same order.

Keep Related Groups Together

Sorting And Grouping

1   In Design view, on the Report Design toolbar, click the Sorting And Grouping button.

The Sorting And Grouping dialog box appears.

2   Click the Keep Together property box, click the down arrow, and select Whole Group from the list.

3 On the Sorting And Grouping dialog box, click the Close button. Click the View button, and click Print Preview.

A complete group now appears on the same page, except where the group itself is longer than a full page.

Customizing Page Numbers

When you used the Report Wizard to create the Sales By State/Province (grouped) report, a text box containing an expression for a page number and total pages was automatically added to your report. You can change the style of page numbering easily by using the Page Numbers dialog box. You can also remove the page number from your opening page.

Create a new text box

In this exercise, you'll delete the page number that the Report Wizard created for you, insert a new page number text box in the center of the page footer, and remove the page number from your opening page.

1 On the toolbar, click the View button down arrow, and click Design View.

2 In the page footer, select the text box containing the page number expression, and then press DELETE.

3 On the Insert menu, click Page Numbers.

The Page Numbers dialog box appears.

4 Select the Page N Of M option, and the Bottom Of Page option. In the Alignment box, select Center.

5 Click the Show Number On First Page check box to clear it, and then click OK.

The new text box appears in the center of the Page Footer section. You can adjust its position if you'd like.

6 Preview your report, and examine the new footer.

7 On the File menu, click Save. On the toolbar, click Close to close the Sales By State/Province (grouped) report.

Preparing Reports for Publication on the Internet or an Intranet

One of the most exciting additions to Microsoft Access 97 is its capability to publish data on the Internet. Lesson 6, "Getting and Working with External Data," discusses sharing data through hyperlinks. Another new feature you can use to export to the Internet is the Publish To The Web Wizard. The Publish To The Web Wizard can be used to create Internet or intranet publications from

Table, Query, or Form datasheets. It can also be used to publish a form or report directly to the Internet or a corporate intranet.

 IMPORTANT You do not need to be connected to the Internet or to an intranet to complete this exercise. The file will be saved to the Windows folder on your computer.

Prepare a report for Internet or intranet publication

In this exercise, you will prepare the Sales by State/Province report for export to a corporate intranet. The report will be exported in an HTML format. This means that the report can be viewed by any program that is capable of reading Internet documents.

1 In the Database window, on the File menu, click Save As HTML.

The Publish To The Web Wizard appears.

2 The first dialog box provides some descriptive information. Read the material, and then click Next.

In the second dialog box, you specify the type of object you want to export.

3 Click the Reports tab, and click the Sales By State/Province box to select it. Click Next.

In the third dialog box, you specify a file to control how the export is formatted.

4 Click Next.

For the purposes of this exercise, you do not need to specify a format. In the fourth dialog box, you specify whether the material you are exporting is dynamic or static. If you were publishing a form for users to fill in, you would select dynamic. When you publish material for viewing only, you select static. Your report is for viewing only.

5 Click the Static (HTML) Publications check box to select it, and then click Next.

In the fifth dialog box, you tell the wizard where to store the material. If you were going to export to the Internet, you would select one of the two options for setting up a WebPost. You are going to save the exported sheet to your local machine.

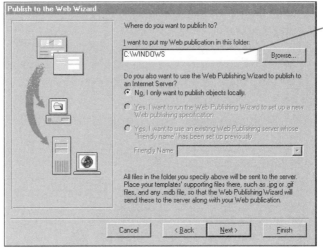

Indicate the folder for storing Web Publications here.

If you have Microsoft FrontPage, Microsoft Word 97, or any other program capable of viewing HTML files, you can now view the exported Internet document.

6 Select the No, I Only Want To Publish Objects Locally option, and in the I Want To Put My Web Publications In This Folder field, type **C:\Windows**

In the final dialog box, you specify whether you want to create a home page and links to all your Web publications.

7 Select the Yes, I Want To Create A Home Page option. In the What File Name Do You Want For Your Home Page field, type **Sweet Lil's**

8 Click Finish.

The Publish To The Web Wizard exports the file to the Windows folder on your computer.

NOTE If you'd like to build on the skills that you learned in this lesson, you can do the One Step Further. Otherwise, skip to "Finish the lesson."

One Step Further: Sorting and Grouping Properties

For quick identification of listings in a report, you can group items by the first letter of their names, much like the letter groupings in an index, and then print the letter as group header. First you'll create a quick report based on the Customer List query, and then you'll change the properties in the Sorting And Grouping window to add a letter at the beginning of each alphabetic group.

Create a new report

New Object

1. In the Database window, select but don't open the Customer List query.
2. On the toolbar, click the New Object down arrow, and select AutoReport.
3. Click the View down arrow, and select Design View.

Set the Sorting and Grouping properties

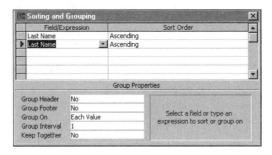

Sorting And Grouping

1. On the Report Design toolbar, click the Sorting And Grouping button.

   The Sorting And Grouping box appears.

2. In the first cell of the Field/Expression column, click the down arrow, and then select Last Name from the list to set the letter at the top of each alphabetic group.

3. Click the second cell of the Field/Expression column, click the down arrow, and then select Last Name from the list to set the actual sorting in the group.

4. Set the properties in the Sorting And Grouping box to match those in the following table. When you have finished, close the Sorting And Grouping dialog box.

Field/Expression:	Last name	Last name
Sort order:	Ascending	Ascending
Group header:	Yes	No
Group footer:	No	No
Group on:	Prefix Characters	Each Value
Group Interval:	1	1
Keep together:	With First Detail	No

By choosing Prefix Characters for the Group On property, and 1 for the Group Interval, you will see only the first letter of each group's last name. By choosing With First Detail for the Keep Together property, a group will not be restricted to one page but will be allowed to run over a page break.

Use an expression in the group header

Now that you have set the properties, you need to create a text box and an expression to display the result.

1   Select the Text Box tool from the toolbox, and drag the tool onto the Last Name Header to create a text box for the Last Name Header of the report.

2   Click the center of the header, and then click the Center button on the toolbar to center the text within the text box. Select the new label, and then press DELETE.

3   In the text box, type =**Left([Last Name],1)** and then press ENTER.

This expression prints only the first letter of the name at the beginning of each new group. The Left function containing the number 1 extracts one character from the Last Name field, beginning on the left. In this case, you will see the one letter that begins all the last names of each group.

Fill/Back Color

4   On the toolbar, click the Fill/Back Color down arrow, and then click a light gray square. Click the Font/Fore Color down arrow, and then click a dark blue square.

5   Preview the report, and then save it as **Customer List (grouped)**

Font/Fore Color

6   On the File menu, click Save.

Finish the lesson

1   To continue to the Review & Practice, on the File menu, click Close.

2   If you are finished using Microsoft Access for now, on the File menu, click Exit.

Lesson Summary

To	Do this
Create a grouped report	In the Database window, click the Reports tab, and then click New. Select a table or query, select Report Wizard, and click OK. To create the report, answer the questions in the dialog boxes.

To	Do this	Button
Change the sort order in a report	Display your report in Design view. On the Report Design toolbar, click the Sorting And Grouping button. In the Field/Expression column, select the field you want to sort. In the field's Sort Order cell, select Ascending or Descending.	
Keep related groups together	Display your report in Design view. On the Report Design toolbar, click the Sorting And Grouping button. Set the Keep Together property to Whole Group.	
Add custom page numbers	Display your report in Design view. On the Insert menu, click Page Numbers. In the Page Numbers dialog box, select the options you want, and then click OK.	
Prepare reports for publication on the Internet or an intranet	On the File menu, click Save As HTML. Follow the instructions in the Publish To The Web Wizard.	

For online information about	On the Help menu, click Contents And Index, click the Index tab, and then type
Creating grouped reports	**grouped reports**
Changing the sorting and grouping order in a report	**change sorting and grouping**
Adding custom page numbers	**page numbers**
Preparing reports for publication on the Internet or an intranet	**Internet, exporting data to Web page formats**

232

Review & Practice

Estimated time
25 min.

You will review and practice how to:

- Add a label to a form.
- Add a toggle button control to a form.
- Add a picture to a form.
- Give your forms a common look and feel.
- Create a detail report with the Report Wizard.
- Create a report that groups data.

Now that you have learned how to give forms and reports a professional appearance, you can apply your new skills to add value to the database.

Scenario

Some of the other managers at Sweet Lil's have heard about the Payroll Form and how professional it looks. The Marketing and Human Resource Departments want you to improve some of their forms. You agree to enhance several forms and create two new reports.

Step 1: Add a Label to a Form

The Marketing Department wants to improve the description of the data on the Box Sales form. You decide to add a label to the Box Sales form to make it more descriptive, and to change a color on the form to make the data easier to read.

1   Open the Box Sales form in Design view.

2   Use the Label tool from the toolbox to create a label control in the header section of the form.

3   Name the label 4th Quarter.

4   Use the Fore Color to change the foreground color to light gray to match the form's title. (Hint: Try using the Format Painter to copy the Box Sales Label format in one step.)

5   Resize the label so the text is easy to read.

For more information about	See
Adding a label to a form	Lesson 10
Changing the size of a control	Lesson 10
Using the Font/Fore Color button	Lesson 10

Step 2: Add a Toggle Button Control to a Form

The Box Sales form does not indicate whether a particular box is a discontinued item, which would be helpful to know. You add a toggle box control to the Box Sales form to display whether the item has been discontinued. You then make the new control match the form's format. You also change the field name so that if you refer to it in another form or query, it has a logical name.

1   Drag the gray line that separates the main form and the subform to just above the subform.

2   Click in the Toggle Button control and then place the cursor just below the Box Name field.

     When you release the mouse, a new toggle button is placed on the form.

3   Change the control source property to the Discontinued field, and the Caption property to Discontinued.

4   Re-size the new control so it's an appropriate size for the caption.

5   Switch to Form view to check your enhancements. If necessary, adjust the label size.

6   In Design view, select the Discontinued toggle button, and change its Fore Color property to dark blue.

7   Change the toggle button Name property from the default field number to Discontinued.

8   Close the Boxes Sales form, and save your changes.

For more information about	See
Adding a Toggle Button control to a form	Lesson 10
Setting the properties of a control	Lesson 10

Step 3: *Add a Picture to a Form*

The Human Resources Department has learned that you can add pictures to forms in the Sweet Lil's database. The department wants you to add the company logo to the Employees form.

1   Open the Employees form in Design view.
2   Use the Image tool in the toolbox to create an image control in the form header section.
3   Insert the Sweet Lil's Logo file from the Practice folder into the control.
4   Look at the picture in the control in Form view.
5   Return to Design view, and set the control Name property to Company Logo.
6   Close the form, and save your changes.

For more information about	See
Adding a picture to a form	Lesson 10
Sizing an embedded object	Lesson 2

Step 4: *Give Your Forms a Common Look and Feel*

The Human Resources Department wants all its forms to have the same look as the Payroll Form. You modify the appearance of one field on the Employee form and then use the Format Painter to apply the format to the fields in the Employees Form.

1   Open the Employees Form in Design view.
2   Change the color of the Employee ID field to dark blue.
3   Use the Format Painter to apply the format to all the fields on the form.
4   Save and close the form.

For more information about	See
Using Format Painter	Lesson 10

Step 5: *Create a Detail Report*

The Production Department wants you to create a report listing the contact names and phone numbers for the suppliers of Sweet Lil's ingredients. The information for the report is contained in the Ingredient Source query.

1 Use the AutoReport: Tabular Wizard to create a tabular detail report based on the Ingredient Source query.

2 Format the report with the Bold AutoFormat, and then preview the report.

3 In Design view, use the Sorting And Grouping button to sort by category.

4 To avoid printing duplicate entries, set the Hide Duplicates property of the Category text box (under the Detail section) to Yes.

5 Preview the report again.

6 Save the report with the name Ingredient Source, and close the report.

For more information about	See
Creating a detail report	Lesson 11

Step 6: *Create a Grouped Report*

Lillian Farber, the company president, wants to reduce box costs again. She wants a report that lists the bonbons in each box along with the cost of each bonbon. She also wants to know the total cost of the bonbons in each box. You will use a Report Wizard to make a report that shows the information.

1 Create a new grouped report by using all the fields in the Bonbons By Box query.

2 Group by Box Name, and use Normal grouping.

3 Sort by Bonbon Name.

4 Sum the Cost of Bonbons field, but do not calculate total percentages.

5 Select the Stepped layout, Portrait orientation, and Corporate style for your report.

6 Name your report **Cost of Boxes**

7 Preview the report, and then save and close the report.

For more information about	See
Creating a grouped report	Lesson 12

Finish the Review & Practice

➤ If you are finished using Microsoft Access for now, on the File menu, click Exit.

Appendixes

If You Are New to Windows 95, Windows NT, or Microsoft Access

If you're new to Microsoft Windows 95 or Microsoft Windows NT version 4.0, and to Microsoft Access, this appendix will show you all the basics you need to get started. You'll get an overview of Windows 95 and Windows NT features, and you'll learn how to use online Help to answer your questions and find out more about using these operating systems. You'll also get an introduction to Microsoft Access.

If You Are New to Windows 95 or Windows NT

Windows 95 and Windows NT are easy-to-use computer environments that help you handle the daily work that you perform with your computer. You can use either Windows 95 or Windows NT to run Microsoft Access—the explanations in this appendix apply to both operating systems. The way you use Windows 95, Windows NT, and programs designed for these operating systems is similar. The programs have a common look, and you use the same kinds of controls to tell them what to do. In this section, you'll learn how to use the basic program controls. If you're already familiar with Windows 95 or Windows NT, skip to the "What Is Microsoft Access?" section.

Start Windows 95 or Windows NT

Starting Windows 95 or Windows NT is as easy as turning on your computer.

1   If your computer isn't on, turn it on now.

In Windows 95, you will also be prompted for a username and password if your computer is configured for user profiles.

2 If you are using Windows NT, press CTRL+ALT+DEL to display a dialog box asking for your username and password. If you are using Windows 95, you will see this dialog box if your computer is connected to a network.

3 Type your username and password in the appropriate boxes, and then click OK.

If you don't know your username or password, contact your system administrator for assistance.

Close

4 If you see the Welcome dialog box, click the Close button.

Your screen should look similar to the following illustration.

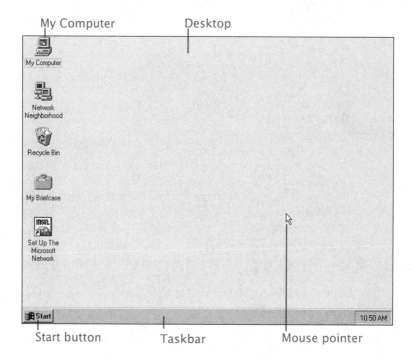

Using the Mouse

Although you can use the keyboard for most actions, many of these actions are easier to do by using a mouse. The mouse controls a pointer on the screen, as shown in the previous illustration. You move the pointer by sliding the mouse over a flat surface in the direction you want the pointer to move. If you run out of room to move the mouse, lift the mouse up, and then put it down in a more comfortable location.

You'll use five basic mouse actions throughout this book.

When you are directed to	Do this
Point to an item	Move the mouse to place the pointer on the item.
Click an item	Point to the item on your screen, and quickly press and release the left mouse button.
Use the right mouse button to click an item	Point to the item on your screen, and then quickly press and release the right mouse button. Clicking the right mouse button displays a shortcut menu from which you can choose from a list of commands that apply to that item.
Double-click an item	Point to the item, and then quickly press and release the left mouse button twice.
Drag an item	Point to an item, and then hold down the left mouse button as you move the pointer.

 IMPORTANT In this book we assume that your mouse is set up so that the left button is the primary button and the right button is the secondary button. If your mouse is configured the opposite way, for left-handed use, use the right button when we tell you to use the left, and vice versa.

Using Window Controls

All programs designed for use on computers that have Windows 95 or Windows NT installed have common controls that you use to scroll, size, move, and close a window.

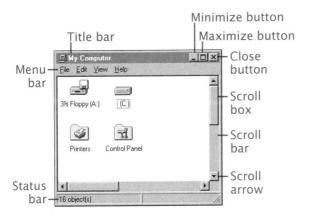

241

To	Do this	Button
Move, or *scroll*, vertically or horizontally through the contents of a window that extends beyond the screen	Click a scroll bar or scroll arrow, or drag the scroll box. The previous illustration identifies these controls.	
Enlarge a window to fill the screen	Click the Maximize button, or double-click the window's title bar.	◻
Restore a window to its previous size	Click the Restore button, or double-click the window title bar. When a window is maximized, the Maximize button changes to the Restore button.	⧉
Reduce a window to a button on the taskbar	Click the Minimize button. To display a minimized window, click its button on the taskbar.	_
Move a window	Drag the window title bar.	
Close a window	Click the Close button.	✕

Using Menus

Just like a restaurant menu, a program menu provides a list of options from which you can choose. On program menus, these options are called *commands*. To select a menu or a menu command, you click the item you want.

 NOTE You can also use the keyboard to make menu selections. Press the ALT key to activate the menu bar, and press the key that corresponds to the highlighted or underlined letter of the menu name. Then, press the key that corresponds to the highlighted or underlined letter of the command name.

Open and make selections from a menu

In the following exercise, you'll open and make selections from a menu.

1   On the Desktop, double-click the My Computer icon.

The My Computer window opens.

You can also press ALT+E to open the Edit menu.

2   In the My Computer window, click Edit on the menu bar.

The Edit menu appears. Some commands are dimmed; this means that they aren't available.

Command is not available.

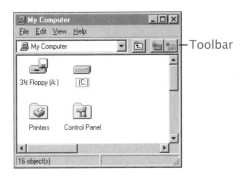

Shortcut key

Command is available.

3 Click the Edit menu name to close the menu.

The menu closes.

On a menu, a check mark indicates that multiple items in this group of commands can be selected at one time. A bullet mark indicates that only one item in this group can be selected at one time.

4 Click View on the menu bar to open the View menu.

5 On the View menu, click Toolbar.

The View menu closes, and a toolbar appears below the menu bar.

Toolbar

6 On the View menu, click List.

The items in the My Computer window now appear in a list, rather than as icons.

7 On the toolbar, click the Large Icons button.

Clicking a button on a toolbar is a quick way to select a command.

Large Icons

8 On the View menu, point to Arrange Icons.

A cascading menu appears listing additional menu choices. When a right-pointing arrow appears after a command name, it indicates that additional commands are available.

243

9 Click anywhere outside the menu to close it.

10 On the menu bar, click View, and then click Toolbar again.

The View menu closes, and the toolbar is now hidden.

11 In the upper-right corner of the My Computer window, click the Close button to close the window.

> **TIP** If you do a lot of typing, you might want to learn the key combinations for commands you use frequently. Pressing the key combination is a quick way to perform a command by using the keyboard. If a key combination is available for a command, it will be listed to the right of the command name on the menu. For example, CTRL+C is listed on the Edit menu as the key combination for the Copy command.

Using Dialog Boxes

When you choose a command name that is followed by an ellipsis (...), a dialog box will appear so that you can provide more information about how the command should be carried out. Dialog boxes have standard features, as shown in the following illustration.

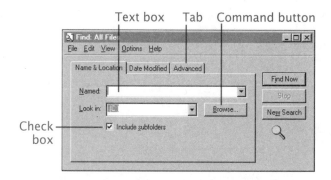

To move around in a dialog box, you click the item you want. You can also use the keyboard to select the item by holding down ALT as you press the underlined letter. Or, you can press TAB to move between items.

Display the Taskbar Properties dialog box

Some dialog boxes provide several categories of options displayed on separate tabs. You click the top of an obscured tab to make it visible.

1 On the taskbar, click the Start button.

The Start menu opens.

2   On the Start menu, point to Settings, and then click Taskbar.

3   In the Taskbar Properties dialog box, click the Start Menu Programs tab.

       On this tab, you can customize the list of programs that appears on your Start menu.

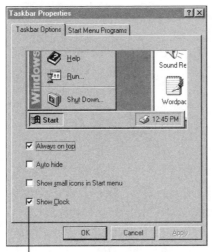

Click here. When you click a check box
that is selected, you turn the option off.

4   Click the Taskbar Options tab, and then click to select the Show Small Icons In Start Menu check box

       When a check box is selected, it displays a check mark.

5   Click the check box a couple of times, and watch how the display in the dialog box changes.

       Clicking any check box or option button will turn the option off or on.

6   Click the Cancel button in the dialog box.

       This closes the dialog box without changing any settings.

Getting Help with Windows 95 or Windows NT

When you're at work and you want to find more information about how to do a project, you might ask a co-worker or consult a reference book. To find out more about functions and features in Windows 95 or Windows NT, you can use the online Help system. For example, when you need information about how to print, the Help system is one of the most efficient ways to learn. The Windows 95 or Windows NT Help system is available from the Start menu. After the Help system opens, you can choose the type of help you want from the Help Topics dialog box.

To find instructions about broad categories, you can look on the Contents tab. Or you can search the Help index to find information about specific topics. The Help information is short and concise, so you can get the exact information you need quickly. There are also shortcut icons in many Help topics that you can use to go directly to the task you want.

Viewing Help Contents

The Contents tab is organized like a book's table of contents. As you choose top-level topics, called *chapters*, you see a list of more detailed subtopics from which to choose. Many of these chapters have Tips and Tricks sections to help you work more efficiently as well as Troubleshooting sections to help you resolve problems.

Find Help about general categories

Suppose you want to learn more about using Calculator, a program that comes with Windows 95 and Windows NT. In this exercise, you'll look up information in the online Help system.

1   Click Start. On the Start menu, click Help.

The Help Topics: Windows Help dialog box appears.

2   If necessary, click the Contents tab to make it active.

3   Double-click "Introducing Windows" or "Introducing Windows NT."

A set of subtopics appears.

4   Double-click "Using Windows Accessories."

5   Double-click "For General Use."

6 Double-click "Calculator: for making calculations."

A Help topic window opens.

7 Read the Help information, and then click the Close button to close the Help window.

Finding Help About Specific Topics

You can find specific Help topics by using the Index tab or the Find tab. The Index tab is organized like a book's index. Keywords for topics are organized alphabetically. You can either scroll through the list of keywords or type the keyword you want to find. You can then select from one or more topic choices.

With the Find tab, you can also enter a keyword. The main difference is that you get a list of all Help topics in which that keyword appears, not just the topics that begin with that word. .

Find Help about specific topics by using the Help index

In this exercise, you use the Help index to learn how to change the background pattern of your Desktop.

1 Click Start, and on the Start menu, click Help.

The Help Topics dialog box appears.

2 Click the Index tab to make it active.

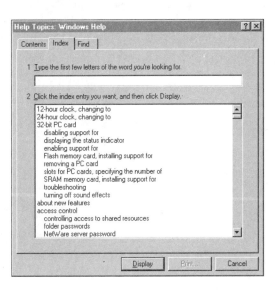

3 In the Type The First Few Letters Of The Word You're Looking For box, type **display**

A list of display-related topics appears.

4 Click the topic named "background pictures or patterns, changing," and then click Display.

The Topics Found dialog box appears.

5 Be sure that the topic named "Changing the background of your desktop" is selected, and then click Display.

6 Read the Help topic.

7 Click the shortcut icon in step 1 of the Help topic.

Shortcut

The Display Properties dialog box appears. If you want, you can immediately perform the task you are looking up in Help.

8 Click the Close button on the Display Properties dialog box.

9 Click the Close button on the Windows Help window.

NOTE You can print any Help topic, if you have a printer installed on your computer. Click the Options button in the upper-left corner of any Help topic window, click Print Topic, and then click OK. To continue searching for additional topics, you can click the Help Topics button in any open Help topic window.

Find Help about specific topics by using the Find tab

In this exercise, you use the Find tab to learn how to change your printer's settings.

1 Click Start, and then click Help to display the Help Topics dialog box.

2 Click the Find tab to make it active.

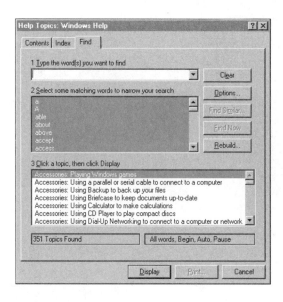

3 If you see a wizard, click Next, and then click Finish to complete and close the wizard.

The wizard creates a search index for your Help files. This might take a few minutes. The next time you use Find, you won't have to wait for the list to be created.

The Find tab appears.

4 In the text box, type **print**

All topics that have to do with printing appear in the list box at the bottom of the tab.

5 In step 3 of the Help dialog box, click the "Changing printer settings" topic, and then click Display.

The Help topic appears.

6 Read the Help topic, and then click the Close button on the Windows Help window.

Find Help in a dialog box

Almost every dialog box includes a question mark Help button in the upper-right corner of its window. When you click this button and then click any dialog box control, a Help window appears that explains what the control is and how to use it. In this exercise, you'll get help for a dialog box control.

1 Click Start, and then click Run.

The Run dialog box appears.

Help

2 Click the Help button.

The mouse pointer changes to an arrow with a question mark.

3 Click the Open text box.

A Help window appears, providing information about how to use the Open text box.

4 Click anywhere on the Desktop, or press ESC, to close the Help window.

The mouse pointer returns to its previous shape.

5 In the Run dialog box, click Cancel.

 TIP You can change the way the Help topics appear on your screen. Click the Options button in any Help topic window, and then point to Font to change the size of the text.

What Is Microsoft Access?

Microsoft Access is a database management product. It is used to create, control, and manipulate one of the most common forms of information system: a database. A database system is a collection of integrated information that describes a particular object or subject. Microsoft Access is a very flexible program that can be used to manage very simple database applications or to build complex corporate management information systems. For example, an individual might use Microsoft Access to create a system that describes professional contacts. The system could then be used to quickly locate phone numbers or e-mail addresses. On the other hand, a corporation could use Microsoft Access to manage all its information requirements, from capturing and recording sales data to publishing sophisticated operations reports.

Microsoft Access is well suited for both creating new database systems and for expanding or upgrading current systems. Microsoft Access can accept data from a wide variety of file formats, which makes it ideal for converting data stored in a different system. Also, the program has an easy-to-master graphical interface, which makes it an ideal tool for less experienced users. More experienced database users, however, become quickly productive with Microsoft Access, because many industry standard tools, such as SQL, are included. Microsoft Access can also share data with the Microsoft SQL Server, which provides a natural bridge between PC and mainframe systems.

The Visual Basic for Applications (VBA) programming language is an integral part of Microsoft Access. Using VBA, you can create very sophisticated programs to control all aspects of how users interact with the database. VBA is also integrated throughout the entire suite of Microsoft Office products, so it is easy to integrate your Microsoft Access database with other Office applications.

Quit Windows 95 or Windows NT

1   If you are finished using Windows 95 or Windows NT, close any open windows by clicking the Close button in each window.

2   Click Start, and then click Shut Down.

The Shut Down Windows dialog box appears.

3   Click Yes.

A message indicates that it is now safe to turn off your computer.

 WARNING   To avoid loss of data or damage to your operating system, always quit Windows 95 or Windows NT by using the Shut Down command on the Start menu before you turn your computer off.

Designing a Database

Good design is a key factor of successful database building. A well-designed database can lead to more efficient use of queries, forms, and reports, and can increase the reliability of the extracted information. In addition, an effectively designed database will be easier to expand as your organization's information requirements grow and change.

Although there are guidelines to assist you in designing your database, there is no such thing as a perfect database design. Designing information systems always involves a degree of compromise. The purpose of this appendix is to provide a general overview of good database design principles. These guidelines should not be viewed as hard-and-fast rules, but rather suggestions for making your database design decisions.

Database Design Process

Although there is no one correct way to create a database, there are some general steps that most professional systems developers follow. These steps generally reflect what is known as the *Systems Development Life Cycle* (SDLC). The SDLC breaks the task of creating a system into stages. In the design stage of the process, you should ask the following questions:

- What are the objectives of the system?
- How should the data be subdivided into distinct entities or topics?
- What are the relationships between these entities?

- What facts about each entity need to be identified and stored to fulfill the system objectives?

A variety of techniques can be employed to answer these questions. One of the best ways is to involve the future end-users of the database. A database, however, may have hundreds or even thousands of users. If the database is very large, you might have to consult representatives of the various user groups, such as a database design committee. This type of committee should include representatives of all significant user groups as well as the organization's top management and information systems professionals.

The design process can be further subdivided into the following stages:

- feasibility study
- entity identification
- assigning attributes to entities
- diagramming entities and relationships

In the feasibility study phase, you must determine whether a database is the best structure for the proposed information system. Although many modern information systems adopt a database approach, there are some instances where a database is not appropriate. For example, if the system requires a large amount of specialized knowledge, it might be more appropriate to create an *expert system*. Expert systems are information systems that use a series of rules and reasoning techniques to emulate human expertise.

Entities vary depending on the company's overall marketing focus.

The main task during the entity identification phase is to completely define all the components of the object or subject that the database will describe. This is a very important aspect of database design, as it will affect the overall direction of the design. For example, the main entities in Sweet Lil's database are: orders, customers, and boxes.

The attributes of entities are those aspects of the components that users will need to know in order to complete their tasks. Two different approaches can be taken to identify attributes. A *task approach* works from the tasks back to the attributes. For example, if you need to fill an order, you would need to first figure out which data items are required to fill an order; the answers to this question are entity attributes. With the *identification approach,* you start by identifying the attributes, and then you identify the tasks that can be accomplished using that set of data. Regardless of which approach is taken, you must develop a complete list of all the data items that need to be included in the system.

Diagramming the entities and relationships determines whether the system can logically lead to the required output. A variety of diagramming techniques are available; however, a discussion of those techniques is beyond the scope of this appendix.

Expanding an Existing Database

Ideally, the initial design of your database will capture all your information requirements. One of the truisms of information systems design, however, is that the only real constant is change. Invariably there will come a point when you need to modify or expand your database. The design process for expanding an existing database is similar to that used in the initial design. It is still necessary to undertake a system study to determine the requirements, entities, and attributes. In a database expansion, however, it is necessary to determine how the expansion will affect the existing database structure. For example, you must determine whether the new data belongs in the same database or if a new database should be created. Here again, there are no hard-and-fast rules, but there are some general guidelines.

When you are expanding an existing database, the basic question to ask is whether the entities being added to the database can be logically related to the existing entities. If there is no logical relationship or if the new entities form a discrete logical unit, they should be assembled in a new database. For example, if Sweet Lil's decides to add a new retail division, the data pertaining to that division should be contained in a new database. If, on the other hand, the information needs were to change as a result of adding a new product line, the expansion could probably be accommodated in the current database.

Adding to an Existing Database

Part 2 of this book is devoted exclusively to the process of adding to an existing database. Tables, queries, forms, and reports can all be added through the Database window. When you decide to add new tables, you should consider whether the new item fits into the existing structure. Although creating new tables is a relatively simple operation, the process of fully integrating them into the database can be quite time-consuming. For example, new relationships probably need to be created, and existing forms and reports might need to be modified. Devoting time to planning and analyzing the impact of the database expansion on existing objects smoothes out the transition to the database's new form.

Expanding by Creating a New Database

If the expansion planning process determines that a new database is warranted, you can use the Database Wizard to help you with its creation. The Database Wizard includes predefined database structures for a wide variety of database purposes. For example, the Database Wizard can create databases for tracking addresses, controlling inventory, and managing assets. Using the Database wizard to create one of the predefined database structures can speed up the development time for your new database. The predefined databases will, however, generally need to be modified to meet your specific requirements.

253

Suppose that you want to create a database to keep track of your music collection. The database will store information about recording artists, individual music tracks, and recordings. The Database Wizard includes a predefined database structure for this application, which you will now use to create your new database.

Create a new database

New Database

You can also click New Database on the File menu.

1 Click the New Database button.

The New dialog box appears.

2 Be sure the Databases tab is selected, and then double-click the Music Collection icon.

The File New Database dialog box appears.

3 In the File Name box, type **My Music Collection**, and then click Create.

The Database Wizard starts. The wizard will ask you a series of questions to customize the predefined database structure to your requirements.

4 The first screen of the Database Wizard provides a summary of the information stored in the database. Read the information, and then click Next.

5 The next screen asks you to specify any optional fields you want to include in the database. Click Yes, select the Include Sample Data check box, and then click Next.

6 The following screen asks you to specify the type of screen display you want for your database. Select Standard, and then click Next.

7 The next screen asks you what style you would like for printed reports. Be sure Corporate is selected, and then click Next.

8 In the next screen, click Next to accept the default title, Music Collection.

9 The final screen allows you to either open the new database, or create it and return to the Database window. If you want to work with the database, be sure that the Yes, Start The Database option is selected, and then click Finish. If you do not want to work with the database at this time, clear the check box, and then click Finish.

 NOTE If you have elected to work with the database, the Switchboard window will open. The Switchboard was created by the wizard to assist you with navigating through the database. To close the Switchboard and return to the Database window, click the Close button in the upper right corner of the Switchboard form. To close the Music Collection database, click the Close button in the upper right corner of the database window

Using Expressions

No matter what type of work you're doing with Microsoft Access, you'll most likely need to use expressions. For example, you might want to calculate a subtotal on a report or design a query that asks for all products that cost $10. Or, you might want to filter a form so that you see the records for only your sales region. In all these cases, you need to create an expression. This appendix provides guidelines for writing expressions and examples of common expressions.

What Are Expressions?

Expressions are formulas that calculate a value. For example, the following expression multiplies the box price by 1.1 (which is the same as raising the price by 10 percent):

=[Box Price] * 1.1

An expression can include *functions*, *identifiers*, *operators*, *literal values*, and *constants*. The following expression contains most of these elements.

Functions help you perform specialized calculations easily. For example, you can use the Avg function to find the average of values in a field or the Sum function to find the total of all values in a field.

Identifiers refer to a value in your database, such as the value of a field, control, or property. For example, [Order Date] refers to the value in the Order Date field.

Operators specify an action (such as addition) to be performed on one or more elements of an expression. Operators include familiar arithmetic operators such as +, −, *, and /, as well as other operators such as =, <, >, &, And, Or, and Like.

Literal values are values that Microsoft Access uses exactly as you enter them. For example, the number 25 and the text value "San Francisco" are literals.

Constants represent values that don't change. For example, the constant Null always means a field that contains no characters or values. A constant might also be True, False, Yes, or No.

Guidelines for Entering Expressions

In some cases, when you enter an expression, Microsoft Access inserts characters for you automatically. For example, Microsoft Access might insert brackets, number signs, or quotation marks. The examples in this appendix show you how to type the entire expression, instead of having Microsoft Access supply additional characters.

Follow these general guidelines when entering an expression.

Element	How to enter	Example
Identifier	Enclose field names and control names in brackets.	[Order Date]
	Use a period (.) to separate the name of a table from a field in the table.	[Boxes].[Box Price]
	If an expression needs to get values from a different database object, use an exclamation point (!) to separate the type of object (Forms), the name of the form (Boxes), and the name of the control on the form (Boxes ID).	Forms![Boxes]![Boxes ID]
Date	Enclose dates in number signs (#). Number signs automatically appear around a date/time value you type in a validation expression or in a criteria expression for a field whose data type is Date/Time.	#10/10/94# #10-Oct-94#

Element	How to enter	Example
Text	Enclose text in quotation marks. If the text doesn't contain a space or punctuation, you can type the text without quotation marks. The marks will then appear automatically.	California, "British Columbia"
Number	Don't enter a currency symbol ($) or a separating comma.	8934.75 (not $8,934.75 or 8,934.75)

Creating Expressions with the Expression Builder

When you want to create a common expression quickly, or when you want help in creating an expression, you can use the Expression Builder. You can start the Expression Builder from places where you would often write an expression, such as in a property sheet or in a criteria box in the QBE grid.

In a property sheet, first you click the property box where you want an expression, and then you click the Build button on the toolbar.

In the Query window, you click where you want an expression, and then you choose Build from the shortcut menu. If the property box or query box where you start the Expression Builder already contains a value, that value is automatically copied into the Expression box.

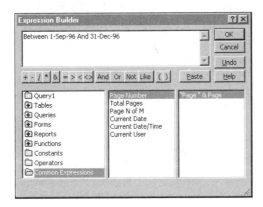

When the Expression Builder appears, you can select types of expressions, field names, and operators, and then paste them into the Expression box. You can also type in any elements you want. To accept the expression you built, choose OK.

Using Expressions in Forms and Reports

You use expressions in forms and reports to get information that you cannot get directly from the tables in a database. For example, you can create expressions that calculate totals, add the values from two fields, or set a default value for a field.

Calculated Control Expression Examples

When you want a form or report to calculate a value, you can create a calculated control that gets its value from an expression. You add the control to your form or report, and then you type an expression directly in the control (frequently a text box) or in the Control Source property box for the control.

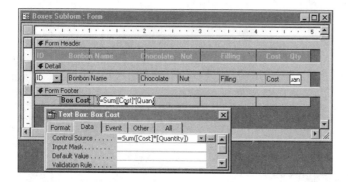

When you type expressions in calculated controls, be sure to include an equal sign (=) to the left of the expression. For example: =[Salary] * 2

When you type a long expression in a property box, you might want to press SHIFT+F2 to display the whole expression at once.

The following table shows some common expressions used for calculated controls.

Expression	Microsoft Access displays
=[Quantity]*[Box Price]	The product of the Quantity and Box Price field values.
=[First Name] &" "&[Last Name]	The values of the First Name and Last Name fields, separated by a space.
=[Bonbon Cost]*1.5	The value in the Bonbon Cost field multiplied by 1.5.
=to Date( )	Today's date.

Expression	Microsoft Access displays
=Page	The page number of the current page.
="Page " & Page & " of " & Pages	The page number of the current page followed by the total number of pages.
="Sales for " &[State/Province]	The text "Sales for" followed by the value in the State/Province field.
=[State/Province Total]/[Grand Total]	The value from the State/Province Total control divided by the value from the Grand Total control.
=Sum([Bonbon Cost])	The sum of the values in the Bonbon Cost field.
=[Orders Subform].Form![Order Subtotal]	The value from the Order Subtotal control on the Orders subform. (To see how to use the expression, refer to the Subtotal control on the Orders form.)
=DatePart("yyyy",[Order Date])	Only the year portion of the date. (The comma is used to separate arguments in a function.)

Validation Expression Examples

You can set validation rules for a field on a form to make sure that you enter the right type of data into the field. To specify a rule, you type an expression in the Validation Rule property box for the control.

The following table shows some typical validation expressions.

Expression	When you enter data, it must
>=Date( )	Be a date that's either today's date or some date in the future.
Between 10 And 100	Be a value between 10 and 100, inclusive.
"USA" Or "Canada"	Match USA or Canada.
Like "[A-Z]##"	Include one letter followed by two numbers (for example, B23).

Using Expressions in Queries and Filters

You use expressions in queries and filters to specify criteria. In queries, you can also use expressions to create fields that are based on a calculation. You don't have to include an equal sign to the left of a query or filter expression.

Criteria Expression Examples

When you're designing a query or filter, you use expressions as criteria. These criteria tell Microsoft Access which records you want to see. You enter criteria for a field into the Criteria box for that field. For example, to find people with customer IDs greater than 100, you'd type the expression >100 in the Criteria box for the Customer ID field.

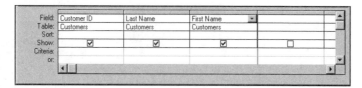

The following examples show some frequently used criteria expressions that you might use in a query based on the Orders table in the Sweet Lil's database.

Field	Criteria expression	Query finds orders
Customer ID	89	For the customer whose ID is 89
Customer ID	>=60	For customers with IDs greater than or equal to 60
Ship City	"Seattle" Or "New York"	For Seattle or New York
State/Province Ship	Not "Ontario"	For all states and provinces except Ontario
Ship Last Name	Like "Mc*"	For names beginning with "Mc"
Ship Last Name	Like "J*son"	For names beginning with "J" and ending in "son"
Carrier ID	Null	That have no value in the Carrier ID field
Order Date	Between 1-Dec-94 And 15-Dec-94	Placed during the first 15 days of December 1994
Ship Last Name	Like [C] & "*"	For last names starting with "C"(for parameter queries only)

Calculated Field Expression Examples

You can use expressions to create new query fields. You enter the expression into a Field box in the QBE grid.

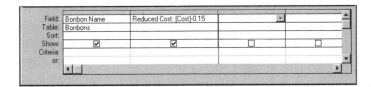

The following examples show some common calculated field expressions.

Name and expression	Microsoft Access displays
Sale Price: [Box Price] * 0.8	The values of the Box Price field multiplied by 0.8 (reduces the values by 20 percent).
Sale Price: CCur([Box Price] * 0.8)	The values of the Box Price field reduced by 20 percent and formatted as currency values (for example, $2,345.50).
Extended Price: [Order Details][Quantity]*[Boxes].[Box Price]	The product of the Quantity field in the Order Details table and the Box Price field in the Boxes table.

For More Information

Although this appendix shows examples of expressions in forms, reports, queries, and filters, you can also use expressions in tables, macros, and modules. You'll find extensive information on expressions in the Microsoft Access online documentation.

For online information about	On the Help menu, click Contents And Index, click the Index tab, and then type
Creating or entering expressions	**expressions**
Entering expressions in forms	**expressions in forms**
Entering expressions in reports	**expressions in reports**
Entering expressions in queries	**expressions in queries**
Entering expressions in filters	**expressions in filters**
Using Expression Builder	**expression builder**

argument   The information that a function uses to produce a new value or perform an action. For example, a new value is displayed when the SUM function adds the argument (A6:A12). An argument consists of numbers, references, text, operators, arrays, or error values.

border   A line that goes around text or tables. You can assign a variety of widths and styles to a border.

both   A logical operator that can be included in an expression to select items that meet more than one criteria.

bound   A property of fields or controls in an Access object, such as a form or report. A bound field or control will be updated when the data that the field or control is bound to changes.

bound control   A control tied to a field in an underlying table or query.

button   [1]A small picture window on a toolbar that you can click to perform an action. Buttons on the toolbar are used to perform the same action as a menu command, such as clicking Copy on the Edit menu. [2]An option in a dialog box, for example, Cancel or OK. [3]The Minimize, Maximize, and Restore control elements used to change the size and position of a window.

calculate   Perform a mathematical operation to determine the contents of a control.

character   An individual letter, number, or symbol corresponding to a key or key combination. Each character can be formatted individually.

check box   A dialog box option that is not mutually exclusive. Clicking a check box inserts or removes an "X."

Clipboard   A temporary holding area in computer memory that stores the last set of information that was cut or copied (such as text or graphics). You transfer data from the Clipboard by using the Paste command. Information remains on the Clipboard until you cut or copy another piece of information.

column   A vertical section of a worksheet or a table.

combo box   A control that allows the user to type a value or select a value from a list.

command button   A control that runs a macro, carries out an event procedure, or calls a Visual Basic function.

control   An object on a form or report that displays data, performs an action, or changes the form's or report's appearance.

criteria   The conditions that control which records to display in a query; the words or values used to determine the data that appears in a data list.

crosstab query   A query that displays summarized values from a single field and rearranges the values into rows and columns.

data   A set of information used by a computer or program.

data type   The attribute of a field that determines the kind of data the field can contain.

data validation   The process of checking if the data being entered meets a specific set of criteria.

database   A collection of data related to a particular topic or purpose, such as a database of customer information. Can also refer to a type of program, such as Microsoft Access, that you can use to organize and manipulate detailed lists of information.

destination   A document or program receiving information that was originally generated in another program. *See also* source.

detail report   A report that provides a more narrow view of a set of data.

embed   To insert an object from a source program into a destination document. *See also* link.

embedded object   Data (such as text or graphics) that you can edit using the full resources of its source program while it is in a destination document. *See also* embed.

expression   A formula that calculates a value. You can use expressions in forms, reports, tables, queries, macros, and modules.

field   An area in a table or form in which you can enter or view specific information about an individual task or resource. On a form, a field is an area where you can enter data.

field selector   A small box or bar at the top of a datasheet column that you can click to select an entire column.

filter   A set of criteria you can apply to data to show specific tasks, records, or resources.

foreign key   A field in a related table that contains the values that match the related fields in the primary key in the primary table.

form   A Microsoft Access database object on which you place controls for entering, displaying, and editing data.

format   Settings that determine the appearance of an object.

group   [1]A collection of objects that are treated and handled as one object. [2]A collection of related programs and documents represented by a single group icon or arranged in a group window. [3]A set of records that contain similar values. [4]A single address in e-mail that can be used to send a message to a predefined group of people.

hyperlink   An object, such as a graphic or colored or underlined text, that represents a link to another location in the same file or in a different file, and that, when clicked, brings up a different Web page. Hyperlinks are one of the key elements of HTML documents.

information   Processed data.

import   The process of converting and opening a file that was created in another program.

insertion point   The blinking vertical bar that marks the location where text is entered in a document, a cell, or a dialog box.

Internet   A worldwide "network of networks," made up of thousands of computer networks and millions of commercial, education, government, and personal computers, all connected to each other. Also referred to as the Net.

join line   A line between fields displayed in field lists in the Relationship window or the Query window that indicates how the fields are matched between the tables.

junction table   A table that provides a link between two tables that have a many-to-many relationship. The junction table provides the relationship between the two tables.

key field   *See* primary key.

link   [1]*See* hyperlink. [2]To copy an object, such as a graphic or text, from one file or program to another so that there is a dependent relationship between the object and its source file. Also refers to the connection between a source file and a destination file. Whenever the original information in the source file changes, the information in the linked object is automatically updated. *See also* embed.

list box   A control that provides a list of values from which you can select.

macro   A series of commands stored as a group, so they can be treated as a single command.

many-to-many relationship   A relationship between two tables in which one record in either table can have many matching records in the other table. *See also* one-to-many relationship; one-to-one relationship.

null field   A field containing no characters.

object   A table, chart, graphic, equation, or other form of information you create and edit. An object can be inserted, pasted, or copied into any file.

object frame   A control used to add, edit, or view OLE objects.

OLE   A Microsoft programming standard that allows a user or a program to communicate with other programs, usually for the purpose of exchanging information. Dragging, linking, and embedding are examples of OLE features. *See also* link; embed.

one-to-many relationship   A relationship in which a record in the main database can be related to one or more records in a detail database. *See also* many-to-many relationship; one-to-one relationship.

one-to-one relationship   A relationship between two tables in which a value in a related table exists in a primary table. The value can occur only once in the related table. *See also* many-to-many relationship relationship; one-to-many relationship.

page footer   Text or graphics that appear at the bottom of every page of a report.

page header   Text or graphics that appear at the top of every page of a report.

parameter   Criteria used to limit the values returned by a query.

primary key   An attribute applied to a field, usually to prevent duplication of a value.

property   An attribute of a control, field, table, query, form, or report that you can set to define one of the object's characteristics.

query   A database object that represents the group of records you want to view. A query is a request for a particular collection of data.

record   A set of information that belongs together and describes a single item in a table or query.

record selector   A small box or bar that appears on the left side of a table, query, or form in Datasheet view. You can select a particular record by clicking on the record selector.

referential integrity   A relationship between two tables designed to prevent the occurrence of values in a related table that do not exist in a primary table.

related   A term indicating that a relationship exists between two records.

relationship   An association between tables that have fields with matching values.

report footer   Text or graphics that appear once at the end of a report and typically contain summaries, such as grand totals.

report header   Text or graphics that appear once at the beginning of a report and typically contain the report title, date, and company logo.

Required property   A property that can be set for a field that will not accept null values.

sort   To automatically reorder text or numbers in ascending or descending order, alphabetically, numerically, or by date.

source   [1] In a Web page, the text page that displays all HTML tags. In Internet Explorer, the source for the displayed Web page can be seen by choosing Source from the View menu. [2] The document or program in which the file was originally created. *See also* destination.

subform   A form within a form.

tab order   A form property that controls how the cursor moves between fields when you press TAB.

table   One or more rows of cells commonly used to display numbers and other items for quick reference and analysis. Items in a table are organized into rows (records) and columns (fields).

value   A number that can be calculated in cells.

wildcard   Special character used in place of any other characters. An asterisk (*) takes the place of one or more characters; a question mark (?) takes the place of one character.

wizard   A tool that guides you through a complex task by asking you questions, and then performing the task based on your responses.

World Wide Web   The collection of available information on the Internet that is connected by links so that you can jump from one document to another. Also referred to as the Web, WWW, and W3.

Index

Index

IMPORTANT—READ CAREFULLY BEFORE OPENING SOFTWARE PACKET(S). By opening the sealed packet(s) containing the software, you indicate your acceptance of the following Microsoft License Agreement.

MICROSOFT LICENSE AGREEMENT

(Book Companion Disks)

This is a legal agreement between you (either an individual or an entity) and Microsoft Corporation. By opening the sealed software packet(s) you are agreeing to be bound by the terms of this agreement. If you do not agree to the terms of this agreement, promptly return the un-opened software packet(s) and any accompanying written materials to the place you obtained them for a full refund.

MICROSOFT SOFTWARE LICENSE

1. GRANT OF LICENSE. Microsoft grants to you the right to use one copy of the Microsoft software program included with this book (the "SOFTWARE") on a single terminal connected to a single computer. The SOFTWARE is in "use" on a computer when it is loaded into the temporary memory (i.e., RAM) or installed into the permanent memory (e.g., hard disk, CD-ROM, or other storage device) of that computer. You may not network the SOFTWARE or otherwise use it on more than one computer or computer terminal at the same time. For the files and materials referenced in this book which may be obtained from the Internet, Microsoft grants to you the right to use the materials in connection with the book. If you are a member of a corporation or business, you may reproduce the materials and distribute them within your business for internal business purposes in connection with the book. You may not reproduce the materials for further distribution.

2. COPYRIGHT. The SOFTWARE is owned by Microsoft or its suppliers and is protected by United States copyright laws and international treaty provisions. Therefore, you must treat the SOFTWARE like any other copyrighted material (e.g., a book or musical recording) except that you may either (a) make one copy of the SOFTWARE solely for backup or archival purposes, or (b) transfer the SOFTWARE to a single hard disk provided you keep the original solely for backup or archival purposes. You may not copy the written materials accompanying the SOFTWARE.

3. OTHER RESTRICTIONS. You may not rent or lease the SOFTWARE, but you may transfer the SOFTWARE and accompanying written materials on a permanent basis provided you retain no copies and the recipient agrees to the terms of this Agreement. You may not reverse engineer, decompile, or disassemble the SOFTWARE. If the SOFTWARE is an update or has been updated, any transfer must include the most recent update and all prior versions.

4. DUAL MEDIA SOFTWARE. If the SOFTWARE package contains both 3.5" and 5.25" disks, then you may use only the disks appropriate for your single-user computer. You may not use the other disks on another computer or loan, rent, lease, or transfer them to another user except as part of the permanent transfer (as provided above) of all SOFTWARE and written materials.

5. SAMPLE CODE. If the SOFTWARE includes Sample Code, then Microsoft grants you a royalty-free right to reproduce and distribute the sample code of the SOFTWARE provided that you: (a) distribute the sample code only in conjunction with and as a part of your software product; (b) do not use Microsoft's or its authors' names, logos, or trademarks to market your software product; (c) include the copyright notice that appears on the SOFTWARE on your product label and as a part of the sign-on message for your software product; and (d) agree to indemnify, hold harmless, and defend Microsoft and its authors from and against any claims or lawsuits, including attorneys' fees, that arise or result from the use or distribution of your software product.

DISCLAIMER OF WARRANTY

The SOFTWARE (including instructions for its use) is provided "AS IS" WITHOUT WARRANTY OF ANY KIND. MICROSOFT FURTHER DISCLAIMS ALL IMPLIED WARRANTIES INCLUDING WITHOUT LIMITATION ANY IMPLIED WARRANTIES OF MERCHANTABILITY OR OF FITNESS FOR A PARTICULAR PURPOSE. THE ENTIRE RISK ARISING OUT OF THE USE OR PERFORMANCE OF THE SOFTWARE AND DOCUMENTATION REMAINS WITH YOU.

IN NO EVENT SHALL MICROSOFT, ITS AUTHORS, OR ANYONE ELSE INVOLVED IN THE CREATION, PRODUCTION, OR DELIVERY OF THE SOFTWARE BE LIABLE FOR ANY DAMAGES WHATSOEVER (INCLUDING, WITHOUT LIMITATION, DAMAGES FOR LOSS OF BUSINESS PROFITS, BUSINESS INTERRUPTION, LOSS OF BUSINESS INFORMATION, OR OTHER PECUNIARY LOSS) ARISING OUT OF THE USE OF OR INABILITY TO USE THE SOFTWARE OR DOCUMENTATION, EVEN IF MICROSOFT HAS BEEN ADVISED OF THE POSSIBILITY OF SUCH DAMAGES. BECAUSE SOME STATES/COUNTRIES DO NOT ALLOW THE EXCLUSION OR LIMITATION OF LIABILITY FOR CONSEQUENTIAL OR INCIDENTAL DAMAGES, THE ABOVE LIMITATION MAY NOT APPLY TO YOU.

U.S. GOVERNMENT RESTRICTED RIGHTS

The SOFTWARE and documentation are provided with RESTRICTED RIGHTS. Use, duplication, or disclosure by the Government is subject to restrictions as set forth in subparagraph (c)(1)(ii) of The Rights in Technical Data and Computer Software clause at DFARS 252.227-7013 or subparagraphs (c)(1) and (2) of the Commercial Computer Software — Restricted Rights 48 CFR 52.227-19, as applicable. Manufacturer is Microsoft Corporation, One Microsoft Way, Redmond, WA 98052-6399.

If you acquired this product in the United States, this Agreement is governed by the laws of the State of Washington. Should you have any questions concerning this Agreement, or if you desire to contact Microsoft Press for any reason, please write: Microsoft Press, One Microsoft Way, Redmond, WA 98052-6399.

The
Step by Step
Practice Files Disk

The enclosed 3.5-inch disk contains time-saving, ready-to-use practice files that complement the lessons in this book. To use the practice files, you'll need Microsoft Access 97 and either the Microsoft Windows 95 operating system or version 3.51 Service Pack 5 or later of the Microsoft Windows NT operating system.

Before you begin the *Step by Step* lessons, read the section of the book titled "Installing and Using the Practice Files." There you'll find a description of each practice file and easy instructions for installing the files on your computer's hard disk.

Please take a few moments to read the license agreement on the previous page before using the enclosed disk.